Executive Job Search for $100,000 to $1 Million+ Jobs

By Wendy S. Enelow

The $100,000+ Job Interview
101 Ways to Recession-Proof Your Career
Best Career Transition Resumes for $100,000+ Jobs
Best Cover Letters for $100,000+ Jobs
Best KeyWords for Resumes, Covers Letters, and Interviews
Best Resumes and CVs for International Jobs
Best Resumes for $100,000+ Jobs
Best Resumes for People Without a Four-Year Degree
College Grad Resumes to Land $75,000+ Jobs
Cover Letter Magic
Expert Resumes for Career Changers
Expert Resumes for Computer and Web Jobs
Expert Resumes for Managers and Executives
Expert Resumes for Manufacturing Careers
Expert Resumes for Military-to-Civilian Career Transitions
Expert Resumes for People Returning to Work
Expert Resumes for Teachers and Educators
Insider's Guide to Finding a Job
KeyWords to Nail Your Job Interview
Resume Winners From the Pros

By Louise M. Kursmark

15-Minute Cover Letter
America's Top Resumes for America's Top Jobs
Best Resumes for College Students and New Grads
Cover Letter Magic
Executive's Pocket Guide to ROI Resumes and Job Search
Expert Resumes for Career Changers
Expert Resumes for Computer and Web Jobs
Expert Resumes for Health Care Professions
Expert Resumes for Managers & Executives
Expert Resumes for Manufacturing Careers
Expert Resumes for Military-to-Civilian Career Transitions
Expert Resumes for People Returning to Work
Expert Resumes for Teachers and Educators
How to Choose the Right Person for the Right Job Every Time
How to Start a Home-Based Desktop Publishing Business
Sales & Marketing Resumes for $100,000 Careers
Sales Careers: The Ultimate Guide to Getting a High-Paying Sales Job

Executive Job Search for $100,000 to $1 Million+ Jobs

Wendy S. Enelow, CCM, MRW, JCTC, CPRW
Louise M. Kursmark, MRW, CPRW, CEIP, JCTC, CCM

IMPACT PUBLICATIONS
Manassas Park, VA

Executive Job Search for $100,000 to $1 Million+ Jobs

ISBN: 1-57023-241-5

Library of Congress: 2005925115

Publisher: For information on Impact Publications, including current and forthcoming publications, authors, press kits, online bookstore, and submission requirements, visit our website: www.impactpublications.com

Sales/Distribution: All bookstore sales are handled through Impact's trade distributor: National Book Network, 15200 NBN Way, Blue Ridge Summit, PA 17214, Tel. 1-800-462-6420. All other sales and distribution inquiries should be directed to the publisher: Sales Department, IMPACT PUBLICATIONS, 9104 Manassas Drive, Suite N, Manassas Park, VA 20111-5211, Tel. 703-361-7300, Fax 703-335-9486, or email: info@impactpub lications.com.

The Authors: Wendy Enelow and Louise Kursmark are both distinguished leaders in the executive job search, career coaching, and resume writing industries, and authors of more than 30 career books. For more than 20 years Wendy has assisted thousands of executive job search candidates in writing resumes and coaching them through the job search process. She is the founder and past president of the Career Masters Institute. She can be contacted at wendy@wendyenelow.com. For more than 15 years Louise has worked directly with her numerous executive-level clients in developing powerful career marketing documents. She can be contacted through her company, www.yourbest impression.com. Professionally active, both authors frequently conduct career seminars and serve as subject-matter experts on a variety of career issues. They have earned several distinguished professional credentials – Master Resume Writer (MRW), Credentialed Career Master (CCM), Job and Career Transition Coach (JCTC), Certified Professional Resume Writer (CPRW), and Certified Employment Interview Coach (CEIP).

Contents

About This Book

Never before in our working lives has the executive job search market been so brazenly fierce and competitive. For every top-level management and executive position there are scores, sometimes hundreds, of applicants, many of whom have excellent qualifications and track records of accomplishment in senior positions. It's a tough market, but one for which you can powerfully position yourself and one that you can successfully penetrate.

Having an outstanding executive resume is a given in these turbulent times. The "stable" company of today is the acquisition of tomorrow, and with any acquisition, merger, IPO, change in ownership, expansion, reorganization, or other major initiative, there will be change. No matter how secure you believe yourself to be in your current position, the truth is that you never know what will happen, and, therefore, you must always be prepared.

Now, ask yourself what you can do beyond the traditional executive resume to distinguish yourself from the crowd of competitors all vying for the same positions. The answer to that question is what this book is all about … the portfolio of executive career documents that you can prepare that will get you noticed and not passed over. These are the documents that savvy executive job seekers are using … job seekers who are getting the interviews and winning the offers.

Consider adding these documents to your resume to create an entire suite of career marketing documents and give yourself a truly competitive career advantage:

- Executive Resume
- Networking Resume
- PowerPoint Resume
- Career Biography/Executive Biography
- Leadership Profile
- Technology Profile
- Marketing Profile
- Training Addendum
- Resume Addendum

- Achievement Summary
- Executive Branding Statement
- Job Proposal
- Special Report
- Reference Dossier
- Executive Cover Letter
- Thank-You Letter
- Web Portfolio

This book will explore these documents in depth, giving you the information you need to create your own and sharing top-flight samples for your review. Once you understand their valuable use in executive job search, you'll wonder how you ever managed your career without them.

CHAPTER 1

The Gateway To Executive Job Search:
Fundamentals of Resume Writing and Job Search That Every Executive Must Know

Open the Gate and Enter

You are about to enter the gateway to executive job search. We're sure you've been there before, because it is extremely unlikely that you've been in the same position or with the same company for a lengthy period of time ... 10, 20, or more years. Those days are long since gone—days when you would be hired in your early twenties, advance through the ranks with one, maybe two, companies, and continue to work there until you retired. It was safe, secure, and comfortable, and there were few if any worries about layoffs, downsizings, reengineerings, reorganizations, merger and acquisition integrations, and the like. Your career life was much simpler then. You knew where you were headed, and most people were satisfied with that.

In 2006 and beyond, it's time to forget all of that! We now live and work in a world of volatility and constant change. Companies are reinventing themselves, new companies are emerging at an unprecedented rate, and globalization has forever changed the entire employment landscape. It's remarkably exciting and offers a limitless range of senior management and executive-level opportunities like we've never seen before. It's a great time to be in the prime of your career, ready and able to take on new challenges, meet new objectives, and deliver impressive results!

What has also changed just as radically is the competitiveness of executive job search. Twenty years ago, an advertisement in the *Atlanta Journal & Constitution* for a CEO of a food manufacturing plant would have generated an average of 50-100 responses. Today, that number may top 500 or even more. Why?

1. **Simply put, there are more people in the job market than ever before as the population of the U.S. and countries worldwide continues to expand.** This is further compounded by the fact that the baby boomer generation and the generation immediately following have saturated the job market over the past two decades. It is predicted by many experts that in

10 to 20 years there will be a significant shortage of workforce talent. However, that is not the current situation or the situation that you will face in the immediate future. Chances are that during your lifetime, the employment market will remain extremely competitive due, in large part, to the sheer numbers of workers (including senior managers and executives).

2. **The phenomenal changes that have occurred in the job market over the past 10-15 years have had a dramatic and sustained impact.** Who ever would have thought that such prominent companies as Enron, Kmart, and Ericsson would be out of business or absorbed into other companies? As we've experienced mergers, acquisitions, reorganizations, downsizings, and other corporate initiatives, our employment market has changed forever. Opportunities do abound, but they are generally not with the large corporations of the past. Rather, opportunities exist in small to mid-size organizations that have survived the corporate decimation of years past and are now poised for strong and steady growth.

3. **Industries have changed, some have disappeared, and other completely new ones have been invented.** Twenty years ago, we could not have imagined some of today's burgeoning industries such as webcasting and online commerce. Successful career management means responding to these changes, learning new skills, experiencing new opportunities, and positioning yourself for opportunities in high-growth industries. Consider the aerospace engineers of 20 years ago. If they did not immerse themselves in new and expanding industries, they most likely would have found themselves out of work along with thousands of others who were impacted during the massive downsizing of the aerospace industry. It is your responsibility to stay on the edge of industry change and innovation.

4. **People are willing to relocate at a moment's notice for an excellent career opportunity.** In years past, that was not the case. People tended to remain in the areas in which they were raised and/or educated, and the number of people relocating was at a minimum. Another unique characteristic of recent generations, many families are willing to live apart for career and/or educational opportunities. Today, people are constantly relocating for the right career opportunity, and "bicoastal marriages" that were extremely rare in the past are becoming increasingly commonplace.

5. **The technology revolution that we've experienced during our lifetime has had a dramatic effect on the entire world of job search.** When it is as easy as pressing a few keys to email a resume to a company, to a recruiter, or in response to an ad, people apply to many more jobs than they have in the past. As a result, employers are flooded with resumes, and one of their first steps is to rigorously weed out anyone who is not a perfect match.

Are You Prepared?

The first question to ask yourself before you begin to launch your search campaign is, "Are you prepared?" Just as with any other project you take on, it is essential that you be fully prepared and organized, with a defined purpose and plan of action. Otherwise, more often than not, you will find yourself wasting precious time and making few strides forward in your job search.

The U.S. Bureau of Labor Statistics states that the average executive job search can last six months or more. Hopefully, you will be one of the fortunate few whose job search moves along more quickly and you will be able to secure a great new opportunity in less time. However, assuming that the average six-month period is what it will take, you certainly do not want to find yourself in a position where you are wasting any time, effort, money, or other resources.

To be fully prepared to launch your executive job search, pay close attention to these four critical action items:

1. **A clear definition of your career objective**—the type of position that you're most interested in, the industry in which you wish to work, the type of company that you want to be employed with, the challenges and opportunities you are seeking, and more. It is virtually impossible to launch an effective executive job search without having a clear and concise understanding of the type or types of positions that you are most interested in. Your objective dictates virtually everything about your job search—how you will "package" yourself (more specifically, what information you will highlight in your resume and other career marketing documents), where you will look for positions (your company, industry, and geographic preferences), and how you will pursue them (the specific job search strategies you will employ).

2. **A clear strategy for how to present yourself** to make you an attractive candidate to your prospective hiring audience (the companies that you want to work for and the executives, owners, and/or investors who will be making the hiring decisions). Today, this is often referred to as branding—communicating your own personal value. But before you can begin to determine your brand, you must know "who" you are and how you want to be perceived in the market.

   Consider this ... a VP of Sales looking to continue as a senior sales executive might create a brand that communicates his unique sales leadership talents (e.g., Senior Sales Executive building new markets and driving double-digit revenue growth). Conversely, if that same VP of Sales is looking for a position in general business management, his brand will be entirely different (e.g., Senior Business Executive creating market value, new revenue streams, and new profit centers). Knowing "who" you are is critical to creating the right brand that will competitively distinguish you in the market.

3. **A clear marketing plan for how to position yourself,** conduct your job search, and successfully compete against other well-qualified candidates. Today's full-blown executive job search requires an integrated marketing approach to position yourself in front of the right companies and hiring executives where your opportunities for employment will be best. When you're planning your search campaign, you'll want to consider a combination of the following job search tools, strategies, programs, and activities to ensure that you are tapping all potential markets and positions:

   - Networking (the single best job search strategy)
   - Advertisements and job postings (print and online)
   - Online resume postings
   - Targeted mailings to companies (print and/or email)*
   - Targeted mailings to recruiters (email recommended)*
   - Targeted mailings to venture capital firms and investor groups (print and/or email)*

   *NOTE: Targeted mailings means just that—targeted, not mass mailings. If you are considering a mailing campaign, the single most critical factor impacting your response rate is your selection of the right target companies, recruiters, and/or venture capital firms. Mailings work best when you are positioning yourself in front of an audience that would be most interested in a candidate with your qualifications. The further you stretch beyond your core expertise, the more difficult it will be to attract a recruiter's or prospective employer's interest.

4. **An executive career marketing portfolio** that will include your resume and may contain various other career marketing documents (e.g., executive career biography, leadership profile, achievement summary, reference dossier). You'll read much more about these documents later in this chapter and throughout the remainder of this book. In fact, that's what this book is all about—demonstrating how to create powerful, well-positioned career marketing documents beyond just an executive resume. And, most important, you'll learn that these documents must be written to support your **current** career objectives, which may or may not coincide with your previous career experience.

   Consider the senior-level executive whose entire career has been in purchasing, logistics, and supply chain management. If her goal is to continue in a similar position, her achievement summary will focus primarily on her successes in those fields. Her reference dossier will include testimonials and letters verifying her relevant contributions, and her career biography will paint the picture of a talented, senior-level purchasing executive. Conversely, if her objective is to transition into a plant operations management position, purchasing and logistics will be just a few of the many management achievements she will highlight in her achievement summary and other career marketing documents. She'll also include information about her success in operations management, technology, training, team leadership, and more.

Putting the Pieces Together

To understand how essential each of the previous four items are, how interrelated to each other they are, and how they will impact every aspect of your job search, let's compare the job search campaigns of two very qualified executives with totally different career paths and totally different objectives.

CANDIDATE #1:	Greg is a 45-year-old Director of Manufacturing Operations with a stellar record of employment with three high-growth computer hardware companies where he has delivered double-digit revenue and profit growth within intensely competitive global markets.
Objective:	*Greg is very clear about his current objective: namely, a similar position — at a higher level — within the same industry. He will consider relocating anywhere along the Eastern seaboard for the right opportunity.*
Strategy:	Greg's #1 strategy is to position himself as a well-qualified, results-driven, senior-level manufacturing executive. As such, his resume and other career marketing documents will focus almost exclusively on his past performance, positions, core management responsibilities, project highlights, and achievements, which, as we all know, are indicative of his future performance and success. He will use a chronological format for his resume that clearly defines the scope of responsibility of each of his positions and his track record of results (e.g., revenue growth, profit improvement, cost reduction, new product development, quality improvement, productivity and efficiency gains, technology implementations, employee leadership performance). Because he is writing to a similar type of company, anyone reviewing Greg's resume and his other career marketing documents should easily be able to understand his contributions and the value he brings to his next employer.
Marketing Plan:	Because Greg is very definite about the type of position and type of company that he is interested in, his marketing plan is very straightforward. Like any savvy executive job seeker, Greg will launch his search with an extensive networking campaign, hoping to leverage his network contacts to uncover unadvertised opportunities. In addition, through extensive research, he will identify the top manufacturers along the Eastern seaboard and then contact the most senior ex-

ecutive at each company (CEO, COO, Chairman of the Board, etc.). In addition, he will contact executive recruiters who specialize in placing senior executives within computer hardware manufacturing companies. Finally, he will dedicate a few hours each week to reviewing online job postings and print advertisements to identify appropriate opportunities. Because his current employer does not know that Greg is pursuing new opportunities, he will not be posting his resume on any job boards so that he can keep his search confidential.

Career Marketing Portfolio:

Greg's career marketing portfolio will consist of an executive resume, a networking resume (abbreviated version to forward to his networking contacts), an executive cover letter (with different versions for use when responding to advertisements, contacting companies, and contacting recruiters), a web portfolio, a leadership profile (a great addition to further substantiate his strong leadership performance), an achievement summary (to further delineate all of his achievements over the years), and a reference dossier (complete with reference letters and full contact information). The web portfolio is particularly important for Greg because he will be looking for opportunities in the high-tech industry of computer hardware manufacturing. Although Greg is not proclaiming himself a programmer, website designer, or software engineer, a web portfolio will clearly demonstrate that he is technologically savvy, a must for anyone in a high-tech industry.

CANDIDATE #2:

Leslie is a 48-year-old Vice President of North American Sales with a major pharmaceutical company. She has been employed with the same company throughout her entire professional career and has earned countless promotions and management awards for her outstanding leadership skills and revenue contributions. However, at this point in her career, she is dissatisfied and wants to leave the industry.

Objective:

Leslie wants to remain in an executive-level sales leadership position, but her industry and geographic preferences are wide open. What is motivating her to make a career change is her desire to tackle new challenges, and she is willing to relocate anywhere within reason to accept such an opportunity.

Strategy:

Leslie's goal is to position herself as a well-qualified sales leader with outstanding skills in sales recruitment and training, nationwide field sales management, customer relationship management, key account development, executive sales presentations, sales negotiations, and sales closings. Because Leslie is unsure of the types of companies and industries to which she will be applying, she will prepare a functional resume that allows her to highlight the wealth of her experience and accomplishments while downplaying the fact that all of her career has been with one pharmaceutical company. The functional resume format is best to use in this situation because it will allow Leslie to isolate her most notable executive sales skills, experiences, and accomplishments from the environment in which they were acquired. Anyone reviewing Leslie's resume will be able to quickly identify her transferable talents and competencies, and not be distracted by the fact that they have all been acquired within the same corporate environment.

Marketing Plan:

Because she is looking at a vast number of sales leadership opportunities, Leslie's marketing plan will be very diverse in scope. She is not bound by geography or industry and, therefore, can apply to virtually any company anywhere in the U.S. As such, she will be utilizing a job search marketing campaign that integrates all core job search channels including networking (the single best strategy to identify hidden opportunities), ad responses, online job postings, online resume postings, and targeted mailings to recruiters specializing in the placement of sales executives regardless of particular industry. She may also consider a small mailing and phone-call campaign to companies that she is particularly interested in working for once she has identified the name and contact information for the senior hiring decision-maker at that organization. Because Leslie's employer knows that she is leaving the company, there is no negative consequence of posting her resume on executive job boards for review by prospective employers.

Career Marketing Portfolio:

Leslie's career marketing portfolio will consist of an executive resume, a networking resume (abbreviated version to forward to her networking contacts), several versions of an executive cover letter (edited to meet the hiring requirements of each particular company that she contacts), an achievement summary (to further highlight her powerful record of sales performance), an executive branding statement (to clearly distinguish her unique sales and customer relationship management brand), and a training addendum (to outline the hundreds of hours of sales, marketing, and leadership training that she has completed). Leslie will use these various documents throughout her search as appropriate in any number of situations.

As you can see from the previous examples, Objective, Strategy, Marketing Plan, and Executive Career Marketing Communications are intimately intertwined and must be the foundation for every successful job search. How can you even begin to develop your Strategy, Marketing Plan, or Marketing Communications if you have not yet clearly defined your Objective? The answer is simple ... you cannot.

Taking it one step further, suppose you have determined your Objective and your Strategy. Can you now just haphazardly launch your search campaign or simply put together a quick resume? Of course not! Rather, you must critically evaluate your Objective and your Strategy, then use that information to determine what your Marketing Plan should be to identify the right opportunities for a candidate with your qualifications and current goals. In addition, you must then create Career Marketing Communications that will effectively position you to meet your strategic objectives for how you wish to be perceived by the hiring audience.

In summary, executive job search requires clarity—clarity in plan and purpose (Objective), presentation (Strategy), positioning (Marketing Plan), and action (Career Marketing Communications). We cannot stress enough how critical these first few steps are to planning and orchestrating a successful executive job search campaign. We've experienced it with thousands of job seekers whom we've counseled, coached, and supported over the past 20 years, and we know from experience that the executives who are most successful in their searches are those who have clarity and direction to guide their campaigns. Take the time that is necessary to uncover these four critical items for yourself and you'll be amazed at how much more efficiently and expeditiously your search campaign moves forward.

The Final Product

Once you have put all the pieces together for your executive job search campaign—your Objective, Strategy, Market Plan, and portfolio of Career Marketing Communications—it will be of tremendous value to you to integrate it all into one document —your Career Marketing Plan. Then, you'll have a single source to which you can refer. Here's an outstanding example of such a product prepared by our colleague, Arnold Boldt of Arnold-Smith Associates in Rochester, NY. (See page 206 for contact information.)

NOTE: If you would like to see the resume and the achievement summary for this executive job seeker, Hillary James Ingraham, please refer to pages 100-102.

CAREER MARKETING PLAN
Hillary James Ingraham

PROFESSIONAL OBJECTIVE: Find a technology company (mid-size to large) that needs motivated leadership, working cross-functionally to support the development of the strategic direction, with the ability to drive the implementation of strategy as Senior Sales and Marketing Executive or General Manager of a business unit.

Preferred Work Functions:
- Sales
- Creating New Revenue Enablers
- Marketing
- Leading an Integrated Organization

Representative Job Titles:
- Vice President Sales and Marketing
- Vice President Sales
- Vice President Marketing
- Business Unit General Manager

POSITIONING STATEMENT: I am a Senior Executive with extensive expertise as a General Manager with P&L responsibilities and Global Sales and Marketing expertise in both Fortune 100 and small global business environments in the technology field. I was successful in the Fortune 100 firm in both mainstream assignments with large revenue responsibilities and start-up units that became mainstream. I accepted the most challenging assignments that others would consider impossible and delivered benchmark results. One of my strengths is quickly building an organization to implement and create innovative solutions in high-stakes situations.

HOW I'M DIFFERENT:

People Competencies	Business Competencies
• Customer Focused—Understand what it means	• Delivering Results in Tough Situations
• People Development—Know how	• Leading Global Sales and Marketing Teams
• Cross-Functional Teamwork—Extensive training	• Designing/Executing Integrated Marketing Plans
• Take-Charge Leader—Know how to lead and take feedback	• Analyzing Markets
• Organizational Design and Building for Implementation—Have done it	• Directing Product Marketing
• Self-Directed Motivator—Knowledge of team enablement	• Improving Sales Management Process
	• Selling to Major Accounts (Fortune 100)
	• Developing and Managing Channels
	• Achieving P&L Targets

TARGET GEOGRAPHIC MARKETS: North Carolina • Northern or Southern California • Seattle, Washington

TYPES OF INDUSTRIES: High Technology • Business Services • Industrial Manufacturing • Financial Services

SIZE OF ORGANIZATION: Mid-size to Large

ORGANIZATIONAL CULTURE: High Integrity • Customer Focused • Creative • Team Wins • People Oriented • Listen to Input and Feedback

TARGET COMPANIES:

A Priority	B Priority	C Priority
Allergan	AtlanticProTech	Countrywide Financial
Beckman Coulter	Diedrich Coffee	Fluor
Broadcom	ICN Pharmaceutical	Water Pik
Epicor	Ingram Micro	West Corporation
FileNet	MicroTech Software	X-Technologies Unlimited
TechWise	Power Wave	
UniTech	Quick Silver	
Western Digital	Rainbow Technologies	

What This Book is All About

Walk into any bookstore or shop any online bookseller today, and you will find scores of books on resume writing. In fact, many of these books have been written by one or both of us during the past several years. But up until now there has been no single book on the market that addresses the full range of documents that can be included in an executive career marketing portfolio. These documents include:

- Executive Resume
- Networking Resume
- PowerPoint Resume
- Executive Career Biography
- Leadership Profile
- Technology Profile
- Marketing Profile
- Training Addendum
- Resume Addendum
- Achievement Summary
- Executive Branding Statement
- Job Proposal
- Special Report
- Reference Dossier
- Executive Cover Letter
- Thank-You Letter
- Web Portfolio

This book will teach you how to strategically write and design these powerful, executive-level career marketing communications—documents that are distinctive, upscale, unique, and competitive. When you have your full executive career marketing portfolio in hand, you'll find yourself in a wonderfully advantageous position in the executive job search market. New doors will begin to open, people will extend you the opportunity for interviews, and you'll find yourself sifting through the many offers you've received to determine which one is right for you!

CHAPTER 2

You Are Your Brand

Clarity, Strategy, and Market Positioning

In Chapter 1, we outlined the four critical action items required to launch an executive job search campaign:

1. **A clear definition** of your career objective—the type of position that you're most interested in, the industry in which you wish to work, the type of company that you want to be employed with, the challenges and opportunities you are seeking, and more.

2. **A clear strategy** for how to present yourself to make you an attractive candidate to your prospective hiring audience (the companies you want to work for and the executives, owners, and/or investors who will be making the hiring decisions).

3. **A clear marketing plan** for how to position yourself in the market, conduct your job search, and successfully compete against other well-qualified candidates.

4. **An executive career marketing portfolio** that will include your resume and various other career marketing documents (e.g., executive career biography, leadership profile, achievement summary, reference dossier).

Now, looking at those items in combination, several concepts become immediately apparent—things that are critical to the success of your entire career marketing campaign.

Defining Your Strategic Message and Market Position

If you were to ask us what we consider the single most important factor in positioning yourself for a successful executive search, we would both agree that strategy is THE key. Who you are, who you want to be (objective), your age, and your salary requirements are the four factors that, when combined, will help you to quickly and accurately identify the optimum strategy for how to market and position yourself.

Suppose, for example, that you're a 32-year-old pharmaceutical sales representative making $75,000 a year (plus bonus) and are now interested in pursuing other field sales positions within either the pharmaceutical or medical device industry. The strategic message you want to communicate to a prospective employer is that you're a top sales producer with a strong record of performance in increasing revenues, capturing key accounts, and building awareness within new business markets. By positioning yourself as a "Top Sales Producer and Key Account Manager," you've instantly communicated your value and established your market position (also known as your brand).

Now, compare that example with the following. In this scenario you're a 52-year-old sales executive in the computer software industry making $200,000 a year (plus bonus) and are now interested in pursuing sales management and leadership positions within a similar industry. In this instance, the strategic message you want to communicate to a prospective employer is that you offer a strong combination of experience and success in sales leadership, key account management, territory management, sales training, and team leadership. By positioning yourself as a "Senior Sales Management and Leadership Executive in Software and Technology Industries," you've instantly communicated your value and established your individual brand.

To help you identify your strategy, take a moment to look objectively at your past career experience and your current career goals. Are they the same? Are they at a higher level? Are you considering a career change? Are you thinking about a change in industry? All of these questions and more are important to answer when defining your strategic market and the specific job search actions you will engage in to tap into that market. Strategy will drive your entire job search process, from what you include in your resume, to the types of positions you will apply for, to the selection of recruiters that you will contact, and much more.

Clarity in Your Message

You must be clear about "who" you are and be certain that your entire campaign focuses on that message. Thus, you must have clarity in your plan and purpose (your objective), clarity in strategy (how you want to be perceived), clarity in market positioning (how and where to conduct your job search), and clarity in communications (the quality of your executive resume and career marketing communications).

Consistency in Your Message

Your message must be consistent from one phase of your search to another. If your objective is a position as a Senior Financial Executive, then your strategy must be to brand yourself as such. Your marketing plan will concentrate on identifying and capturing senior-level financial positions, and your resume and entire career marketing portfolio will boldly communicate the fact that you are a talented financial executive who brings value, integrity, leadership talents, and bottom-line financial results.

Communicating Your Message

Job search is NOT the time for modesty! When you are writing your resume and other career marketing communications, your objective is to create documents that communicate a hard-hitting, clear, consistent, and strategic presentation of your unique value — your brand. Consider the following characteristics of well-crafted executive job search documents. They are:

- Sales and marketing tools written to sell you — the executive job seeker — into your next position.
- Distinctive communications that present a clear and concise picture of who you are and the value you bring to an organization.
- Dynamic documents that clearly communicate your professional skills, qualifications, knowledge, talents, accomplishments, and successes.
- Visually attractive presentations that communicate a professional image.

In summary, all of the information presented in this chapter boils down to just one thing — clearly defining your value and then creating/promoting your unique brand within the executive job search market. Branding, a well-known concept as it relates to products, technologies, services, and companies, is a relatively new idea in the context of executive job search. As the market has become increasingly competitive and individuals are constantly searching for new strategies and techniques to differentiate themselves, executive branding has begun to emerge as a critical tool in facilitating successful search campaigns.

Building Your Brand

There is no better way to introduce you to the concept of personal branding as it relates to executive job search than to begin with an excellent article by one of our most talented and respected colleagues, Deborah Wile Dib of Advantage Resumes / Executive Power Coach in New York.

Seven Steps to a Branded Executive Resume That Attracts Interviews! *by Deborah Wile Dib*

Today's most successful executives are branded commodities — visible and respected leaders with a unique selling point, a marketable value proposition, and a history of innovation, contribution, and thought leadership. These leaders understand the power of branding and its ability to help them outcompete for the best jobs and best compensation. They know that branding is no longer an option in high-stakes executive careers where personal branding and a personally branded resume are critical tools for growth and career control.

Use these seven steps to produce an interview-generating resume that reflects your brand, proves your value, and markets your potential!

1. **Understand that the new branded resume must:**

   - ❑ Be built around a strong personal brand and value proposition.
   - ❑ Be accomplishment driven—show a record of profit-making and cost-saving accomplishments that prove past successes and predict future contributions.
   - ❑ Show intangible and tangible value.
   - ❑ Build chemistry and show at least a dash of charisma (the type that gets people motivated and excited to do seemingly impossible work).
   - ❑ Be long enough to deliver the critical information that decision makers need to make an initial assessment of suitability.
   - ❑ Demonstrate leadership, vision, change management, thought leadership, courage (and ability to make and implement tough decisions), ethics and integrity (critical in today's executive market), and the ability to execute.
   - ❑ Prove agility and flexibility to proactively meet the lightning-fast changes in the marketplace and to create and deliver shareholder/stakeholder value.

2. **Think about these positioning questions:**

   - ❑ **Gap Analysis**—What do employers in my market need/want? Do I have it? How can I prove it?
   - ❑ **Benefit/Differentiator**—Why hire me? What can I offer that my competition can't?
   - ❑ **$$**—How have I/will I create growth, profit, and shareholder value?
   - ❑ **Chemistry**—What is my emotional appeal and culture fit?
   - ❑ **Irresistible**—What *one* thing could seal the deal?

3. **Then develop preliminary resume and interview content using these and other brand-defining questions to guide you:**

   - ❑ What are my top five business/leadership skills?
   - ❑ What have I done that best demonstrates each of those skills with bottom-line, strategic performance?
   - ❑ Can I write CARS (challenge/action/result/strategic importance) success studies of each of these and then speak of them in a concise, enthusiastic, and compelling manner?
   - ❑ What do my peers and staff routinely say about me? Do I have a reputation in the marketplace, press, media, etc? What is it?
   - ❑ What parts of my job do I love? Do my best accomplishments reflect that enjoyment?
   - ❑ What is my management style? How do I interact with my team, core management group, or board of directors?
   - ❑ Do my accomplishments and skills have value in my target market?
   - ❑ Can I answer the question "Why should I hire you?" with a compelling value proposition that makes me irresistible to my targeted employers?

4. **Begin the resume with a profile that is a response-generating sales tool, not a cluster of clichéd phrases. Your profile:**

   - ❑ Must be focused around personal branding and the target market.
   - ❑ Must show uniqueness with interest, vigor, excitement, and a sense of possibility and personality.
   - ❑ Should have a verbal "executive snapshot" with basic information in one or two sentences—years and type of experience, industry focus, types of companies, etc.
   - ❑ Has to strongly predict future success and do that based on solid examples of current and past successes.
   - ❑ Should have a cluster of three or so accomplishments that tie in with the resume's target and strategy.
   - ❑ Will often give a sense of work style and ideals—a mission statement about what makes you an outstanding executive.

5. **Compose body copy that is strategic, tight, and clean with concise, telescopic writing. Your copy should:**

   - ❑ Be strategic and aligned with the needs of the marketplace.
   - ❑ Not list every job and every nuance of every job, BUT it should *always* resonate with executive accomplishment—leadership, strategy, problem solving, change management, thought leadership, agility, and more.
   - ❑ Be filled with "executive speak"—the industry-specific language that executives in your industry use. This creates credibility. The lack of it creates concern.
   - ❑ Follow each company listing with a one- or two-line snapshot of the firm's size, main scope, marketplace position, etc. This frames the executive's place and scope in that company.
   - ❑ Have a descriptor for each job or position cluster that gives the "nuts and bolts" information on the job—revenue managed, budgets created/managed, direct and indirect reports, reporting lines (example: "Reported directly to the CEO."). Five or so areas should do it—no laundry lists needed!

6. **Build your employment case with a resume of relevant "WOW" accomplishments. Your accomplishments should:**

   - ❑ Be the main content of your resume—a great resume is light on "responsible for" skills and heavy on "what I did with what I was responsible for" accomplishments.
   - ❑ Be clustered in segments that follow two or three branding concepts—the brand attributes that reflect you and will mean the most to the reader. For example, a CIO might have a cluster of accomplishments under the heading "Major Technology Projects & Contributions" and another cluster under "Strategic Business Management."

❏ Be "front-loaded" with the main "grabber" at the beginning of the sentence. Decide what that key "WOW" factor is. Is it a big number result, or is it the thing that led to the result?

❏ Define and support the "connectors" in a career transition, making the case for your suitability for the new target.

7. **Be quality-driven! Plan on multiple revisions. Be sure to review and determine/check/ decide:**

❏ Are descriptions clear?

❏ Is there a better way to organize information?

❏ Be sure accomplishments are front-loaded.

❏ Is branding clear and consistent with a defined differentiator?

❏ Are there enough numbers and ROI facts—have you "dollarized" your contributions?

❏ Is there a clear message of value creation—profit building, change management, etc.?

❏ Is there enough punch to get interest for an interview?

❏ Is the format appropriate? Elegant? Clean? Readable?

❏ Can you truly say you've done your best for yourself and that you are fully pleased with the result?

Deb Dib is a certified career management coach, certified personal brand strategist, nationally certified resume writer and featured contributor to 21+ career books. She is a careers industry leader who has delivered knowledge and power to senior executives at the C-suite, president, V, and director levels since 1989. www.executivepowercoach.com; email: deborah.dib@advantage resumes.com

Before we move on from Deb's article on executive branding as it relates to resume strategy, design, and writing, it is important to note that these same concepts are just as critical when you are developing all of the other materials in your executive career marketing portfolio (e.g., leadership profiles, career biographies, accomplishment summaries, technology profiles). Your brand must be constant, from one document to the next, so that the entire portfolio of your materials communicates the same message of brand value, accomplishment, and performance.

As you review all of the samples in this book, you will note that for each executive job seeker profiled, all of his/her materials are clear and consistent in delivering the message, *"This is who I am, this is my brand, these are my most notable achievements, and, in sum, this is the value I bring to your organization."*

Building Your Brand Through Nontraditional Channels

Your overall performance in your management and executive positions is the foundation upon which you have built your brand and established yourself within the market. In addition, there are several other indirect marketing efforts that you can engage in that will further solidify your brand and provide you with a strong and sustainable market position. Although none of these activities will necessarily generate a job interview or offer today, they are vital to your long-term career management efforts. Specifically, these activities will:

- Strengthen your credibility.
- Increase your professional visibility.
- Expand your market reach and recognition.
- Provide you with a distinct advantage over your competition.

Writing Articles

Years ago, getting articles published could be quite difficult. Over the past few years, however, as the Internet has exploded, the opportunities for publishing have increased remarkably. Thousands and thousands of websites are constantly searching for content; many will be happy to post your articles to increase their online intellectual property and perceived value to their site visitors. Certain websites will pay for content while others do not. However, your purpose in writing these articles is not to make a few hundred bucks here and there. You are writing them to communicate your expertise and increase your name recognition/visibility.

Because there are so very many websites, you must use some discretion in publishing online to be sure that your articles are on the right websites. For example, if you're a Quality Assurance Executive, consider submitting an article to the ASQ (American Society for Quality) website. If you're a Senior Marketing Executive, try the American Marketing Association's website. Publishing on an obscure site that no one ever reads may not be worth the effort and will not deliver the value that you may be anticipating; however, you might find that you need to establish a track record as a writer before your work will be accepted by the better-known sites. If this is the case, then do your very best work for the lesser-known sites and let those articles serve as your entrée to more highly visible and well-recognized sites.

Speaking at Professional Meetings and Conferences

There is little more that you can do to establish your credibility than to present at a professional conference or meeting. We all know that "only experts speak," so by presenting at these types of public events, you are immediately communicating the message that you are an expert. Maybe someone in the audience will return to the office and tell the CEO that they just heard a great presentation on new trends in integrated logistics management. Or perhaps the CEO himself will be in the audience, impressed with your knowledge and your ability to speak publicly. Next time he's in the market for a Logistics Executive, who will be the first to come to mind? Use public speaking platforms as a vehicle to increase your market visibility and further substantiate your brand differentiation.

Sharing Market, Product, Technology, and Industry Experience

Often, giving something away is a great way to earn recognition. Suppose you've devoted the past six years of your career to transitioning start-up health care ventures into profitable, well-established corporations. Through this experience, you've learned the "tricks of the trade." Why not communicate that information to other health care organizations in need of strong developmental and organizational leadership? Consider writing a short bulletin on "The Top 10 Strategies for Transitioning From Start-Up to Profitability Within Today's Competitive Health Care Market." Send that document out to 10, 20, or 50 companies you would be interested in working for, without even mentioning that you're in the market for a new position. By doing so, you've clearly demonstrated that you bring value to the organization and are an expert in your chosen profession or industry. In many instances, they'll contact you immediately to establish connections and perhaps inquire as to your availability! One word of warning ... be sure that you are sharing NEW knowledge and not simply reiterating what everyone in the industry already knows.

Serving on Boards of Directors, Committees, Task Forces, and Leadership Councils

It is vital to make yourself visible within your professional community. You can do this through high-level board affiliations or through volunteer contributions to professional associations, executive committees, and the like. These efforts serve to increase your market visibility and expand your network of contacts. It might be that both you and the president of Turner Technology serve on the task force of a new technology R&D venture. What a tremendous opportunity for you to develop a collegial relationship that could serve you both well over the years to come. Even community-based associations can be valuable in terms of developing relationships with civic and industry leaders who, in turn, may be the link to executive opportunities you may not be aware of.

The above activities will give you a recognizable brand with strong market presence and should not be taken lightly. Although they will require some work, time, and effort, the rewards to be gained are tremendous. Evaluate each of the activities, determine which are appropriate for you, your career, and your search campaign, and then initiate the efforts necessary to establish the contacts, book the events, develop the article content, and proactively transition yourself into a visible executive brand within your industry and/or profession.

CHAPTER 3

Your Executive Job Search Guide: Critical Information Every Job Seeker Must Know

Before we delve any further into how to strategize, design, and write your executive resume and all of your other career marketing documents, it is essential that we first explore several critical items about executive job search in general. Consider this section your job search primer, giving you fundamental, valuable information to help you plan and conduct a successful search campaign. Some of these concepts may be familiar to you; others will not. Pay close attention, for all are valuable in helping you to accelerate your search campaign, generate more interviews, and get more offers.

Sell It to Me; Don't Tell It to Me

When you boil it down to the basics, job search really is nothing more than sales and marketing. You have a product to sell—yourself—and you want to do all that you can to make your product as attractive as possible to your buying audience. Think of yourself much like the new, most expensive PDA on the shelf at Radio Shack. You're surrounded by four other models of PDAs, all of which are good, but not quite as good as you are and certainly not with the same array of talents/capabilities. To get noticed on that shelf, you must have the best packaging, best merchandising, and best display possible.

Now, picture yourself as the product and the same concepts hold true. You want the best packaging (resume and job search materials), best merchandising (integrated job search campaign), and best display (interviewing expertise). One of the most critical items in giving you that competitive advantage over all of the other "products" is your ability to "sell" your expertise rather than just "tell" your background. Here's a quick and easy example:

- "Tell" … Full management responsibility for one of Ryder Dedicated Logistics Company's largest warehousing operations. Achieved all financial objectives.

- "Sell" ... Full strategic planning, operating, marketing, and P&L responsibility for a $225 million, 5-site, 260-employee, dedicated logistics and warehousing operation for Ryder Dedicated Logistics. Closed 2004 at 12% under expense budget and 22% over revenue goal to end the year with a 15% gain in net profit contribution.

Can you see the difference in impact when you "sell" the benefits of the product (you) as opposed to simply telling the features? Integrate the "sell-versus-tell" concept into all phases of your search—when writing your executive resume and other career marketing documents; when networking to identify new opportunities; when interviewing via phone, video, or in person; and in all of your job search follow-up activities. It will make a measurable difference in how your hiring audience perceives you and the number of opportunities and offers that come your way.

Executive Resume Formats

For as long as resumes have existed (particularly in their current state over the past 20 years), there has been an ongoing debate about the use and effectiveness of a chronological resume versus a functional resume versus the more recent, combination-style (hybrid) resume. To better understand the differences between them and to help you determine which is right for you, let's explore the pluses and minuses of all three.

Chronological resumes provide a step-by-step path through your career. Starting with your current or most recent position, chronological resumes are written backwards, from most recent to past, allowing you to put the emphasis on your current and most recent experiences. As you progress further back in your career, job descriptions are shorter with an emphasis on achievements and notable projects.

Chronological resumes are the resume style preferred by the vast majority of employers and recruiters. They are easy to read and understand, clearly communicating where you have worked and what you have done. Unless your particular situation is unusual, a chronological resume is generally the best career marketing tool for executive job seekers.

Functional resumes focus on the skills and qualifications you offer to a prospective employer. It is this type of information that is brought to the forefront and highlighted, while your employment experience is briefly mentioned at the end. Individuals who might consider a functional resume are career changers, professionals returning to work after an extended absence, individuals who have been in the job market for a lengthy period of time, or candidates who are 55+ years of age. If you fall into one of these categories or a related category, you will want to focus your resume on your specific expertise, qualifications, and competencies rather than the specific chronology of your employment experience.

Functional resumes are much less frequently used. Many corporate human resource professionals and recruiters look at these resumes with less interest, believing that the candidate is hiding something or attempting to "change reality." Be extremely careful if you decide this is the right style for you (which it might very well be), and be sure to include your complete job history at the end of your resume.

The most recent trend in resume writing is to combine the structure of the chronological resume with the skills focus of the functional resume. By starting your resume with a career summary, you can begin with a heavy focus on the qualifications and value you offer (functional approach), and then substantiate it with solid, well-written, and accomplishment-oriented position descriptions (chronological approach). Many of the resumes in this book reflect this new **combination-style (hybrid) resume**, which is well-received by both recruiters and corporate human resource professionals. Combination-style resumes give you the best of both worlds—an intense focus on your qualifications combined with the strength of a solid employment history. They are powerful marketing tools.

The Power of Keywords

You have probably read and heard a lot in recent years about keywords and their importance in job search. Keywords are critically important for executive job seekers, and the reason might surprise you.

Most people consider keywords important to integrate into their resumes, cover letters, and other job search communications because of the expanding use of resume scanning technology. For most job seekers, that is accurate. If you happen to be a 23-year-old recent college graduate applying for management training opportunities with major banking and financial institutions nationwide, the keywords you integrate into your resume are extremely important. In this situation, chances are that your resume will be scanned and a keyword search performed long before human eyes will ever review it or meet you. Keywords are used to evaluate candidates' skill sets to determine if they have the right qualifications for a particular position.

For senior managers and executives, however, scanning has much more limited applicability, particularly when you are going directly to companies for hiring opportunities. Chances are that human eyes are going to read your resume on many more occasions than electronic eyes. Executive recruiters, on the other hand, will tend to scan your resume into their system so that it is accessible to all recruiters within that organization. For the latter, keywords do become a more significant concern for executive job seekers.

With that said, it is certainly important that you integrate your keywords appropriately throughout your resume so that when scanning does become relevant to your search campaign, you are prepared. Note that keywords do not have to be integrated into one single section in your resume. Scanning technology will pick up your keywords and keyword phrases no matter where they are positioned in your resume (e.g., Career Summary, Professional Experience, Publications, Technical Qualifications, Project Highlights, Accomplishments & Results).

Where we believe keywords are of most value to executive job seekers is in the messages that they communicate. By using just one keyword or one keyword phrase, you are able to powerfully communicate a wealth of information. Suppose you included a sentence in your resume or executive career biography that mentioned your expertise in customer relationship management. With the use of that one phrase—customer relationship management—you are communicating to your reader that you may have experience in customer acquisition, customer service, product/service presentations, price negotiations, order fulfillment, key account relations, customer retention, customer satisfaction, and more. Let keywords work to your advantage by integrating them throughout all of your career marketing communications. Then, give them a try during your interviews and you will find they are equally powerful tools in verbally communicating the strength of your experience and the vast array of your executive talents.

Write in the First Person

All too often we come across executive resumes, cover letters, career profiles, achievement summaries, and more that are written in the third person. This is not our recommended strategy. Your job search is all about YOU and, therefore, must be written in the first person (while dropping the "I's" whenever possible). Here's a great example:

First Person: Revitalized non-performing sales region and restored to profitability within 10 months.

Third Person: John Smith revitalized a non-performing sales region and restored it to profitability within 10 months.

See the difference? In the first example, you are taking credit for and owning the achievement. In the second example, someone else—John Smith—is taking credit. The latter takes ownership away from you and is not the manner in which you want to present yourself during your executive search.

The Resume "Objective" Controversy

One of the greatest controversies in resume writing focuses on the use or omission of an Objective. There are three questions to ask yourself that will help you decide whether or not you need an Objective on your resume.

1. **Do you have a specific objective in mind?** A specific position? A specific industry? If so, you can include a focused Objective statement such as: "Seeking an upper-level management position in the Pharmaceutical R&D industry" or "President/CEO of an emerging telecommunications company." As you can see, each of these Objective statements clearly indicates the precise position the candidate is seeking.

2. **Is your objective constant?** Will your objective stay the same for virtually all positions you apply for and all the resumes you submit? If so, include a focused Objective such as that outlined in #1 above. If not, do not include an Objective. You do not want to have to edit your resume each and every time you send it. It's a time-consuming process and stalls the flow of resumes out your door.

3. **Is your objective unclear?** Are you considering a number of opportunities? Are you interested in a number of different industries? If your answer is YES, do not include an Objective statement, for it will be unfocused and communicate little of value. Think about an Objective such as: "Seeking a senior management position where I can lead a company to improved revenues and profits." Doesn't everyone want to help a company make money? These are useless words and add no value to your resume. They do not tell your reader who you are or what you are pursuing.

Remember, every time you forward a resume you will also be sending a cover letter. If you do not include an Objective statement on your resume, let your cover letter be the tool that communicates your objective in that specific situation to that specific employer or recruiter.

Following are three sample Objective formats you can choose from if you determine that an Objective is right for you.

PROFESSIONAL OBJECTIVE:

Challenging Executive Sales Management position in the Utilities Industry.

EXECUTIVE CAREER GOAL:

C-Level Executive Management position in International Commerce where I can apply my 15 years' experience in Investment Finance, International Banking, and International Trade.

OBJECTIVE: SUPPLY CHAIN EXECUTIVE — TECHNOLOGY INDUSTRY

For many executive job seekers, Objectives are simply not necessary. Consider this: When you write an Objective, you are telling your reader what you want **FROM** them. When you start your resume with an Executive Summary or Executive Career Profile, you are telling your reader what you can do **FOR** them, what value you bring to their organization, what expertise you have, and how well you have performed in the past. In both, you are writing about the same concepts, the same professions, or the same industries. However, the Career Profile is a more effective, more executive, and more hard-hitting strategy for catching your reader's attention and making an immediate connection. And isn't that the point of your resume? Your goal is to intrigue a prospective employer to (1) read your resume, (2) invite you for an interview, and (3) offer you a position.

To demonstrate this concept, compare the two examples below:

> Example #1:
> **PROFESSIONAL OBJECTIVE:** Senior-Level Corporate Financial Management Position

> Example #2:
> **EXECUTIVE CAREER PROFILE:**
>
> **Financial Management Executive** with a top-flight, 15-year career with Dow Chemical, American Express, and Microsoft. Expert in mergers, acquisitions, joint ventures, and international corporate development. Personally transacted more than $200 million in new enterprises, slashed $14 million from bottom-line operating costs, and contributed to a 33% increase in corporate valuation. Astute planner and negotiator. Wharton MBA.

In both of these examples, is it clear that the individual is seeking a senior-level financial management position? Yes, they are both communicating the same overall message—namely, that the candidate is a qualified finance executive.

Now, ask yourself which is a stronger presentation. Obviously, the Executive Career Profile is stronger. It is more dynamic, more substantive, and clearly communicates the success of the candidate. Finally, ask yourself if you started your resume with an Executive Career Profile as presented above, would you need an Objective that stated your goals? Probably not. The Career Profile paints a clear and concise picture of who you are. It is not necessary to include a statement above the Career Profile saying, "I want a job as a such-and-such."

Over Age 50?

If you are above age 50, you'll want to give some extra thought to how you will position yourself in your search campaign, particularly with regard to your resume and other career marketing communications. You certainly do not want to start your resume by announcing that you have 30, 35, or more years of experience. You might perceive that such a statement communicates you are an extremely well-qualified candidate, but in fact it can have the reverse impact and put you out of the running because the hiring company thinks you are "too old." This is particularly relevant for senior managers and executives who have been working for decades and are becoming increasingly concerned that their age may be thwarting their job search efforts.

First, and most important, let's get one thing straight: Chances are slim to none that a company is going to hire a CEO, CFO, or other senior executive who is only 30 years of age! That may happen in the rapidly expanding technology markets due largely to the technology expertise of our younger generations. However, most organizations that are recruiting for top-level talent are looking for candidates who have experience and who are not 30 or 35 years old. So, begin by letting yourself off the hook and realizing that your age is not necessarily a negative but, rather, a positive that demonstrates your years of experience and track record of success. That is what companies are looking for ... individuals who can deliver positive results today and in years to come.

With that said, let's take a fresh look at the "over-50" age issue and how you can best manage that during your search campaign. Most important, you must remember that your resume and other job search documents are NOT intended to tell your entire life story. Rather, they are to be used to sell the highlights of your career and your accomplishments, open doors, and generate interviews and offers. That's it! No resume or leadership profile is ever going to get you a job. If well crafted, however, it should get you an interview.

If you're 50 or older and concerned that your age is impeding your search, consider the following two strategies when writing your executive resume and other career marketing communications:

1. **Do not date your education.** Simply list your degrees and colleges. If prospective employers want to know when you graduated, they'll ask you during the interview. And, at that point, it's fine to divulge the information; you already have your foot in the door and your age won't be used to screen you out.

2. **Consider going back 15 years or so in your employment history**, or to where there is a natural break (e.g., different company, different position). Then, summarize your older experience briefly at the end so you can highlight the relevant and important information while downplaying specific dates. Here are three potential formats you can use that allow you to positively leverage different aspects of your earliest career experience:

   - **To highlight fast-track career promotion:** "Promoted through a series of increasingly responsible management positions with HyLab Technologies, a $200 million laser products R&D firm."

   - **To highlight the reputation of your employers:** "Previous professional experience includes several key management positions with DataTech, IBM, and HP."

   - **To highlight notable achievements:** "Reduced operating costs 22% in the first year and an additional 11% in the second year while HR Director for Chase Manhattan Bank's International Division."

Taking Your Resume and Career Marketing Documents Global

If you're considering international employment opportunities, then you must understand the following:

1. The words "resume" and "CV" (curriculum vitae) generally refer to the same thing—a document that highlights your professional and educational experience. The terms are often used interchangeably. When there is a difference, a CV is typically longer with

more detail about publications, speaking engagements, affiliations, continuing education, and the like.

2. Research each country to identify their standards for how to present your employment experience—in chronological order (from past to present) or reverse chronological (most recent to past). The latter is most often used in the U.S.; the former in many other countries. If no specific guidelines are recommended for a particular country, use reverse chronology.

3. Detail your specific educational credentials, licenses, and certifications if there is any possibility that these items will not be clearly understood in another country. This means including course/program name, university, location, numbers of course hours, and specific course highlights.

4. Be sure to use industry-specific and job-specific terminology that will be known the world over. These will most likely be referred to as keywords that are representative of both your profession and your industry.

5. If you are submitting your resume in English, be sure to find out if the country in which you're applying uses "American" English or "British" English. There is a significant difference in the spelling of many words. Note that U.S. companies use "American" English in all of their offices worldwide.

6. Include all of your foreign language skills as well as out-of-the-U.S. experiences (e.g., traveling, working, and/or living abroad). If you prepare your resume in a foreign language, be sure to also prepare one in English, because many companies will expect you to be able to conduct business in both their native language and in English.

7. If your resume is produced in a language other than English, be sure to have a native speaker of that language carefully review your resume. This will avoid the potential for major errors and ensure that your document is culturally correct.

8. Know that different countries use different size paper. For example, the paper standard in the U.S. is 8 ½ x 11 inches; the paper standard in Europe is 210 x 297 mm (known as "A-4"). Use the "page set up" function in your word processing software to select the correct size paper and automatically reformat your document. This is important whether you're mailing paper resumes or emailing electronic resumes.

9. Work permits and visa regulations vary greatly from country to country and may take months to acquire. Be thorough in investigating requirements for specific countries by contacting each country's embassy in the U.S. for detailed information. This process

will be expedited if (a) the country has a shortage of professionals with your particular skill set or (b) you are transferred to that country by your current employer.

Working abroad offers you a tremendous opportunity to strengthen and expand your professional skills and qualifications, while offering you and your family an outstanding cultural exchange experience. If you decide to pursue an international career track, know that flexibility, patience, and the willing acceptance of differing cultural and business norms will be vital to your success.

Networking That Works for You

Creating a structured plan and process is vital to any successful venture, whether launching a new business, orchestrating an organizational turnaround, or managing your job search networking campaign. It is critical that you clearly identify your market (your network contacts), develop a personalized network marketing plan, and build an administrative process/system to manage it all. Keeping track (whether on your computer or paper) of all of your contacts is critical or, inevitably, you'll misplace a name, forget to follow up when promised, and potentially miss out on a great opportunity.

First and foremost, however, you must remember the MOST IMPORTANT concept underlying the networking process:

> *Ask your network contacts for their HELP and other referrals, not for a job!*
> *People are delighted to help you; very few will have jobs to offer to you.*

Tier #1 Contacts

Contacts: Hottest prospects and people you know best (e.g., other executives and senior managers, current and past colleagues, current and past managers, vendors, consultants, recruiters with whom you have an established relationship, bankers, venture capitalists).

Process: More often than not, your initial contact with these individuals will be via phone … a quick call to announce that you're in the job market and would appreciate any advice, assistance, recommendations, referrals, and the like.

Follow-Up 1: At the end of each conversation, tell your contact that you'd like to send a resume and other material for them to have on file, and ask if they prefer mail, fax, or email. Immediately forward your resume with a brief, friendly cover letter, thanking them for any help they can offer and mentioning the types of positions and/or industries in which you are interested.

Follow-Up 2: If you have not heard back from any of your contacts within two weeks, give them a quick call and inquire if they've had a chance to review your resume and if they have any recommendations or referrals.

Tier #2 Contacts

Contacts: People whom you know casually and with whom you may or may not have an ongoing relationship. This list will largely fall into the same categories as outlined in the Tier #1 contacts; it's simply that you do not know these individuals as well. This tier may include commercial realtors and developers, local newspaper publishers, attorneys, accountants, investors, Chamber of Commerce directors, state licensing personnel, and others who know what's happening within a particular business community and/or may have clients who would be interested in your talent.

Process: Your initial contact with these individuals will most likely be 50% by phone and 50% by mail/email, depending on your level of comfort in these relationships and ease in connecting with each individual. Obviously, whenever possible, it's best for the initial contact to be via phone, allowing you to establish a more personal relationship. However, if that's not possible, mail or email contact is fine. Your conversation will be a bit more formal than with your Tier #1 contacts, but your objective is the same: to quickly communicate that you're in the job market and would appreciate their help.

Follow-Up 1: If you've called a prospective networking contact, follow up immediately by sending a resume and any other career marketing documents that are appropriate. For those you are contacting initially by mail or email, be sure to send your resume and any other relevant career marketing information along with your initial correspondence. Do not wait to hear back from them and then forward your information. "Strike while the iron is hot" and forward all of your information at the first contact.

Follow-Up 2: If you have not heard back from any of your contacts within three weeks, give them a quick call and inquire if they've had a chance to review your resume and if they have any recommendations or referrals.

Tier #3 Contacts

Contacts: People who have been referred to you by your Tier #1 and #2 contacts. Chances are that you will not know these individuals at all, and you'll be making a "warm" contact (leveraging the name of the individual who recommended that you contact them).

Process: Your initial contact with these individuals will most likely be 50% by phone and 50% by mail/email, depending on your level of comfort and ease in connecting with each individual. Again, whenever possible, it's best for the initial contact to be via phone for a more personal and more immediate relationship. Your conversation will be a bit more formal than with your Tier #1 and #2 contacts, but, as before, your goal is to quickly communicate that you're in the job market and would appreciate their help.

Follow-Up 1: If you've called a prospective networking contact, follow up immediately by sending a resume and any other career marketing documents that are appropriate. If you've mailed or emailed a new contact, be sure to send along your resume and any other relevant career marketing information when you initially contact them. Do not wait to hear back from them and then forward your information.

Follow-Up 2: If you have not heard back from any of these contacts within three weeks, give them a quick call and inquire if they've had a chance to review your resume and if they have any recommendations or referrals.

Technology and Its Impact on the Executive Job Search

Technology has revolutionized how job seekers look for new positions, how companies select candidates and hire, how recruiters work, how employees work, and more. In essence, technology has impacted the entire employment and hiring process, and is anticipated to have even more profound effects on hiring, employment, and lifelong career management in the years to come.

Two of these impacts were discussed earlier—the large increase in resumes and applications for specific opportunities, and the emerging role of keywords and keyword scanning. Another huge impact has resulted from the proliferation of email, which now is often the preferred method for communication between candidates, companies, recruiters, and others involved in the job search process. Email allows for immediate response and follow-up and, in turn, accelerates certain components of the employment and hiring process. With just a click here and there, you can instantly forward your resume and reference dossier in response to an advertisement, forward additional information that a recruiter or hiring authority has requested, send an immediate thank-you letter after an interview, follow up with a quick note to learn the status of a job opening, and so much more. Email has eliminated many of the communication barriers that previously existed in job search, providing a real-time forum that is immediate and easy to manage.

The other major influence that technology has had on job search is the evolution of the resume into its new, tech-based formats: scannable, electronic, and web-based. The following information will help you understand each and how you can best use each in your search.

Scannable – The scannable resume can be referred to as the "plain-vanilla" resume. All of the things that you would normally do to make your printed resume look attractive—bold print, italics, multiple columns, sharp-looking typestyle, and more—are stripped away in a scannable resume. You want to present a document that can be easily read and interpreted by scanning technology.

The need for a separately formatted resume for scanning purposes has rapidly diminished as technology has advanced (improving ability to read traditional paper resumes) and electronic applications have increased. We don't think you will need to produce a separate, scannable version of your resume; but if for some reason you need one, simply print the ASCII text format that is described in the next section. It is certainly "plain vanilla," and it is 100 percent scannable.

Electronic – Your electronic resume can take three forms: word processing file, PDF file, and ASCII text file.

Your most useful format will be the word processing file—preferably a Microsoft Word (.doc) file. Whenever possible, send this file as an attachment to your email. Because the vast majority of businesses use Microsoft Word, it is the most acceptable format and will present the fewest difficulties for your recipients.

If your resume has an unusual format or you are sending it to someone who does not have Microsoft Word, consider sending a PDF (portable document format) file. This format will keep the layout of your resume intact and is readily viewable by most recipients. If you don't have Adobe Acrobat (the software used to create PDF formats) on your computer, you can find a number of Internet sites that will convert your Microsoft Word file to PDF format for free. We like http://gobcl.com, but there are many others. Be aware, however, that PDF files cannot be easily read by resume scanning software nor input into resume storage systems, and, therefore, they are not the preferred format for most people.

The third format you can use to send your resume electronically is an ASCII text file, which is easy to create. Simply open your Microsoft Word file, resave it as a text file (.txt file extension), and close the file. That's it! Now, open the file and you will see that your resume has been stripped of formatting and now appears in Courier font with all text left-justified. Take a few minutes to review the document to be sure there are no odd characters or conversion glitches, then save the file for when you need a text-only format that you can cut-and-paste into online job applications and recruiter websites. You can also paste the text into the body of an email if you are unable to send your nicely formatted resume as an attachment.

Web-Based – Also known as a web portfolio, this newest evolution in resumes combines the visually pleasing quality of the printed resume with the technological ease of the electronic resume. You host your web resume on your own website (with your own URL) to which you refer prospective employers and recruiters. Now, instead of seeing just a "plain-vanilla" version of your emailed resume, with just one click a viewer can access, download, and print your web resume—an attractive, nicely formatted presentation of your qualifications.

What's more, because the web resume is such an efficient and easy-to-manage tool, you can choose to include more information than you would in a printed, scannable, or electronic resume. Consider separate pages for achievements, technology qualifications, equipment skills, honors and awards, management skills, and more, if you believe they would improve your market position. Remember, you're working to sell yourself into your next job!

If you are in a technology-intensive industry, you might want to take your web resume one step further and create a virtual multimedia presentation that not only tells someone how talented you are, but also visually and technologically demonstrates it. Web portfolios are outstanding tools for communicating "proof of performance" and are an emerging trend that supports lifelong career management.

One final word about technology and its phenomenal impact on today's job search market: Don't let it intimidate you! Except for multimedia web portfolios, none of the things that we've discussed are particularly complex, nor do they require that you be a technology genius. They are easy-to-use technologies that will be critical in helping you prepare and execute your executive search campaign. If you're stumped, there are talented career professionals nationwide who have extensive technology expertise as it relates to job search, hiring, and employment. If you can't manage the technology yourself, find a technology partner who can guide you through the process.

Two Resume Essentials

We have purposely not given you a formula for writing your resume and other career marketing documents. There are no rules for resume writing, and your unique materials must reflect your unique brand and value. But there are two "musts" that we want to emphasize as the final key points in this chapter.

No Errors

Your resume must be perfect in its grammar, spelling, and punctuation. We know you know this—this is one resume-writing truth that has remained constant over the years—but we reiterate it here because so many of the resumes we see contain careless errors that create a poor first impression. Don't let this happen to you.

Easy-to-Read Format

If your resume is hard to read, no one will read it. It's that simple. Busy recruiters and employers don't have the time or the patience to wade through tiny type, edge-to-edge text, or dense paragraphs. They'll put your resume to the side and never look at it again.

Follow these tips for making your resume and related materials inviting to your readers:

- Use a reasonable font size. For most fonts, 10, 11, or 12 point is ideal reading size.

- Keep paragraphs short—ideally, no more than 4 or 5 lines.

- Limit length of lists—ideally, no more than 5 or 6 bullet points should appear in a row without some kind of visual break to let the reader absorb the material.

- Allow ample white space—blank space at the margins and between sections that serves as a "breather" for the reader.

- Use formatting enhancements such as bold type, italics, horizontal lines, shading, and boxes appropriately to identify key sections of your resume and guide your reader through the document.

Bottom line, strive for a clean, uncluttered, distinctive, and executive appearance so that readers can concentrate on the content and quickly perceive the value you offer.

CHAPTER 4

Building Your Executive Job Search Community

Job search used to be a relatively direct process between you and the hiring company. You would submit a resume or application, interview directly with the company, and, perhaps, be offered the opportunity. There were virtually no "middle men" involved in the process.

Today, however, that has changed dramatically and there are many players in the executive job search community, each with unique qualifications and expertise. The ones whom you will most frequently encounter include:

- Career Coaches
- Career Counselors
- Resume Writers

- Executive Recruiters
- Contingent Recruiters
- Outplacement Consultants

These individuals (and companies) can be of tremendous value to you as you plan and orchestrate your executive job search campaign. Now, let's explore each of these "new" job search partners, who they are, the services they offer, and their potential contributions to your successful search for a powerful executive opportunity.

Building Your Community

Career Coaches

Career coaching is an exciting and growing occupation, the newest phenomenon in the employment industry. Just as professional athletes have coaches, so now can you, the career professional, have your own coach who will guide you in making the right decisions for yourself and your career. Coaches don't simply give you the answers but, rather, coach you to reach your own conclusions and take your own actions. They are there to:

- Help you explore and better define your professional talents, tools, and competencies.
- Address personal issues impacting your career progression.
- Help you clearly identify your immediate and long-term career objectives.
- Discuss and resolve obstacles to employment and career success.

- Guide you in developing both short-term and long-range executive career strategies.
- Assist you in developing, executing, and managing a successful job search campaign.
- Prepare you to competitively interview, negotiate compensation, and evaluate job offers.

In addition, many coaches offer services beyond the immediate job search and are available to support you throughout your career with ongoing guidance in long-term career planning, management, and advancement. Whether you meet with your coach once a week, once a month, or once a year, it's great to have someone in your court, encouraging you towards professional success and achievement.

Do YOU need a career coach?

Are you clear about your objectives? Are you encountering obstacles you can't overcome? Are you marketing yourself effectively? Do you simply need someone on your team? If yes, then you might consider hiring a career coach. Their services can be invaluable in helping you execute a successful search campaign.

Recommended Credentials:
Career Management Fellow (CMF)
Certified Career Management Coach (CCMC)
Certified Employment Interview Professional (CEIP)
Credentialed Career Master (CCM)
Job & Career Transition Coach (JCTC)
Master Career Coach (MCC)
Professional Certified Career Coach (PCCC)

Career Counselors

Career counseling is a well-established and well-respected industry that has existed far longer than career coaching. In fact, for decades, colleges and universities have offered on-site career counseling services to their students, and private career counseling practitioners can be found nationwide. Career counselors tend to be:

- Well-credentialed with graduate degrees, licenses, and professional certifications.
- Qualified in the administration and interpretation of various career testing and assessment instruments (valuable information as you plan your long-term career path).
- More focused on the "front-end"—career testing, assessment, analysis and planning—than the "back end" of the search—resume writing and the actual process of job search (e.g., mailings, Internet postings, etc.).
- Highly skilled problem solvers, crisis managers, and facilitators, able to help you identify your career direction and proactively move forward.

Do YOU need a career counselor?

Do you know what you're hard-wired to do? Do you know what motivates and excites you? Do you know your natural abilities, interests, behaviors, and values? Getting to know yourself can be a valuable tool for lifelong career success. Career counselors can help you find those answers.

Recommended Credentials:
- Certified Professional Counselor (CPC)
- Licensed Professional Counselor (LPC)
- Nationally Certified Career Counselor (NCCC)
- Nationally Certified Counselor (NCC)

The differentiation between career coaching and career counseling is becoming increasingly more vague with significant cross-over between these two areas of specialization. In particular, many career counselors now offer career coaching services in order to expand their areas of expertise and their portfolio of client services.

Resume Writers

Don't be fooled into thinking that professional resume writers are "glorified" secretaries or administrative assistants. They are not! Rather, resume writers are well-qualified professionals who have often worked for years with senior-level job search candidates and are trained to write documents that get the attention of hiring managers, HR executives, and recruiters. They are talented writing professionals who, in fact, generally do much more than just write resumes. Many also write executive career biographies, leadership profiles, achievement summaries, technology profiles, executive cover letters, thank-you letters, and a host of other documents that you may need while facilitating your executive search campaign. The minor investment you will make in hiring a professional resume writer can be worth tens of thousands of dollars in your pocket by getting you in front of decision-makers faster than you would be able to accomplish on your own.

For the most impact, be sure that you work with a writer who has experience in your profession and industry. That way you can feel confident that they know the "right" keywords, resume formats, and more that will get you noticed and not passed over.

Do YOU need a resume writer?

Does your resume focus on your career achievements and successes? Does it communicate your value? Are the right keywords included? Can you feel the energy of the document? Is the visual presentation top-of-the-line? If you answered "no" to any of these questions, then, yes, you need a professional resume writer.

Recommended Credentials:
- Certified Professional Resume Writer (CPRW)
- Certified Resume Writer (CRW)
- Master Resume Writer (MRW)
- Nationally Certified Resume Writer (NCRW)

Executive (Retained) Recruiters

Always remember the guiding principle of job seeker and recruiter relationships—"The recruiter is NEVER working for you." The recruiting firm works for, and is PAID BY, the company that has hired them and, as it should be, recruiters' alliances are with those companies. Never be fooled into thinking a recruiter is out there marketing you to prospective employers. That is an extremely rare circumstance!

With that said, retained recruiters are an outstanding addition to your job search community because they have the jobs! However, recruiters are of value to you only if you find the right recruiters, those who specialize in your profession and/or your industry. The closer the match, the better the potential opportunities. Remember, recruiters are hired to find a specific person with specific qualifications to perform specific tasks. They are generally not out-of-the-box thinkers.

Do YOU need executive recruiters?

Yes! And the more you have in your corner, the better. There is no exclusivity in these relationships, so work with as many recruiters as possible. The more who know about you, the more opportunities.

Contingent Recruiters

Don't rule out contingent recruiters too quickly, even if you are a $100,000+ candidate. The world of recruitment has changed dramatically over the past few years, largely as a result of the Internet and online job search capabilities. One of the many changes is the cross-over between contingent and retained assignments. Use any and all recruiters who specialize in your industry and profession. It makes no difference to you how they get paid!

Do YOU need contingent recruiters?

Yes! The more people on your team, the better.

Outplacement Consultants

Outplacement exploded onto the scene in the early and mid 1980s following the tremendous changes (downsizings, reorganizations, reengineerings, mergers, acquisitions, and more) that occurred in the workplace. Best described as "one-stop shopping," outplacement companies provide a wealth of services to transition the unemployed executive through the job search process to his/her new position. You get coaching and counseling as needed, resume writing assistance, training in interviewing and salary negotiations, contact information for companies and recruiters, and more. You also may get an office and both receptionist and secretarial support services. For many senior-level job seekers, this is a service that can't be beat.

Do YOU need an outplacement consultant?

The answer to this question is not clear-cut because of the large dollars involved. What's more, many of the "traditional" outplacement services are no longer necessary because most executives now have their own computers and are email and

Internet savvy. If your employer has offered to pay for your outplacement, ask yourself if you actually need all the services that the outplacement company offers. If not, consider asking your employer to give you the money to use as you feel appropriate in your search. If you're paying for outplacement yourself, be as sure as you can that the ROI will be well worth the fees.

If you are considering working with a career services professional, check qualifications and references to be sure that you are hiring an individual who:

- Is well-informed about your profession and your industry.
- Has a track record of success working with other senior-level executives and $100,000+ candidates.
- Has solid credentials—professional certifications, licenses, publications, academic degrees, and more.

Executive Job Search Success Teams

It is extremely difficult to achieve your goals in isolation. Knowing this, successful people constantly surround themselves with other successful and positive people who can help guide them and support them in achieving their personal and/or professional goals. Your job search is no different. You can either go it alone or benefit from the combined expertise and support of a team working with you to keep you positive and on track, provide sound advice and honest feedback, help you set realistic goals, and then keep you accountable for them.

Your Job Search Success Team should be made up of individuals whose opinions you respect and who are positive, accessible, and straightforward. They should have insight, knowledge, or expertise that is in line with your career goals for today, tomorrow, and in the future.

To begin, contact five to seven people whom you would like to have on your Executive Success Team to discuss your job search and how you could benefit from their support. If they agree, simply arrange a mutually convenient time and regularly scheduled commitment to meet in person or via phone. They can review your resume, cover letter, executive profile, and other career marketing communications with an objective eye; make networking contacts on your behalf; share leads with you; recommend alternative career options you might not have considered; educate you regarding new market opportunities; provide valuable feedback in response to your specific concerns; and help you move towards action.

Whom Do You Want On Your Executive Success Team?

- **Mentor.** If you have been fortunate enough to have developed a solid relationship with a mentor, this individual should serve as the foundation for your Executive Success Team. Hopefully, this is someone who has known you well for years and is quite familiar with the depth and scope of your career, track record of performance, innate talents, and achievements.

- **Past and Present Managers.** If you've had a particularly positive working relationship with any of your past managers, invite one or two to join your Success Team. Again, these individuals should be quite familiar with your qualifications. They will be able to share career insights that might be obvious to them but which you've never thought of yourself.

- **Professional Peers.** This will generally be a large group of individuals from which you will need to select one or two. When evaluating whom to approach, consider the time they have available to assist you, their particular style and how it meshes with yours, and other contacts they may have that could potentially be of value in your search campaign. Ask yourself if they are giving and supportive or "all business" with little time left over.

- **Banker, Accountant, or Financial Consultant.** These individuals can be valuable additions to your Executive Success Team, particularly if they are well connected in the professional communities in which you plan to focus your search campaign. Further, because these individuals often work on a consulting or contractual basis with many clients, they may be aware of opportunities and career options that you might never have considered.

- **Vendors/Suppliers.** Vendors/suppliers tend to know a great deal about what's going on internally at their client companies. Use this information to your advantage by inviting a vendor with whom you have a particularly strong working relationship to join your Team and share his/her expertise with you.

- **Family Friends.** Think about whom you and your family know. Do you have personal relationships with key corporate players? Or perhaps there are family relationships that have existed for years or even decades? These could be individuals with whom you've never associated professionally but know quite well from the golf course, country club, Rotary Club, condo association, daycare center, and the like. Carefully review this list of people to determine who would be valuable additions to your Executive Success Team.

A Few More Words Of Advice ...

1. **Be sure that there is a good mix of people on your Executive Success Team.** Your Team will be of limited value if everyone comes from the same industry, same profession, and/or same geographic area. You want diversity of ideas and input.

2. **It is best to meet with your Success Team individually or in small groups of two to four.** If you assemble everyone at one time, it is often difficult to absorb the valuable information that every member has to share with you.

3. **Be sure that you're the one who pays for meals, greens fees, and the like.** Your Team is there to support you and your career efforts, not your pocket!

4. **Surround yourself with smart, caring, and helpful people.** Before you approach anyone, ask yourself if they are supportive and have the time available to share with you.

CHAPTER 5

Your Library of Executive Job Search Documents

Before we move on to the remaining chapters of this book, where we discuss each type of executive job search document in detail and provide accompanying examples, we want to give you an easy reference guide to all the documents and how they can best be used during your executive search. Refer to the chart on the next several pages for a quick overview of each type of document, its purpose, and its intended use.

Pay special attention to the "When to Use" column and you will notice that many of these documents can be used for a broad range of job search activities. However, we are not suggesting that you follow an "all documents, all the time" strategy. Instead, carefully consider the specific opportunity, the nature of your contact, and your purpose for each step of the process. Then, use the documents that best support your strategy for each particular contact.

In the following chapters, we have provided examples along with an explanation of how the individual job seeker used the various documents. This will help you understand the best situations and strategies for sharing your materials so that they are effective tools in moving your job search forward.

Document	Definition/Purpose	When to Use
Executive Resume (CHAPTER 6)	A powerful, distinctive, well-written, and well-designed presentation of your executive capabilities, achievements, and relevant professional experience	• Response to advertisement/posting • Direct employer contact • Direct recruiter contact • Networking contact (Tier 3; see Chapter 3 for more information on networking) • During the interview
Networking Resume (CHAPTER 6)	A "slimmed-down" version of your executive resume for distribution to networking contacts who are at least somewhat familiar with your professional career history.	• Networking contact (Tier 1 & Tier 2; see Chapter 3 for information on networking)

PowerPoint Resume
(CHAPTER 6)

Presentation format that communicates highlights of your career. Great for use during a "public" presentation such as a panel or group interview and as a quick reminder of your competencies as part of your interview follow-up.

- During the interview
- Interview follow-up
- Second and third round of interviews

Career Biography
(CHAPTER 7)

Narrative format that provides an overview of your executive career and distinguishing highlights.

- Response to advertisement/ posting
- Direct employer contact
- Direct recruiter contact
- Networking contact
- During the interview

Leadership Profile
(CHAPTER 8)

Specifically focused document that demonstrates and verifies your executive leadership talents, key positions, track record of performance, notable achievements, professional activities and contributions, and core skill sets.

- Response to advertisement/posting
- Direct employer contact
- Direct recruiter contact
- Networking contact
- During the interview
- Interview follow-up

Technology Profile
(CHAPTER 8)

Specifically focused document that demonstrates and verifies the strength of your technology expertise; generally used by individuals in technology professions or technology-intensive industries.

- Response to advertisement/posting
- Direct employer contact
- Direct recruiter contact
- Networking contact
- During the interview
- Interview follow-up

Marketing Profile
(CHAPTER 8)

Specifically focused document that demonstrates and verifies the strength of your marketing, business development, product development, and related expertise.

- Response to advertisement/posting
- Direct employer contact
- Direct recruiter contact
- Networking contact
- During the interview
- Interview follow-up

Resume Addenda
(CHAPTER 8)

Optional add-on pages that communicate depth, scope, and volume of professional, managerial, technical, executive, and leadership activities.

- Response to advertisement/ posting (only when specifically requested)
- During the interview
- Interview follow-up
- Second and third tound of interviews

Achievement Summary **(CHAPTER 9)**	Distinctive document that clearly and concisely communicates the most significant highlights of your executive career.	• Response to advertisement/posting • Direct employer contact • Direct recruiter contact • Networking contact • During the interview • Interview follow-up
Executive Branding Statement **(CHAPTER 10)**	Precisely worded statement that identifies and communicates your specific executive brand — your unique value.	• Response to advertisement/posting • Direct employer contact • Direct recruiter contact • Networking contact • During the interview • Interview follow-up
Job Proposal **(CHAPTER 11)**	Persuasive communication that makes the case for hiring you for a specific opportunity.	• During the interview • Interview follow-up
Special Report **(CHAPTER 12)**	Your original work, a thoughtful document that shares information about a very specific/finite topic to solidify your position as a subject-matter expert.	• Response to advertisement/posting • Direct employer contact • Networking contact • During the interview • Interview follow-up
Reference Dossier **(CHAPTER 13)**	Written testimonials of your notable contributions, achievements, honors, awards, and performance from third-party references.	• During the interview • Interview follow-up • Second and third round of interviews
Executive Cover Letter **(CHAPTER 14)**	Well-written and carefully targeted introduction that accompanies every resume that you send.	• Response to advertisement/posting • Direct employer contact • Direct recruiter contact • Networking contact
Thank-You Letter **(CHAPTER 15)**	Mailed or emailed communication that can fulfill several purposes: to thank the interviewer for the opportunity, share additional information that will further strengthen your candidacy, provide additional information as requested by the interviewer, and overcome any objections identified during the interview	• Interview follow-up (all stages)

Web Portfolio (CHAPTER 16)	Expanded online presentation, lengthier and more in-depth than a traditional executive resume, allowing you to present — on individual web pages — detailed information about your career, employment experiences, competencies, achievements, project highlights, education, certifications, publications, and more.	(When "technologically" appropriate:) • Response to advertisement/posting • Direct employer contact • Direct recruiter contact • Networking contact • During the interview • Interview follow-up • Second and third round of interviews

CHAPTER 6

Writing Executive Resumes

In Chapter 3 we provided you with strategies and specific guidelines to help you write a powerful executive resume, and we discussed how to use your resume and other career marketing documents for an effective search. In this chapter we will show you examples of the executive resume in three of the formats we have mentioned:

- **Traditional executive resume**—a distinctive, well-written, and well-designed presentation of your executive capabilities, achievements, and relevant professional experience
- **Networking resume**—a "slimmed-down" version of your executive resume for distribution to networking contacts
- **PowerPoint resume**—presentation format that communicates career highlights

There are two key points to give special thought to as you write your resume(s) and then decide which to use for a particular contact or opportunity.

1. Focus on Your Target

The more you know about your target positions, industries, and potential employers, the better equipped you will be to create a document that is truly on point. You won't be tempted to clutter up your resume with irrelevant information, and you can easily review it from the perspective of what is most important for the distinct role, at the particular company, in the specific industry you are targeting.

For example, if you are interested *only* in the plastics industry, where you've worked your whole career, you should use industry-specific language to paint yourself as the inside expert that you are. In this case, being seen as a real "plastics expert" is a plus! But if you want to move to a new industry, you will need to use more generic language to describe your industry background so that you can position yourself more broadly—perhaps as an "operations expert" or a "sales and marketing exec." Review your resume from the perspective of the person reading it, and be sure you have painted the right picture of "who" you are and how you want to be perceived.

2. Focus on Your Recipient

As you adapt your traditional resume for additional formats such as a networking resume or PowerPoint resume, use your knowledge of the target audience and the recipient to guide your decisions about what is the most important information to present.

For example:

- If you are preparing a networking resume to circulate to fellow members of the board of a nonprofit organization, be sure you include that leadership role on the resume. It will serve as a reminder to them (if they need it) and will connect back to them if, for example, they share the resume with a business contact who does not know you personally but knows them and their board involvement.

- If you are creating a PowerPoint resume to present during a panel interview, add meaningful names and data to your achievement statements. Perhaps you can show that you beat out one of the company's prime competitors, or sold to one of their key targets, or have worked extensively with C-level executives in a field they would like to penetrate.

In both of these examples, this specific information might not appear on your traditional resume. The additional formats give you the opportunity to expand and add details that are meaningful to your intended audience.

Examples

We begin by showcasing a traditional executive resume—the foundation for the other resume formats we have discussed in this chapter. Then we provide two additional examples that pair the traditional resume with either a networking resume or a PowerPoint resume, so you can see how the additional version was built from the original document and how the two complement each other while serving different purposes for the job search.

EXAMPLE 1: Executive Resume: Meredith Rockwell (pages 46-47)
(Writer – Louise Kursmark)
For this operations executive's resume, the all-important numbers and results stand out through effective formatting that includes eye-catching tables on both pages of the resume.

EXAMPLE 2: Executive Resume and Network Resume: Tony J. Raymond (pages 48-51)
(Writers – Michelle Dumas and Dan Dorotik)
A traditional, three-page executive resume was written for this individual who had progressed to the CIO level and was now seeking a position as a COO, CIO, or VP. Because networking played a primary role in his job search, he created a one-page network resume that he handed out at the many networking events he attended. He also sent the network resume to his many personal and professional contacts, preceded by a phone call. When a

network contact generated a specific job opportunity, Tony sent his full resume and formal cover letter to the hiring authority.

Both of Tony's documents emphasize his broad combination of operations, technology, and supply chain management experience.

EXAMPLE 3: Executive Resume and PowerPoint Resume: Jordan Thomas (pages 52-61)
(Writer – Tracy Parish)
The two-page executive resume begins with a powerful testimonial taken from a respected business publication. This same quote is used to introduce the PowerPoint resume, which repeats some basic information from the executive resume (career history and education) while adding additional quotes, a brief personal statement, and a project highlight page that was selected for its relevance to the particular opportunity. Jordan could easily customize this page for different opportunities or add pages to present multiple projects. The slide-show PowerPoint file, emailed to a recruiter or top executive, gave them quick access and a strong visual image of Jordan's key information.

MEREDITH ROCKWELL

301-745-7299 • rockwell@yahoo.com
759 Harbor Court, Unit 5A, Baltimore, MD 21229

OPERATIONS EXECUTIVE

Building & Leading World-Class Manufacturing & Distribution Organizations
Lean Manufacturing • Six Sigma (Black Belt) • Continuous Process Improvement

Repeatedly turned around unprofitable operations and delivered continuous improvement in process, cost, quality, safety, and productivity. Achieved "impossible" performance improvements in demanding industries by clearly communicating vision, instilling team culture, and igniting competitive drive. Drove major projects, programs, and initiatives from planning through tactical execution; mastered advanced methodologies, processes, and technologies and aligned change efforts with business goals.

EXPERIENCE AND ACHIEVEMENTS

BIGBOX, INC., Baltimore, MD   2004–Present

Operations Manager / Six Sigma Black Belt

Drove measurable performance improvements in the operation of BigBox's 1-million-sq.-ft. distribution center, supporting corporate imperative to slash operating costs that resulted in BigBox's first quarter of profitability and set the stage for continued profitable growth.

Manage productivity, safety, and quality for distribution center employing more than 350 during peak seasonal production. Lead Black Belt projects and mentor Green Belt teams to drive continuous-improvement initiatives deep into operational structure.

- Created a daily planning model and performance-review process to focus improvement activities on performance gaps. Increased throughout per labor hour **33%** and order accuracy **44%**.
- Quickly boosted order-picking productivity **12%** by establishing performance expectations and associate accountability.
- Led 2 DMAIC Black Belt projects that delivered savings of **$260K**, reduced errors by **50%**, and found a permanent solution for a recurring problem—subsequently applied at 3 national distribution sites.
- Developed an innovative learning-curve model that accurately predicted productivity of temporary associates hired for peak holiday season. Deployed across all 3 shifts for entire operation—enabled JIT staffing to meet high-volume delivery goals with **zero** overtime and **52%** improvement in inventory accuracy over prior year.

KLEIN AUTO SYSTEMS, Baltimore, MD   1992–2004

Program Group Manager, Climate Systems Division, 2000–2004

Turned around unprofitable business unit, aggressively applying Lean Manufacturing and Six Sigma (DFSS, DMAIC, DFM/A) methodologies to reduce costs and increase both productivity and profitability in a QS 9000 production environment. Managed P&L, new business development, product development, manufacturing engineering, strategic planning, and sales forecasting for $60MM, 300-employee division producing climate-control systems for major automotive accounts.

- Slashed production costs for existing products; landed new business; reconfigured line from batch to lean continuous flow for greater productivity. Results:

	Sales	*Pretax Net Profit*	*Models Assembled*	*Inventory Turns*
1996	**$12.6MM**	(3.4%)	4	36
1999	**$16.7MM**	10.4%	4	64
2003 Plan	**$31.8MM**	23.4%	8	100+

Program Group Manager, Climate Systems Division, **KLEIN MANUFACTURING**, continued

- Eradicated #1 cause of expansion-device warranty claims and shaved **10%** off warranty costs.
- Provided organizational leadership to downsizing initiative, driving **$2MM (15%)** from operating cost per year with minimal effect on customer satisfaction.
- Prepared and presented numerous sales and technical presentations. Led team presentation to the division's largest customer that secured new programs valued at **$32MM.**
- Landed and successfully launched multiple programs for customers such as Daimler-Chrysler, GM, Ford, Peterbilt, Kenworth, International, John Deere, and JCB.

Program Manager, Off Highway Group, 1997–2000

Restored profitability, steadily improved operating performance, expanded market penetration, and diversified product offerings for sustainable growth. Completed training at Toyota Supplier Support Center and introduced Lean Manufacturing to the Group.

Led a team of 7 in new business development, manufacturing engineering, customer service and sales forecasting; accountable for P&L.

- Added **$1.6MM** to the bottom line; improved product throughput **46%** with only **25%** increase in labor; **eliminated** production set-up time.

	Sales	Pretax Net Profit	Models Assembled	Model Families	Average Lot Size	Productivity
1993	$6.2MM	(9.3%)	3	2	7.4	79%
1996	$10.1MM	10.1%	10	6	6.4	95.1%

- Earned sole-supplier status with John Deere and built construction-equipment business from **$0** to **$3MM** yearly.
- Eliminated an unprofitable OEM product line after aggressive attempts to revitalize the line were unsuccessful. Maintained favorable relationship with the customer.

Engineering Manager, 1996–1997

Managed 3-person staff in system design, development, testing, manufacture, and commercial input. Served as primary customer contact in landing **$1.3MM** in sales and a new customer for the division.

Senior Design Engineer, 1994–1996

Spearheaded product redesign of an existing HVAC system for a key account. Reduced part count **40%** through DFM/A techniques and achieved **$900K** annual cost reduction.

Manufacturing Engineer, 1992–1994

Developed and installed manufacturing processes for 4 new products.

EDUCATION

Black Belt, 2004   BigBox, Inc.
MBA, 1997   Loyola of Baltimore
BS Operations Management, 1992   University of Maryland

TONY J. RAYMOND

28 High Street ▪ Los Angeles, CA 04390
Home: (309) 453-9087 ▪ Cell: (309) 453-1068 ▪ Email: tjraymond@email.com

SENIOR MANAGEMENT EXECUTIVE
OPERATIONS / TECHNOLOGY / SUPPLY CHAIN MANAGEMENT

Results-driven information technology and operational executive offering more than 20 years of experience and success in driving operational growth, leading full-scale start-up and turnaround efforts, optimizing supply chains, and building best-in-class technology infrastructure. Valuable depth of leadership experience; recognized visionary and agent for change with documented ability to take initiative and orchestrate reengineering activities that revive stagnant operations and preserve shutdown of under-performing organizations. Astute negotiator and confident decision-maker. MBA degree.

Selected Achievements:
~ Championed successful launch of new company, new plant, new business unit, and multiple new product offerings ~
~ Corporate officer involved in successful turnaround and restructuring of bankrupt company ~
~ Led international procurement globally, including Japan, Singapore, Malaysia, Mexico, Germany, UK, and Finland ~
~ Repeatedly produced dramatic cost savings and revenue increases valued in the 10's of millions ~

Selected Core Competencies:

- Operations & General Management	- Supply Chain Optimization	- Change Management
- Technology Infrastructure Planning	- International & Domestic Procurement	- Mergers & Acquisitions
- P&L Management	- Kaizen / Lean Manufacturing	- Team Building & Leadership
- Start-up & Turnaround Operations	- ISO9000 – 9001/9002	- ERP Implementation

PROFESSIONAL EXPERIENCE

Concepts Nationwide, Inc. ▪ Los Angeles, CA   **2002 – Present**
Fourth largest provider of convention and meeting services nationwide, with $550+ million in annual revenues.

CHIEF INFORMATION OFFICER (2002 – Present)
VICE PRESIDENT, STRATEGIC SUPPLY MANAGEMENT (2003 – 2004)
VICE PRESIDENT, FINANCE (2002)

Promoted to become company's first CIO and provide business insight and perspective in the turnaround and restoration of company's IT infrastructure and organization plagued by poor connectivity, lack of standards, weak leadership, and broken processes. Hold full P&L responsibility for internal software organization Management Technology America (MTA) and provide leadership for cross-functional team of 52. Develop IT strategic roadmap and short-/medium-/long-term goals to establish vision for all aspects of technology infrastructure. Manage daily operations of all IT systems (99.99% uptime), administer $6.5 million budget, and formulate policies/procedures that support technology aims.

Recruit talent and develop team, accelerating promotion of top-performing staff and creating "culture of excellence." Solidify relationships with vendors and partner companies; function as liaison between IT and business users to ensure effective 2-way communications. Work with senior management colleagues to secure buy-in for plans; serve at the forefront of key transitional initiatives through company's frequent M&A activities.

- **Set up MTA as company's core internal IT organization** and created strategy to consolidate multiple software systems into standard program, reversing prior history of fragmented functions to produce unified pricing, targeted customer analysis/marketing, centralized fleet management, and shared service center.

- **Generated over $15+ million in first-year sales** by implementing project management portal using Sharepoint and B2B site. Deployed Vertex Taxware that resulted in $600,000 savings, Absolute Software for asset management, .NET software into Las Vegas branch, digital dashboard for management exception reporting, and VoIP/wireless tools.

- **Merged 17 general databases into single database,** overseeing 15-month project that served as key factor in driving $14 million overall company savings, along with migration of acquired company's systems and back-office consolidation. Converted 33 branches from legacy system to MTA over 3-month period.

Professional Experience

- **Negotiated $28.8 million in annual savings** on $225 million procurement spread for supply management organization. Returned $1.4 million in obsolete parts, negotiated 6-figure savings on voice/data, facilitated sharing of $250,000 in goods between branches, and secured 10% reduction on cell phone charges.

- **Secured 51% headcount reduction and $3.5 million annual savings** by consolidating 3 back offices; reduced IT headcount from 71 to 52 between 2002 and 2004, with total savings of $1.4 million.

- **Decreased IT budget 40% over 2-year period** through outsourcing of data center, email, hardware/software break fix, disk imaging, and DSL migration. Implemented Dell outsourced IT desktop and help desk support that improved service to 85% of calls answered within 45 seconds and 70% problem resolution within first 3 minutes.

Parker Corporation ▪ Cabrillo, CA   1999 – 2002
$48 million managed service provider, web host, and value-added reseller organization.

VICE PRESIDENT, SUPPLY CHAIN MANAGEMENT

Tasked with building supply chain organization from the ground up for start-up B2B Internet security business. Hired and directed staff in procurement, inventory planning, sourcing, and order fulfillment functions. Oversaw design, installation, management, and monitoring of firewall/security, web site/application hosting, virtual private networks, and e-commerce services. Designed web-based RFPs and online bidding, negotiated supplier agreements with high-profile companies, and handled A/R duties.

- **Developed and staffed entire organization;** established all policies and procedures, implemented entire supply chain (including inventory plan), and integrated third-party logistics with 2-hour, 24x7 response time.

- **Negotiated supplier contracts that led to $5 million in savings,** securing deals with EMC, Nokia Internet Services, CheckPoint, Cisco, Sun Microsystems, Dell, IBM, Compaq, RSA Security, and Equant Integration Systems. Negotiated all domestic and global freight contracts/forwarders.

- **Led team that cut outstanding receivables from $6.9 million to $3.7 million,** reducing DSO from 91.9 to 61.8 days over 5-month period. Earned formal recognition and bonus award for efforts.

- **Served as key architect in design of e-market supply chain solution,** including new installs, sparing, procurement, and logistics. Negotiated and implemented Virtual Private Network product offering, including third-party integration.

Allied Electric, Inc. ▪ Seattle, WA   1995 – 1999
$2.2 billion supplier of inverters, servo drives, and numerical control cabinets.

DIRECTOR, MATERIAL CONTROL (1997 – 1999)
MANAGER, MATERIAL CONTROL (1995 – 1999)

Recruited for newly created position to direct staff of 12 in production procurement, shop-floor scheduling, production receiving, and warehousing; earned promotion to lead team in plant-wide management of procurement, scheduling, service, and stockroom functions for $290 million operations, with direct reporting responsibility to VP of operations. Prepared and administered annual budget of $105 million, with $40+ million global procurement from Far East. Managed operational, financial, and HR functions, including team building/leadership workshops with interdisciplinary teams from Customer Service, Engineering, Product Management, Sales, HR, and Operations divisions.

- **Reduced finished goods inventory from $49.3 million to $37.7 million,** achieving goal over 8-month period; averaged 12% annual cost reduction from 1996 to 1999.

- **Cited for key role in $25 million sales increase** by implementing both make-to-order and lean manufacturing, reducing inventory and increasing service levels as additional results.

- **Created strategies that led to 99% inventory accuracy,** eliminating physical inventory for first time in company's history. Implemented vertical/horizontal shuttle storage systems and reduced warehouse space 80%.

Professional Experience

- **Staffed and developed organization from the ground up,** wrote and implemented policies and guidelines, and implemented ISO 9002 procurement/materials procedures.

- **Guided team in selection and process mapping for SAP manufacturing module;** served as team member for selection of Peak Technologies Warehouse Management System.

- **Participated in 3 major committees:** heading up manufacturing process and module for new software implementation, outlining entire supply chain for Yaskawa, and leading sales operations process.

Industrial Technology Corporation ▪ New York, NY   1989 – 1995
$21 billion industry leader in industrial technology.

MATERIALS MANAGER

Brought on board to establish materials organization, hiring/training all employees and setting up all internal processes and systems. Led team in procurement, planning, order fulfillment, transportation, and vendor control activities affecting company's $125 million manufacturing plants. Guided purchase of castings, machined parts, electrical and electronic components, sheet metal, bushings, and bearings; managed budget of $60 million.

- **Spearheaded turnaround initiative that addressed out-of-control quality and delivery problems,** increasing on-time shipments from 41% to 97%.

- **Headed team that negotiated firm pricing contracts and secured $750,000 in savings.** Collaborated with group for successful start-up of Automated Tape Library System, establishing complete supply line.

Integrated Media ▪ Chicago, IL   1983 – 1989
$5.3 billion world leader in integrated media and entertainment solutions.

MANAGER, PURCHASING (1985 – 1989)
BUYER SPECIALIST (1985)
BUYER (1983 – 1985)

Progressed through series of fast-track promotions. Directed purchases of all raw materials, equipment, vital supplies, and services, with $47 million annual budget as Purchasing Manager. Negotiated all contracts and capital purchases for $22 million funnel line expansion; purchased production materials and electrical/electronic components for picture-tube plant.

EDUCATION & CREDENTIALS

MBA in Leadership and Change Management, 1999
UNIVERSITY OF WASHINGTON ▪ Seattle, WA

BSBA in Production/Operations and Materials Management, 1983
UNIVERSITY OF ILLINOIS ▪ Urbana-Champaign, IL

Training:
Project Planning, Dimensions of Leadership, Essentials of Communicating with Diplomacy and Professionalism

Presentations:
Optimizing IT Business Value, Leveraging Technology for Competitive Advantage and Beyond Theory

Technology Skills:
Comprehensive list of technology competencies and areas of expertise is available for review.

TONY J. RAYMOND

28 High Street ▪ Los Angeles, CA 04390
Home: (309) 453-9087 ▪ Cell: (309) 453-1068 ▪ Email: tjraymond@email.com

---

SENIOR MANAGEMENT EXECUTIVE
Operations / Technology / Supply Chain Management
Start-up & Turnaround Operations / Mergers & Acquisitions / Lean Manufacturing

Visionary and results-driven executive offering more than 20 years of experience and success in driving operational growth, leading full-scale start-up and turnaround efforts, spearheading change initiatives, optimizing supply chains, and building best-in-class technology infrastructure. Valuable depth of leadership experience. Astute negotiator and confident decision-maker.

Selected Achievements:
~ Championed successful launch of new company, new plant, new business unit, and multiple new product offerings ~
~ Corporate officer involved in successful turnaround and restructuring of bankrupt company ~
~ Led international procurement globally, including Japan, Singapore, Malaysia, Mexico, Germany, UK, and Finland ~
~ Repeatedly produced dramatic cost savings and revenue increases valued in the 10's of millions ~

MBA in Leadership and Change Management, 1999 ▪ University of Washington
BSBA in Production/Operations and Materials Management, 1983 ▪ University of Illinois

---

PROFESSIONAL HIGHLIGHTS

CHIEF INFORMATION OFFICER ▪ Concepts Nationwide, Inc. ▪ Los Angeles, CA   2002 – Present

Championed turnaround and restoration of company's IT infrastructure and organization plagued by poor connectivity, lack of standards, weak leadership, and broken processes. Manage $6.5 million budget, 52-person team, and P&L performance for internal software organization Management Technology America (MTA).

- Generated over $15 million in first-year sales with new project management portal using Sharepoint and B2B site.
- Merged 17 general databases into single database, helping drive $14 million overall company savings.
- Negotiated $28.8 million in annual savings on $225 million procurement for supply management organization.
- Secured 51% headcount reduction and $3.5 million annual savings by consolidating 3 back offices.
- Reduced IT headcount from 71 to 52 between 2002 and 2004, with total savings of $1.4 million.
- Decreased IT budget 40% over 2-year period through strategic outsourcing.

VP, SUPPLY CHAIN MANAGEMENT ▪ Parker Corporation ▪ Cabrillo, CA   1999 – 2002

Built supply chain organization from the ground up for start-up B2B Internet security business. Developed and staffed entire organization; established all policies and procedures, implemented entire supply chain, and integrated third-party logistics with 2-hour, 24x7 response time.

- Structured and negotiated supplier contracts that led to $5 million in savings.
- Led team that cut outstanding receivables from $6.9 million to $3.7 million over 5-month period.
- Served as key architect in design of e-market supply chain solution.

DIRECTOR, MATERIAL CONTROL ▪ Allied Electric, Inc. ▪ Seattle, WA   1995 – 1999

Led team in plant-wide management of procurement, scheduling, service, and stockroom functions for $290 million operations. Controlled annual budget of $105 million, with $40+ million global procurement from Far East. Managed operational, financial, and human resource functions. Implemented ISO 9002 procurement/materials procedures.

- Slashed finished-goods inventory from $49.3 million to $37.7 million, achieving goal over 8-month period.
- Cited for key role in $25 million sales increase by implementing both make-to-order and lean manufacturing.
- Created strategies that led to 99% inventory accuracy, eliminating physical inventory for first time.

MATERIALS MANAGER ▪ Industrial Technology Corporation ▪ New York, NY   1989 – 1995

Established Materials department from scratch, hiring all employees and setting up internal processes and systems. Headed procurement, planning, order fulfillment, transportation, and vendor control activities. Managed $60 million budget.

- Spearheaded turnaround initiative that addressed out-of-control quality and delivery problems.
- Guided team that negotiated firm pricing contracts and secured $750,000 in savings.

* Early career (1983 – 1989) in progressive buying and purchasing management positions with Integrated Media.

JORDAN THOMAS

SENIOR TECHNOLOGY EXECUTIVE

> **"CIO Jordan Thomas not only cleaned up Ace's messy systems but also helped it launch two new business lines."**
> "ALL HAIL TO THE CHIEFS," *Inc. Technology Magazine*, Fall 2004

PROFESSIONAL EXPERIENCE

ACE CONSULTANTS, INC. – Torrance, CA (2003 to 2005)
CIO / Vice President of Operations and Technology

Specially selected to re-engineer processes, resolve long-standing problems, and streamline business functions to increase efficiency and profitability. Implemented technology plans; upgraded servers, PCs and applications; formed strong relations with the consulting firm; and improved overall business operations. Further enhanced client services, employee productivity, and revenue by implementing strategic IT and process improvement plans, while concurrently developing policies and launching new lines of business. Reduced paperwork/delays by 90%.

- Featured in *Inc. Technology Magazine* in Fall 2004 for company contributions; achieved what 2 predecessors were unable to accomplish.
- Integrated new technology to allow centralized storage of computer files and data-sharing capabilities, resulting in increased efficiency/accuracy while improving customer service.
- Provided Internet access and faxing capabilities to all desks and upgraded email system.
- Launched support for telecommuting by integrating Citrix server, laptops, and Palm Pilots.

FRANKLIN RESOURCE GROUP, INC. – Pasadena, CA (2000 to 2003)
Vice President / Client Administrative Services

Achieved a complete 360-degree turnaround in unsatisfactory client relationships for the largest department of a company specializing in executive compensation and benefits consulting for top corporate clients. Reached a near 100% customer-satisfaction rating.

- Achieved a 75% reduction in report errors, staff overtime, and employee turnover.
- Realized a 20% client growth rate with minimal staffing increases.
- Successfully designed a comprehensive, state-of-the-art new client system to administer variable non-qualified deferred compensation plans.

IBM / MARKETING AND SERVICES DIVISION – Los Angeles, CA (1991 to 2000)
Project Manager (1998 to 2000)

Promoted to direct fee-based client projects. Oversaw a broad range of key responsibilities in managing daily operations, including strategic planning; project phase development; scheduling; staff training, development, guidance, and supervision; subcontractor management; vendor negotiations and relations; testing; follow-up; customer support; and client satisfaction.

- Selected to manage a pioneering 3-year project developing a student information system for the nation's second largest school district.
- Launched and led a nationwide, 5-month project involving 40 team members in 8 major cities executing an application migration project for a major U.S. bank. Worked under stringent deadlines, completing the project on time and under budget with an exceptional client satisfaction rating.

1011 Western Avenue • Madison, IL 61345 • 618-449-2200 • jthomas@earthlink.net

JORDAN THOMAS

Page Two of Two

IBM / MARKETING AND SERVICES DIVISION – continued
Systems Engineer (1991 to 1998)

Recruited to manage both the sales and implementation phases of all IBM products and services for large, multi-industry, national accounts. Oversaw all aspects of client relations. Served as a central point-of-contact in providing information and resolving issues at all levels.

- Met all set company goals; sold and implemented $10 million annually.
- Secured an $8 million bid to replace a large competitive data center installation at a high-profile oil company and headed up the 18-month implementation project.
- Successfully expanded existing account by 30% 6 years straight with the nation's largest tax-processing company.
- Received 4 IBM Symposiums and a National Division Manager's Award; consistently achieved top ratings for customer satisfaction.

EDUCATION & TRAINING

UNIVERSITY OF SOUTHERN CALIFORNIA – Los Angeles, CA
MBA in Finance and Marketing
Graduated magna cum laude

BS in Mechanical Engineering
Graduated summa cum laude

ADDITIONAL PROFESSIONAL TRAINING: Business • Project Management • Leadership • Finance • Management • Sales • Customer Service • Product Information / Education • Various Technologies

COMMUNITY LEADERSHIP

UNIVERSITY OF SOUTHERN CALIFORNIA – Los Angeles, CA
Alumni Mentor (1995 to Present)

1011 Western Avenue • Madison, IL 61345 • 618-449-2200 • jthomas@earthlink.net

53

To view information on a key candidate for a
Technology Executive Position,
please go to the tool bar above and click
"Slide Show,"
then "View Show."

JORDAN THOMAS

1011 Western Avenue • Madison, IL 61345 • 618-449-2200 • jthomas@earthlink.net

"The President handed his special assistant the technology plan and said 'Here you go. Make this happen.' Eighteen months after Thomas's arrival, Jones promoted him to vice-president of operations and technology."
– Article Titled "All Hail to the Chiefs," *Inc. Technology Magazine*, Fall 2004

Persistence and patience...
"They can't tell me it can't be done."

Allow me to introduce myself.

You can probably tell by the opening statement that I like to swim upstream. I am not afraid of change, nor am I hesitant to express my opinion (tactfully, of course.) As a complement to that, I am also very adept at handling potentially hostile situations and achieving mutually satisfying results.

So why hire me? Integrity, values, and ethics. You will find my integrity to be unparalleled, my values to be well defined, and my work ethic to be solid. In a nutshell, I don't make excuses or beat around the bush; I simply make things happen.

Continuing Automatically...

"CIO Jordan Thomas not only cleaned up Ace's messy systems but also helped it launch two new business lines."

—Ibid

Continuing Automatically...

JORDAN THOMAS

1011 Western Avenue • Madison, IL 61345 • 618-449-2200 • jthomas@earthlink.net

Professional Impact

"Two years after Thomas joined KPI, his work is visible everywhere: not only in the freshly upgraded network and technical standards but also in the employees' ease in using those systems. Under his guidance the company developed security and backup procedures, something it never had before, as well as a telecommuting program... 'We are benefiting from Jordan's experience, his discipline, his ability to work with people, and especially his ability to bring the needed change to our organization.'"

– Ibid

Continuing Automatically...

JORDAN THOMAS

1011 Western Avenue • Madison, IL 61345 • 618-449-2200 • jthomas@earthlink.net

Career History

ACE CONSULTANTS, INC. – Torrance, CA (2003 to 205)
CIO / Vice President of Operations and Technology

FRANKLIN RESOURCE GROUP, INC. – Pasadena, CA (2000 to 2003)
Vice President / Client Administrative Services

IBM / MARKETING & SERVICES DIVISION – Los Angeles, CA (1991 to 2000)
Business Systems Executive / Project Manager / Systems Engineer

Continuing Automatically...

JORDAN THOMAS

1011 Western Avenue • Madison, IL 61345 • 618-449-2200 • jthomas@earthlink.net

Relevant Project Highlight

Centralized Storage Project (Ace Consultants, 2005)

- Computerized the filing/data storage of company's records of complex technology projects, to include:

    ✓ Technology specifications, hardware, software and tools

    ✓ Contract terminology with auto-reminder system for billing and payment tracking

    ✓ SLA details and tracking mechanism, with reminders mid-cycle to prevent costly service lapses

    ✓ Company-wide desktop access with multi-layer security features

    ✓ Consolidated reporting functions including trend identification

Continuing Automatically...

JORDAN THOMAS

1011 Western Avenue • Madison, IL 61345 • 618-449-2200 • jthomas@earthlink.net

Education and Training

UNIVERSITY OF SOUTHERN CALIFORNIA – Los Angeles, CA
MBA in Finance and Marketing (1989)
Graduated magna cum laude

BS in Mechanical Engineering (1982)
Graduated summa cum laude

Continuing Automatically...

Thank you for your time and professional courtesy in reviewing this material.

For further information or to schedule a personal interview, please contact:
Jordan Thomas at 618-449-2200

To Exit, Please Press ESC

CHAPTER 7

Writing Executive Career Biographies

The executive biography has a powerful pedigree, having long been used to profile board of directors members, prominent public figures, high-level speakers, and the most senior executives of a company. In the world of executive job search, some executive recruiters prefer to present their candidates using the biography format rather than the more traditional resume. The senior-level job seekers profiled later in this chapter used their biographies for diverse purposes during their career transition. You, too, may wish to develop this format and put it to good use during your search.

Most commonly known as an executive biography, this document can also assume other titles, including:

- Executive Profile
- Career Profile
- Professional Profile
- Candidate Profile
- Values Statement
- Capabilities Statement

Whatever we might choose to call it, the smooth narrative format of a biography reads very differently than the choppier, harder-hitting resume. Although typically just one page long, the bio is chock-full of information and must be well written and appropriately spaced and formatted so that it is inviting to the reader. After all, if no one takes the time to read your bio, it will not be of much value during your search!

If you are considering preparing an executive biography for yourself, review the samples that follow in this chapter and use these guidelines to create a document that is meaningful, compelling, and useful.

1. Lead with your executive brand

What are you known for? It is important to communicate this critical distinguishing information in the opening paragraph. Your brand—your unique value—is what makes you memorable and sets you apart from other well-qualified candidates.

2. Hit the high points

After the opening paragraph, most biographies follow a chronological or reverse-chronological format. Because your most impressive achievements probably occurred later in your career rather than during your first few years in the workforce, we recommend reverse-chronological. To write these paragraphs, consider each of your positions or each of your company tenures. What was the most important thing you accomplished at each? Be sure this is prominently featured in the appropriate paragraph. Too much detail will bog down your readers, so prepare crisp summaries highlighted by memorable results and notable achievements.

3. Include affiliations, community activities, and personal and family information

While your resume needs to be hard-hitting, your bio can be a bit softer and more personal. Many executives choose to include a brief paragraph giving family and personal information, although this is optional. The bio is also a great place for you to expand on any community affiliations or activities that have been meaningful to you. Of course, board-level positions should be mentioned as well.

4. Keep it short and focused

Resist the urge to write your entire life story! One-page bios are the norm, although later in the chapter you will see a superb example of a two-page biography. Remember that, like all of the career marketing materials you are preparing, your bio is a positioning statement that should be carefully designed to draw attention to your professional capabilities, accomplishments, and long-term potential.

Examples

Following are three distinctive, effective resume-and-bio pairs that showcase accomplishments and individuality. As you read each document, notice how the bio fleshes out some of the resume information and how the resume provides a deeper level of detail about career activities. When read together, each pair of documents paints a cohesive picture of a highly qualified executive.

EXAMPLE 1: Executive Resume and Executive Biography: Michael K. Edwards
(pages 65-67)
(Writer – Laurie Smith)
These documents were written to position Michael for a general management role. As such, they present strategic and bottom-line contributions as well as specific results in his functional area of supply chain management. Michael used his bio most often with his networking contacts but occasionally combined it with his resume and cover letter to create a total presentation package that he sent to a company or a recruiter.

EXAMPLE 2: Executive Resume and Executive Biography: Anthony Moorefield
(pages 68-71)
(Writer – Gayle Howard)
Because his resume was a somewhat lengthy and detail-rich three pages, Anthony used his one-page executive biography as a networking tool and a pre-screening device for executive recruiters. When interest was shown, he forwarded the full resume. Both separately and combined, the documents reinforce three things: Anthony's international experience, his high-level business ethics, and his willingness to make tough decisions.

EXAMPLE 3: Executive Resume and Executive Biography: Thomas Webster
(pages 72-77)
(Writer – Michelle Dumas)
After leaving the bank where he had spent his entire career, Thomas was pursuing two different targets: leadership of an investment fund or leadership of a small business. He used his two-page executive biography for both of these targets, most extensively within his network and with groups of private investors. When he became CEO of a small investment company, he used his executive biography to help secure investment funding and adapted portions of the bio for his company's marketing materials.

Michael K. Edwards

1598 Pleasant Hill Drive
Los Angeles, CA 90023

medwards1289@yahoo.com

Residence: 213-538-2248
Mobile: 213-389-4589

MANUFACTURING EXECUTIVE – OPERATIONS ❖ GENERAL MANAGEMENT

More than 15 years of success driving efficiency and bottom-line performance of manufacturing operations in both high-volume and custom production environments in U.S., Europe, Pacific Rim, and Mexico. Special focus on optimizing purchasing, materials management, production, and supply chain management processes. Key contributor throughout career to enterprise strategy. Proven performer in high growth, reorganization, consolidation, turnaround, and facility relocation situations, with results including:

- ❖ Reengineered operations, slashed costs by $Millions, and reduced headcounts with no customer impact.
- ❖ Turned around under-performing organizations and managed P&L for improved margins and bottom line.
- ❖ Automated processes and streamlined decision making with state-of-the-art planning and information systems.
- ❖ Enhanced customer service and delivery for dramatically increased customer satisfaction and confidence.
- ❖ Improved key account and vendor relationships, and negotiated numerous multi-million dollar contracts.

Management Style: Foster quality-oriented, customer-focused culture of accountability and teamwork with common vision, high camaraderie, and open communication. Equally comfortable providing strategic input as member of senior management team and rolling up sleeves to identify and resolve production problems on factory floor.

PROFESSIONAL HIGHLIGHTS

ELECTRONIC SPECIALTIES, Los Angeles, California   2003–Present
Privately held international manufacturer of precision fittings and clamps.

Vice President, Procurement
Reporting directly to COO, served as one of senior management team's 5 core members, playing corporate-wide role in strategic planning. As sole procurement officer for company, supported rapid, double-digit percentage growth in business volume and manufacturing capacity. Directed all tactical and strategic aspects of procurement including production material ordering/scheduling and non-integrated MRP and scheduling systems.

Made key contributions to corporate strategic initiatives and planning, with special focus on improving inventory management/costs and fully leveraging capabilities of MRP and scheduling systems:

- Chaired Supplier Consolidation Committee and led development of materials component of strategic plan.
- Optimized inventory turns and investment in raw materials and finished goods by documenting and streamlining internal VMI system and its interaction with multiple non-integrated systems. Supplied data to MIS to enable automation.
- Standardized processes for external suppliers, and negotiated blanket contracts for 4%+ annual savings.
- Reduced raw and finished goods storage requirements 77% while increasing capacity and output by 45%, supporting 50% increase in production equipment while maintaining stocking levels allowed to customers.

PRECISION INDUSTRIAL PARTS, INC., Fresno, California   1997–2003
$25 million niche manufacturer of custom injection molded parts for OEMs.

General Manager (1998–2003); Materials/Purchasing Manager (1997–1998)
Recruited to apply purchasing, materials management, and strategic planning skills to help drive turnaround of struggling operation; contributions prompted promotion to multi-plant operating and P&L responsibility for company's 3 manufacturing facilities in US and Mexico within 2 years. Reporting directly to President, directed staff of 17 and workforce of 517. Played key role in establishing vision, corporate culture, and short-/long-term strategic plans and goals.

Working closely with team in highly visible, hands-on role, transformed Cardex job shop to state-of-the-art, system-driven organization through contributions spanning all areas of this international operation:

- Planned and executed move of Mexican operations to new facility, including full build-out and meeting tough regulatory/permit challenges. Moved and re-certified all manufacturing lines with zero customer impact.
- Applied Kaizen continuous improvement principles to material logistics and manufacturing operations, and initiated and led ISO-9000 effort for both Mexico and U.S. plants, achieving first level UL audit.

- Restored customer confidence and brought on-time shipment and delivery to 95%+ within first 8 months, while reducing customer response time more than 80% with automated customer support process and bid/quote system.
- Negotiated blanket contracts for key product components, saving $1.4 million first year and 3%–5% annually thereafter, while working with team and vendors to reorganize materials, purchasing, and planning processes in 3 months.
- Replaced "job shop" planning with integrated MRP system, and adapted systems for Y2K with zero issues.
- Secured key $14 million, 3-year customer contract, and managed quotation process yielding 70% of sales.
- Championed implementation of supplier-held inventories, reducing on-hand inventory by 50% in single year.

HPC ELECTRONICS, Phoenix, Arizona   1995–1997
$29 million producer of connectors and cables for OEMs.

Purchasing Manager
Recruited to bring order to procurement process as part of positioning struggling company for acquisition. Managed procurement, sourcing, planning, subcontracting, and international source development for 3 manufacturing locations (Ireland, Mexico, U.S.). Established and structured completely new department with staff of 5.

Executed rapid turnaround of costs and profitability in severely limited cash flow environment prior to acquisition:

- Quickly created low overhead Procurement/Parts Planning function including ISO-9001 certified/audited process.
- Resolved 6 open supplier legal disputes at no cost to company in 2 months.
- Identified/delivered immediate cost savings exceeding $600K, with additional $1.4 million identified for 1996.
- Provided support key to introduction of strategically critical new product 8 months ahead of schedule.
- Restructured Purchasing Department and instituted cross training to enable 35% headcount reduction.

EXCEL PRODUCTS, INC., Santa Fe, New Mexico   1992–1995
International manufacturer of marine parts, with sales in excess of $290 million.

Director of Purchasing
Reporting to COO, directed staff of 13 in annual purchases of $140 million+ in raw materials, fabricated parts, and equipment. Developed offshore sourcing in China, India, Taiwan, Japan, and Malaysia. Managed parts planning and new product development and introduction. Only non-executive team member included in plant/corporate-level strategic planning.

Consistently exceeded all objectives, earning maximum bonuses and recognition in every area measured:

- Saved $15 million+ during tenure through aggressive process improvements that reduced costs 8%+ annually.
- Automated materials planning with new BPCS MRP system, while nearly tripling raw material inventory turns.
- Reduced product introduction time 25% by implementing team concept in cooperation with Engineering.

PREVIOUSLY: Starting at Excel as entry-level Buyer, consistently supplied creative cost-saving and process-improvement ideas that garnered multiple awards and fast-track promotion to Senior Buyer and then Director of Purchasing in only 4 years.

EDUCATION & TECHNICAL EXPERTISE

B.S. – Business Management, California State University, Northridge, 1988
Technical/Process Background: Process Reengineering, EMI (Early Manufacturing Involvement), JIT (Just In Time) Manufacturing, CFM (Continuous Flow Manufacturing), VMI (Vendor-Managed Inventory), EDI (Electronic Data Interface), DFM (Design for Manufacturing), TQM, Kaizen, ISO 9000, KanBan, Supply Chain Management, Program Management.

PROFESSIONAL AFFILIATIONS

Institute of Supply Management (ISM), American Production and Inventory Control Society (APICS)

Michael K. Edwards

Driving Efficiency and Bottom-Line Performance of International Manufacturing Operations

Michael Edwards brings to the table a bottom-line oriented, hands-on approach to business that has enabled him to improve productivity, customer satisfaction, and profitability of diverse manufacturing operations in both custom production and high-volume environments throughout the U.S., Mexico, and the Pacific Rim. Applying a strong general business acumen and leadership skills along with in-depth knowledge of purchasing, materials management, and supply chain processes, he is as at home rolling up his sleeves to resolve issues on the factory floor as he is in making key contributions to corporate strategy as a member of the senior management team. Mr. Edwards has delivered outstanding results in the face of multiple reorganization, consolidation, turnaround, and facility relocation challenges.

Recently at Electronic Specialties, Inc., Mr. Edwards helped this privately held international manufacturer of precision fittings and clamps to support its rapid business growth and the increased manufacturing capacity that this requires. As one of a 5-member core management team, he led development of and provided strategic input as subject matter expert for the materials component of the corporation's strategic business plan, while serving as catalyst in planning an enterprise-wide supplier consolidation initiative. As sole procurement officer for the company, his focus on optimizing VMI (vendor-managed inventories) and fully leveraging the capabilities of disparate and un-integrated MRP and scheduling systems enabled a 77% reduction in raw and finished goods storage requirements, while capacity and output increased by 45%.

Previously, at Precision Industrial Parts, a $25 million niche manufacturer of custom injection molded parts for use in various OEM products, Mr. Edwards drove turnaround of a struggling operation and held full P&L responsibility as General Manager of the company's three manufacturing facilities that employ more than 500 in the U.S. and Mexico. The transformation accomplished here from a Cardex job shop to a state-of-the-art, system-driven organization was truly remarkable, spanning all areas of this international operation. Mr. Edwards also accomplished relocation of the company's Mexican operations to a new facility amid tough regulatory challenges, and re-certified all manufacturing lines in a manner totally transparent to the customer.

At HPC Electronics, a $29 million producer of connectors and cables for OEMs, Mr. Edwards executed an immediate turnaround of costs and bottom-line profitability through multiple initiatives that helped pave the way to acquisition of the company at outstanding shareholder value. Contributions to this successful acquisition include quick resolution of multiple legal disputes with suppliers (at no cost to the company), identification of $2 million in cost savings to be achieved within a year, and escalating introduction of a mission-critical product by 8 months.

With Excel Products, Inc., a leading manufacturer of marine parts, Mr. Edwards participated in strategic planning at plant and corporate levels, and his contributions again touched numerous areas. Highlights include more than $15 million in cost reductions, nearly tripling raw material inventory turns, a 25% reduction in product introduction time, and automation of materials planning with a state-of-the-art MRP system.

After graduating with a B.S. in Business Management from California State University, Mr. Edwards joined Excel and advanced rapidly from entry-level buyer to Director of Purchasing. He captured multiple company awards and, at this early point in his career, participated at corporate level in strategic planning efforts.

Mr. Edwards's career evidences exceptional management skill with both human and physical resources that invariably results in higher efficiency, lower costs, and improved employee morale. He views people management as his forte, and he thoroughly enjoys and excels at developing and promoting his employees while creating a customer-focused, service-oriented organization. Mr. Edwards offers a winning combination of skills proven in diverse settings to deliver concrete operational results and increased profitability.

****

Anthony Moorefield

18 Eloura Lane
Rocklin, CA 95677

■ ■ ■
Email: moorefield@hotmail.com

Telephone: (916) 624-8735
Mobile: (916) 509-9900

——— SENIOR EXECUTIVE ———

Chief Executive Officer ■ Managing Director ■ General Manager

Performance excellence, an unrelenting results focus, and aggressive implementation over two decades have become career hallmarks underscored by an indelible commitment toward ethical business practices and superior service. As an acknowledged change agent, expertise has been honed in delivering change that exceeds business objectives for cost containment and productivity, while uniting teams to a common purpose. Characterized by board members and executive peers as a corporate "straight shooter"—expert in taking action and leading from the front through a rich blend of market insight, sharp-eyed pragmatism, financial acuity, and visionary leadership.

Value Offered:

- Financial Management
- Organizational Restructuring
- Profit and Loss Management
- ROI Strategies
- Sales and Marketing Campaigns

- Change Management
- Strategic Marketing
- Profit Margin Increases
- Relationship Building
- Revenue Growth Initiatives
- Team Coaching

- Compliance Direction
- Business Start-ups
- Corporate Networking
- Public Speaking
- Sales Forecasting
- Strategic Vision

——— Benchmarks & Milestones ———

- Delivered 2.5% profitability increase against a backdrop of tumultuous cultural change that rejected unethical processes in favor of genuine competition. Despite substantial internal and procedural changes to the business culture, sales were delivered virtually to target.

- Instigated a transparent communications program that outlined new expectations for responsible corporate citizenship, and the necessity to comply with newly devised policy and structure.

- Doubled sales to $10 million in just 24 months, through a series of improvements that tracked field force performances, exited unproductive team members, and provided genuine incentives for delivering results. Results were delivered 3 years ahead of projection.

——— Career Summary ———

NOMAD HALL, Malaysia, New Zealand, Vietnam, Singapore — 1/1997–Present

Chief Executive Officer, Malaysia — (3/2004–Present)
Managing Director, Nomad Hall New Zealand — (3/2002–2/2004)
Managing Director, Nomad Hall Vietnam — (2/2000–2/2002)
Manager, OTC Integration, Nomad Hall Nutrition Singapore — (7/1998–12/1999)
Regional Manager Medical Nutrition, Nomad Hall Nutrition Singapore — (1/1999–1/2000)
Regional Manager, SE Asia Medical Nutrition, Nomad Hall Nutrition Singapore — (1/1997–12/1998)

MAXHELM AUSTRALIA PTY LTD — 10/1995–12/1996
Sales and Marketing Manager, Medical Nutrition

BRADY AUSTRALASIA PTY LTD — 1/1992–10/1995

Product Manager, Medical Nutrition — (2/1995–10/1995)
Product Specialist, Anesthetics — (8/1994–1/1995)
Product Manager, Pharmaceuticals — (6/1994–10/1994)
Manager, Pacific Islands — (3/1992–12/1993)
Marketing Services Manager — (1/1992–10/1994)

TRAVEL INCORPORATED — 10/1989–12/1991
Project Manager — (7/1991–12/1991)
Project Manager — (1/1991–6/1991)
Executive Assistant to Managing Director — (10/1989–12/1990)

NOMAD HALL, Malaysia, New Zealand, Vietnam, Singapore
Chief Executive Officer, Malaysia

The plan to steer a new vision, mission, and strategy in the first 100 days as CEO was immediately placed "on hold" when confronted with an organization in disarray. A recently failed internal audit exposed a multitude of infrastructure and internal control issues, while a lack of organizational transparency had bred suspect ethical behaviors and a divided staff. Clearly, immediate action was critical.

Reviewed alternatives and opted to steer a culture of renewal focusing on restoring internal and external reputations, elevating morale, and reinforcing the importance of business ethics and formalized processes for genuine long-term prosperity.

Early Contributions:

- Gathered evidence of unscrupulous promotional strategies and breaches in codes of conduct and severed ties with individuals responsible. Initiative eliminated deceitful practices, enabling a new generation of business to flourish.

- Instigated a transparent communications program that outlined new expectations for responsible corporate citizenship.

- Launched an aggressive program for managing poor performances with zero salary increases and deadline-dependent performance improvement plans.

Immediate Results:

- Delivered 2.5% profitability increase against a backdrop of tumultuous cultural change that rejected unethical processes in favor of genuine competition. Despite the substantial internal and procedural changes to the business culture, sales were virtually delivered to target, and expenses cut by 4.8%.

- Revolution of change prompted high scores on employee satisfaction surveys that quizzed staff on levels of management transparency, expectations management, and ethical behaviors.

Additional Accomplishments:

- Pioneered a consumer-centric analysis of existing sales tactics used by sales and marketing teams in Malaysia for the first time in the company's history. Partnered with market consultants to validate assumptions and receive customer feedback that provided greater insights for improved customer/product alignment and targeted marketing.

Managing Director, Nomad Hall New Zealand

A history of over-promising and under-delivering had damaged marketplace reputations and with undisciplined leadership, staff morale had plummeted. New Zealand's tough reimbursement environment ensured that the country was one of the hardest markets for pharmaceutical companies to operate within.

Key Contributions:

- Streamlined finance, logistics, human resources, IT, and medical functions by closing New Zealand's operations and sourcing from the Australian affiliate.

- Reduced top-heavy executive management structure, reducing senior management headcount by 30%.

- Cut product "write-offs" by 80% and slashed working capital from 35% to 20%.

- Elevated team morale through open, honest management style that took action and listened to issues. Introduced a reward and recognition program centered on "*Catching people doing good things,*" a highly popular idea that quickly spread across the organization.

- Introduced incentive scheme for representatives that was considered instrumental in exceeding 2003 targets by 4%—the first time in 7 years a target was met or exceeded. Increased sales-per-representative from $NZ 1.6 million to $NZ 3.7 million.

1/1997–Present
(3/2004–Present)

SNAPSHOT

Company: **Asian-based healthcare company. Revenues derived from pharmaceutical research and development, over-the-counter medicines, generic medicines, medical nutrition, animal health, baby food, and lenses.**

Customer base: **medical clinics, retail pharmacies, government/private hospitals.**

Direct Reports: **9 (Country Finance Officer, HR Manager, Head of Sales, Therapeutic Franchise Head Central Nervous System, Medical Manager, Drug and Regulatory Affairs Manager, Product Manager CVS, Associate Product Manager CVS, Senior Administrative Assistant.**

(3/2002–2/2004)

SNAPSHOT

Position summary: **Engaged to turn business around within 3 years and develop and implement market strategies that focused on attractive pricing to meet government purchasing requirements.**

Revenues: **$15 million.**

Customer base: **medical clinics, retail pharmacies, government/private hospitals.**

Managing Director, Nomad Hall New Zealand (continued)

- Instrumental in reversing government decision to refuse reimbursement for a revolutionary product that arrested the progression of a crippling disease. Campaign gained momentum and, with 5,000 emails received within the first 72 hours of the campaign, government altered its stance to reach a funding contract agreement four months later in a deal worth $NZ 130 million over 10 years.

Managing Director, Nomad Hall Vietnam   (2/2000–2/2002)

- Doubled sales to $10 million in just 24 months, through a series of improvements that tracked field-force performances, exited unproductive team members, and provided genuine incentives for delivering results. Results were delivered 3 years ahead of projection.

- Transformed sampling and attention-grabbing gimmick promotions into a series of slick, professional, and sophisticated marketing strategies focused on delivering continual medical education to doctors.

- Doubled sales of calcium supplements in just 12 months by instigating a new screening test for bone density—an indication of osteoporosis.

- Delivered 30% profit through the sale of a manufacturing site.

- Sourced funding and sponsored project for the successful company achievement of GMP accreditation—the first Vietnamese-based pharmaceutical manufacturing plant to accomplish this standard of excellence.

- Identified and mentored six high-potential employees, all of whom progressed to prominent international assignments or leadership roles.

SNAPSHOT

Environment: **Combination of representative office operations and 100% foreign-owned company with pharmaceutical manufacturing plant.**

Position summary: **Oversaw $5 million operation employing 160. Developed strategic plans, OTC/FMCG competencies in marketing and sales, and mentored high-performing talent.**

Manager, OTC Integration, Nomad Hall Nutrition Singapore   (7/1998–12/1999)
Regional Manager Medical Nutrition, Nomad Hall Nutrition Singapore   (1/1999–1/2000)
Regional Manager, SE Asia Medical Nutrition, Nomad Hall Nutrition Singapore (1/1997–12/1998)

- On a shoestring budget, successfully launched medical nutrition business in New Zealand, Malaysia, Thailand, and Indonesia during the Asian financial crisis. Reinvested restructuring savings of $US 1.5 million into the larger markets.

- Propelled sales from $3 million to $20 million, focusing resources and energies on large markets to drive growth. Identified suitable partner for entry into Japanese market.

Prior Engagements

- Maxhelm Australia Pty Ltd (10/1995–12/1996). **Sales and Marketing Manager, Medical Nutrition.** Launched new medical nutrition range in Australia, exceeding financial objectives by more than 50%.

- Brady Australasia Pty Ltd. (1/1992–10/1995). **Product Manager Medical Nutrition, Product Specialist Anesthetics, Product Manager Pharmaceuticals, Manager Pacific Islands, Marketing Services Manager.** Introduced discipline in marketing team for cost-center management, budgeting, and forecasting. Managed $7.5 million marketing expenses within budget. Established and steered eightfold increase in revenues in the Pacific Island region.

- Travel Incorporated (10/1989–12/1991). **Project Manager CTAL, Project Manager, Executive Assistant to Managing Director.**

Education

Bachelor of Science, Business Administration
University of California at Los Angeles

Anthony Moorefield

EXECUTIVE BIOGRAPHY
Chief Executive Officer

Anthony Moorefield is Chief Executive Officer of the Malaysia division of global pharmaceutical leader Nomad Hall, and a veteran of the healthcare industry with more than fourteen years' management-level experience in operations, sales and marketing, and product management of medical nutrition, anesthetics, pharmaceutical, and over-the-counter products.

Starting his career in pharmaceuticals as Brady Australasia's Marketing Services Manager, Anthony quickly progressed through the professional ranks within the firm. Reveling in his reputation as a business evangelist and troubleshooter—then as now, Anthony demonstrated his ability to eliminate organizational "bloat," establish progressive policies, generate unparalleled revenues, and meet aggressive competitors head-on with a strong mix of sophisticated marketing prowess and his enviable strengths in forging long-lasting customer alliances.

New challenges beckoned for Anthony in 1995 when he accepted the role as Sales and Marketing Manager for Medical Nutrition products with Maxhelm Australia, an assignment that saw him launch a new product range to market and exceed all financial forecasts by an impressive fifty percent. It was an exceptional achievement for the fifth entrant in an already overcrowded market that treated products as commodities.

As company recognition grew, Anthony accepted the role of Regional Manager of SE Asia's Medical Nutrition division with Nomad Hall Singapore in 1997; a career phase that has been hallmarked by goal achievement and professional progression to the present day.

Representing the Nomad Hall Group at senior management level in Vietnam, New Zealand, Singapore, and now as Chief Executive Officer of Nomad Hall Malaysia, Anthony has consistently left each division in an infinitely improved position than when he commenced. He has proven his influence in lobbying governments on behalf of the industry and company and "cracked" tough markets such as New Zealand, where he steered his team to deliver sales improvements for the first time in seven years.

A dealmaker and astute businessperson, Anthony is best known for his capacity to facilitate change. Adopting a transparent communications style and achieving the type of willing and enthusiastic acceptance that is not only rare in most organizations, but at times almost unprecedented, Anthony stands as an example of integrity: strong on business ethics and relentless in his pursuit to clean up practices that have been operating outside business boundaries. In just twelve months as CEO of Nomad Hall Singapore, Anthony rid the business of unethical procedures, flushed out those with poor reputations, and made it clear to vendors, customers, team members, the field force, and partners that the business operates on a par with industry best practice—backed by a renewed customer-centric focus and a relentless will to succeed.

Possessing an intuitive knowledge of people, and an inherent ability to recognize and nurture talent, Anthony has consistently injected business with a team of smart, resourceful, and intuitive professionals to compete with polished presentations, superior product knowledge, and the authority to make a deal. Several individuals have rewarded his faith and mentorship by progressing to leadership and international appointments throughout the company.

While steering organizational change is Anthony's passion, it is his talent for capitalizing on opportunities and identifying internal control flaws that has elevated his management profile. An analytical and strategic mindset underscores management decision making, ensuring visionary leadership is supported with pragmatic business understanding.

Anthony attributes a great deal of his success as a negotiator, communicator, and senior manager to his powers of persuasion and his ability to get things done. He is keen to drive similar results for his next employer.

Anthony Moorefield is a Board Member of the Singapore Pharmacy Association and has also served as a Board Member of industry associations in Vietnam and New Zealand. He holds a bachelor's degree in Business Administration from the University of California.

18 Eloura Lane
Rocklin CA 95677

Email: moorefield@hotmall.com

Telephone: (916) 624-8735
Mobile: (916) 624-9900

THOMAS WEBSTER

90 Colonial Village
Portsmouth, NH 92098
Residence: (603) 762-6209 ▪ Office: (603) 762-0034 ▪ E-mail: twebster@email.net

---

SENIOR FINANCIAL & GENERAL MANAGEMENT EXECUTIVE
President/Chief Executive Officer ▪ General Manager ▪ Investment Fund Managing Director

---

Visionary, entrepreneurial-minded executive noted as an expert rainmaker, aggressive deal maker, and motivational leader bringing a rare level of business acumen and record of achievements developed over a rich 20-year career in the commercial banking arena. Growth- and results-focused; expert knowledge of business financing tools coupled with the core management qualifications to transform failing companies and capitalize on market opportunities.

Building businesses, leading turnaround of troubled companies, working in diverse industries and with 1,000s of business models, and delivering sustained profitability and growth in
dynamic economic conditions.

PROFESSIONAL HISTORY

Nation Financial Bank – Boston, MA   1982 – 2004
Progressed through a series of fast-track, performance-based promotions—entry-level to division president—during a 2-decade period of frequent change, variable economic conditions, and 5 acquisitions/mergers. Produced extraordinary P&L growth and commissioned with increasing executive authority and responsibility over past 7 years.

	2004	2003	2002	2001	2000	1999
P&L	$73.7 million	$57.8 million	$52 million	$21.3 million	$18.6 million	$17.6 million
Increase	27.5%	11.2%	144%	14.5%	5.7%	--

PRESIDENT, COMMERCIAL BANKING (2002 – 2004)

Following national consolidation and reorganization into territories, promoted to provide executive management for the fastest growing market territory (covering Massachusetts, New Hampshire, and Maine) with $7 billion assets. Held full decision-making authority in a matrix environment for 2,400 employees and $73+ million P&L. Retained title of Massachusetts state president and led 13 direct reports comprising New Hampshire and Maine state presidents and line and functional managers throughout Massachusetts.

Challenges:

Tasked with leading development, growth, and improved financial performance of a newly formed territory made up of 3 uniquely different markets and business cultures:

New Hampshire   Shared top market positioning with single major competitor (40% each); challenged to devise new client and employee retention strategies to sustain and strengthen market share.

Massachusetts   Held largest share of the market (27%) but challenged aggressively for dominant position by 3 national competitors.

Maine   Overpowered by competitors and holding minimal market share (6%). Turnaround and transformation required through divestiture/reinvestment of capital or acquisition/growth to increase market share and strengthen future viability.

Actions:

Spearheaded visibility-boosting strategies to forge new business and outpace the competition by solidifying "top-of-the-mind" awareness with key referral sources. Leveraged marketing, sponsorships, and philanthropy to connect with influential constituents. Capitalized on unique opportunities presented by the 2002 Winter Olympics to boost name recognition with Olympics-themed promotions and campaigns.

Selected Results:

▪ Delivered $73+ million in commercial banking direct contribution, ranking as the 3rd most profitable of 13 territories nationwide and achieving #1 ranking on all relative return/profitability measures, including ROA, ROI, and revenue per FTE.

72

<u>MASSACHUSETTS STATE PRESIDENT</u> (2002 – 2004)

Senior executive directing all operations of MA's 2nd largest bank with $6 billion assets, 1,500 employees, and 83 branch locations. Chaired a 10-person paid advisory board, guided 11 direct reports, controlled $2.8 million total philanthropy/marketing/sponsorship budget, and represented the bank as spokesperson for all government, public, and media relations. Held P&L authority for commercial banking business and matrix management oversight of nationally reporting local business lines.

Challenges:

Faced with dispirited, merger-worn employees and a disconnected product line with no apparent alignment to corporate vision. Required immediate intervention to create an empowering, cohesive work atmosphere and to rebuild pride and value among employees and customers.

Actions:

Championed development of the bank's first statewide common vision for success and aggressively promoted the vision to achieve employee engagement. Created processes to utilize collective goals as a guide for future direction and all critical decisions; realigned business lines to parallel and support the vision. Fostered positive public relations, built brand value, established a team atmosphere, and minimized unwanted employee turnover by initiating new:

- Community Outreach Campaigns
- Volunteer Community Projects
- Media Relations Strategies
- Sports Marketing Sponsorships
- Quarterly Employee Performance Reviews
- 360-Degree Employee Reviews

Selected Results:

- Captured share away from market-leading competitor and grew deposits 8.86% in spite of declining economic conditions and a contracting market base.

- Rekindled growth momentum, accelerated brand value, and revitalized employee morale and enthusiasm to pursue achievement of common goals; facilitated an empowering, team-focused atmosphere that rewarded community involvement and top-quality customer service.

- Profiled in a feature article as one of "MA's Top CEOs" by MassachusettsBiz magazine, October 2003.

■■■■■■■

<u>EXECUTIVE VICE PRESIDENT</u> (1999 – 2002)

Charged with P&L and full general management authority for the Massachusetts Commercial Banking Division encompassing a $3.5 billion loan portfolio, 7 direct reports, and 70 employees in 8 statewide locations.

Challenges:

Confronted with a problem-plagued, recently merged division requiring mediation of infighting, improved management reporting systems, standardized performance measures, and led development of a common vision to drive success in the rapidly expanding economy and a fiercely competitive market.

Actions:

Consolidated and merged 3 locations to streamline operations and improve cost efficiency. Created scalable sales management, risk management, and budget management control systems designed to keep pace with projected growth. Spearheaded development of new products, businesses, and strategic investments to ramp business growth ahead of the competition. Executed market research and authored business plan to capitalize on the state's fast-growing high-tech industry.

Selected Results:

- Attained #1 market share in the state against larger, entrenched competition.

- Grew 2 niche businesses from scratch that boosted portfolio $602 million; headed development of a national ski resort finance business and a highly specialized public finance portfolio.

- Cut direct expenses $1.7 million and reduced headcount by 15 full-time employees.

73

Executive Vice President continued

- Boosted closing ratio 55% through implementation of new processes that pre-empted the competition.

- Initiated a $2.5 million strategic investment in a local mezzanine capital fund to provide senior debt and financial service products to local mid-market companies involved in M&A activities; substantially enhanced bank's referral network and reputation.

■■■■■■■

SENIOR VICE PRESIDENT (1996 – 1998)

Took over leadership of recently merged team composed of 8 vice presidents, 3 associate vice presidents, and 1 credit analyst covering the eastern region of New England. Oversaw P&L and all general management functions for $11.7 million annual business.

Challenges:

Charted cultural and technical integration of recently merged region, focusing efforts to build personal credibility and trust with the team and to forge a highly effective and motivated group.

Actions:

Instituted processes to recognize individual success and performance. Assigned valued projects to top producers and shared referral network to funnel business through team members. Introduced group-specific advertising as a step to drive accelerated growth.

Selected Results:

- Led team to #1 ranking among all peer groups; earned recognition as experts on corporate finance frequently quoted in periodicals and invited as panel members and speakers.

- Grew revenue 55% to high of $27.3 million in 1998 from initial $17.6 million in 1996.

■■■■■■■

VICE PRESIDENT (1988 – 1995)

Promoted to accelerate growth of the bank's commercial portfolio. Built high-impact client relationships and personally forged more than a dozen key relationships that have grown to become the bank's most profitable house accounts. Completed extensive national sales training programs, including Xerox, Dale Carnegie, and Strategic Selling. Won top sales and business development awards and assigned as leader on many new major client initiatives. Worked extensively with equity sponsors on M&A transactions.

Selected Results:

- Produced more than 1,000% growth over 7 years, building the commercial portfolio to a height of $287 million from initial $26 million.

- Pioneered 27 client relationships as the foundation of a new portfolio that has since grown to $237 million; pinpointed and capitalized on market inefficiencies by creating a product that forged entry into the credit enhancement market for public debentures issued by Massachusetts special districts.

- Negotiated, structured, and established financing to lift Attitash Associates out of bankruptcy with no impairment to direct creditors and continued access to new capital for growth to current standing as a publicly funded, world-renowned ski resort.

- Collaborated in the national consolidation of dialysis centers and led senior debt financing by introducing an industry-first, innovative patient cash-flow borrowing base. Performed enterprise valuations and played instrumental role in building company value to levels that achieved eventual sale for $130 million.

- Nurtured and advanced projects of critical importance to the Boston community; headed negotiations and financing and was a primary leader in interactions with major league baseball authorities and the stadium vote that enabled expansion of the Baseball Club into the Boston market.

ASSISTANT VICE PRESIDENT (1987 – 1988)

Managed banking activity for the Structured Finance Group's portfolio. Handled credit agreements, credit amendments/waivers, treasury management activities, foreign exchange transactions, interest rate swaps, and other financial derivatives. Represented the bank to the creditor's committee in the Omni Airlines bankruptcy.

■■■■■■■

COMMERCIAL LOAN OFFICER (1986 – 1987)

Recruited aggressively to join one of several lending departments; selected the Structured Finance Group as a critical step to shift career into commercial banking. Executed complex financial modeling and audited clients' cash conversion cycles. Devised a client relationship profitability model that was later adopted as the bank's standard.

■■■■■■■

CREDIT DEPARTMENT MANAGER (1983 – 1986)

Achieved performance-based promotion into management role that was a turning point in career. Led dramatic turnaround of a previously mis-managed and severely troubled team, capturing attention of the senior management and accelerating future promotions to executive levels. Headed a 15-person team in all analysis and monitoring of the bank's credit decisions portfolio. Forged complete restructuring of group to replace under-performers, renew motivation, and correct functional deficiencies of the team. Raised performance standards to new highs, recruited several key hires, reduced training costs 42%, and eliminated unwanted turnover.

■■■■■■■

SENIOR CREDIT ANALYST (1982 – 1983)

Performed analysis of credit decisions and client portfolios. Progressively assigned to projects of increasingly larger scope and complexity.

EDUCATION & CREDENTIALS

M.B.A., MARKETING ■ University of New Hampshire, Durham (1985)
B.S.B.A., FINANCE ■ University of Southern Maine, Portland (1977)

Chartered Financial Analyst, Level I (CFA)
Certified Cash Manager (CCM)

AFFILIATIONS & AWARDS

Corporate Boards	-	Chairman, Nation Finance Bank Community Advisory Board
	-	Advisory Board, Boston Capital Partners (private mezzanine fund)
Community Boards	-	Executive Committee/Co-chair of Public Affairs, Boston Metro Chamber of Commerce
	-	Board of Trustees, Mile High United Way
	-	Chairman of Strategic Planning Committee, Junior Achievement
	-	Executive Committee/Chairman of Fundraising, I Have a Dream Foundation
	-	Steering and Selection Committee, Citizen of the East
	-	Founding Board and Executive Committee, Second Century Fund
	-	Board of Directors, New England Forum
Awards	-	Leadership Boston (Group of 40 emerging business and community leaders)
	-	2001 Allied Award, Women's Vision Foundation
	-	1999, 2000, 2001 Boston Business Journal, Who's Who in Business and Finance

THOMAS WEBSTER

90 Colonial Village
Portsmouth, NH 92098
Residence: (603) 762-6209 ▪ Office: (603) 762-0034 ▪ E-mail: twebster@email.net

SENIOR FINANCIAL & GENERAL MANAGEMENT EXECUTIVE

Executive Profile

Thomas Webster brings a vast wealth of experience and deep insight born from an extraordinary commercial banking career providing a rare insider view of thousands of business models spanning virtually all industries to each venture he touches. As the son of a working-class family and a first-generation college graduate, Thomas's 20+-year journey from carpenter's apprentice, to recovery specialist with the U.S. Small Business Administration, to his most recent role as president of a $7 billion, three-state, 2,400-employee commercial bank has been driven by innovation, vision, and a true passion for challenge.

NATION FINANCIAL BANK ▪ Boston, MA ▪ 1982 – 2004

President, Commercial Banking (2002 – 2004)
Massachusetts State President (2002 - 2004)
Executive Vice President (1999 – 2002)
Senior Vice President (1996 – 1998)
Vice President (1988 – 1995)
Assistant Vice President (1987 – 1988)
Commercial Loan Officer (1986 – 1987)
Credit Department Manager (1983 – 1986)
Senior Credit Analyst (1982 – 1983)

Excelling in a dynamic environment of frequent change, five acquisitions and mergers, and variable economic conditions, Thomas refined his unique and highly effective management style. Best characterized by commitment to "collective vision," his decisive yet flexible brand of leadership has proven superior in fostering collaboration and partnerships, engaging employees to work toward common goals yet encouraging proactive response to changing market, economic, and business demands.

Applying a visionary, entrepreneurial-driven focus, Thomas Webster is perhaps best known for his value as a trusted advisor and source of counsel to his customers. Forging close, personal relationships, Thomas encourages open communication and brainstorming and has worked hand-in-hand with company executives and business leaders to overhaul, fine-tune, implement, and execute a diversity of business plans. Becoming a partner in the business process, he has played an instrumental role in successful new venture launches, bankruptcy workouts, operational restructuring and turnaround, consolidation and merger, and national expansion and growth projects.

With an energy fueled by the thrill of the challenge, Thomas's leadership and inherent business savvy have been equally beneficial to Nation Financial Bank. Throughout his tenure he was valued for his achievements in developing and building multimillion-dollar business lines from the ground floor, rekindling growth momentum in stagnant markets, and driving expansion and business success in all economic cycles – boom/bust, growth/recession. An aggressive, hands-on deal maker and rainmaker, he has delivered against all challenges, meeting or surpassing every profit and budget target for 20 consecutive years and driving extraordinary increases in direct profit contributions for the past seven years.

	2004	2003	2002	2001	2000	1999
P&L	$73.7 million	$57.8 million	$52 million	$21.3 million	$18.6 million	$17.6 million
Increase	27.5%	11.2%	144%	14.5%	5.7%	--

…Continued…

THOMAS WEBSTER

A native of Maine, in 1982 Thomas made his home in the Portsmouth, New Hampshire, area where he and his wife of 25 years continue to raise their two children today and where it is common to find Thomas at his children's dance recitals and soccer matches. With an adventuresome spirit carried over from his college days when he was legendary on campus for living in a tepee for over a year, or perhaps from surmounting his fear of heights to indulge his passion for skydiving, Thomas encourages his children to overcome their own imagined limitations and boundaries, and enjoys yearly white-water rafting trips with them.

Sincerely committed to the City of Boston and the surrounding area, and genuinely believing in the importance of giving back to the community that has nurtured his family and contributed to his career success, Thomas Webster is a well-known and respected community leader and participant in numerous community events. Active on various corporate and community boards, Thomas was awarded affiliation in the 40-member "Leadership Boston" group, was the 2001 recipient of the "Allied Award" from the Women's Vision Foundation for his work in advancing the issues of women in the workplace, was featured three times in the *Boston Business Journal,* and was profiled as one of Massachusetts's top CEOs in the October 2003 issue of *MassachusettsBiz* magazine.

Corporate	-	Chairman, Nation Finance Bank Community Advisory Board
Boards	-	Advisory Board, Boston Capital Partners (private mezzanine fund)
Community	-	Executive Committee/Co-chair of Public Affairs, Boston Metro Chamber of Commerce
Boards	-	Board of Trustees, Mile High United Way
	-	Chairman of Strategic Planning Committee, Junior Achievement
	-	Executive Committee/Chairman of Fundraising, I Have a Dream Foundation
	-	Steering and Selection Committee, Citizen of the East
	-	Founding Board and Executive Committee, Second Century Fund
	-	Board of Directors, New England Forum

Thomas launched his career by earning his B.S.B.A. degree in Finance from the University of Southern Maine in 1977, and attained an M.B.A. in Marketing from the University of New Hampshire in 1985. He has since earned his credentials as a Chartered Financial Analyst, Level 1 (CFA), and a Certified Cash Manager (CCM).

Known for his intelligence, determination, charismatic personality, and influential leadership, Thomas Webster has earned the respect of the community, his employees, his customer, and his peers for his willingness to roll up his sleeves and do whatever needs to be done to succeed. He is not daunted by challenge but, rather, enthused by new opportunity. Thomas believes in long-term vision and works tirelessly to achieve and surpass his goals.

CHAPTER 8

Writing Profiles and Addenda

A separate document profiling specific leadership, technology, marketing, training, or other strengths is an ideal way to present vital information that will support your current career goals. Most often used as a one-page addendum to the resume, the profile creates a snapshot that is sharply focused on one key aspect of your qualifications.

Keep these guidelines in mind as you develop your own profile documents.

1. Focus, focus, focus

Remember, your resume is designed to present the full scope of your career information, and it might encompass two, three, or more pages. In contrast, your profile should focus on just one thing, whether it's your leadership skills, technology expertise, marketing successes, training experience, or specific industry knowledge. Decide which facet of your expertise you wish to call attention to; then pull out the experiences, activities, and accomplishments that relate most closely to that specific area.

2. Get to the point

A snapshot is a quick view — not an entire album! We recommend that you keep your profile to one page.

3. Organize for readability

Break down the information in your profile into distinct areas and use headings to call them out. This will make it easier for readers to skim the page and quickly gain an overview of what you have to offer.

Examples

In the following examples, each profile was prepared and used for a different purpose. See how well each one correlates with the executive resume yet pulls the reader's attention to the right information to support a specific goal.

EXAMPLE 1: Resume and Technology Profile: Robert Martin (pages 80-83)
(Writer – Phyllis Shabad)

Robert's three-page resume provides ample evidence of his strong executive competencies and technology leadership. As a companion piece, the technology profile zeroes in on specific knowledge, industry recognition, and successes related to technology. It finishes with a powerful case study, a perfect illustration of all of the expertise listed above. Robert used the profile as a resume addendum or when asked, during an interview, about his specific technology experience.

EXAMPLE 2: Resume and Leadership Profile: Jennifer Brown (pages 84-86)
(Writer – Michelle Dumas)

Jennifer's one-page leadership profile helped her to market both herself, as an employee, and the consulting services that she offered while searching for her next opportunity. Both the resume and the leadership profile clearly express her expertise and her ability to add value in today's increasingly complex global business environment. The format of her leadership profile makes it useful either as a resume addendum or as a stand-alone marketing piece.

EXAMPLE 3: Resume and Training Addendum: Jonathan Diaz (pages 87-89)
(Writer – Tracy Parish)

The Training Addendum that accompanies this executive resume is a great strategy for presenting material that is important but just too voluminous to include on a resume. The addendum adds credibility to Jonathan's quality and training expertise, providing a lot of detail that still can be easily skimmed. Jonathan included this addendum with his resume on occasion, but more often he provided it during an interview as documentation for his credentials.

EXAMPLE 4: Resume and Marketing Profile: Blaire Weyland (pages 90-93)
(Writer – Phyllis Shabad)

Blaire's Marketing Profile supports her resume, which at three pages is rich with the accomplishments of a successful 15-year career. While several of the items included in the profile were mentioned in the resume, such as her e-zine development and C-TPAT certification manual, when presented as a comprehensive list in the addendum they take on new force and meaning. Blaire used the addendum either when sending her resume or as a leave-behind following interviews.

EXAMPLE 5: Resume and Leadership Profile: Melissa Thomas (pages 94-97)
(Writer – Louise Garver)

Formatted like a more traditional executive biography, this profile focuses on Melissa's leadership capabilities as demonstrated by her career successes. It was prepared as part of her resume package at the specific request of an executive recruiter, who wanted to present Melissa for a position as president of a biotech company. Thus, it was important to downplay her specific industry experience and highlight her industry-spanning leadership skills. The strategy worked, and Melissa was offered the position.

ROBERT M. MARTIN

CHIEF TECHNOLOGY OFFICER • E-COMMERCE DEVELOPMENT • BUSINESS GROWTH ACCELERATION

Senior technology executive with deep experience managing architecture, planning, and e-commerce initiatives for global leaders in the shipping and logistics, voice and data networking, and energy industries. Defined and implemented enterprise-level plans that deftly addressed tactical and strategic needs. Synthesized stakeholder contributions into an enterprise and modular architecture built for business growth. Resilient, pragmatic thinker with a disciplined style in communicating across functions to develop, manage, and execute a vision and roadmap. Trilingual: fluent in English, French, and German.

NOTABLE:

▶ Created global vision linking IT to business goals, leading PBB to high-tech, market-leading position in shipping and logistics.

▶ Captured new segment of customer base at little cost with cutting-edge web site that both automates and personalizes services.

▶ Drove exponential sales growth by developing world-class, high-demand services that markedly surpass those of competitors.

▶ Transformed costly "stovepipe" solutions with little re-use value into affordable gateway congruent with client needs.

AREAS OF EXPERTISE

STRATEGIC PLANNING ▼ MISSION-BUILDING ▼ IT CONSOLIDATION & CENTRALIZATION
MIS MANAGEMENT ▼ TEAM BUILDING & LEADERSHIP ▼ BUSINESS & TECHNOLOGY TURNAROUND STRATEGIES

Development Life Cycle • Supply Chain Management • Architecture & Planning • Infrastructure Development • CRM Initiatives
Financial /Billing /Yield Management Systems • E-Commerce Frameworks • Database & Messaging Systems • EAS Integration
Network Management • P&L Oversight • Cost Controls • QA / QC Processes • Global Procurement • Market Analytics
R&D / Prototype Solutions • Product Development & Evaluations • Legacy Systems • Knowledge Management
Vendor Relations • Global Contract Negotiations • Staff Development • Succession Planning • Productivity Enhancements

EXECUTIVE PERFORMANCE AND VALUE

CONCEIVED OF AND LED STRATEGIC PLAN THAT BECAME BLUEPRINT FOR ALL FUTURE TECHNOLOGY INITIATIVES AT PBS

As CTO, developed cohesive IT strategy to support five-year strategic business imperatives of PBS Global, including a migration to evolve legacy systems into strategic architecture and a global methodology to achieve effective, repeatable processes. Met financial objectives to reduce IT costs as a percentage of revenue while also improving service levels.

Value and Results

- Collaborated with all IT divisions and key internal/external clients to develop the mission statement and brand IT's guiding principles, values, roles, and services. Used key business stakeholders as well as business, application, technical, and physical architects from Asia, North America, Latin America, and Europe to launch these initiatives.
- Elicited feedback to identify and document key requirements, IT functionality gaps, and internal and external constraints. Mapped back to the business objectives with recommendations for meeting them at affordable and sustainable costs.
- Realized dramatic improvements in standardization of business and IT processes, creation of a PBS global IT organization, and improved ability to sustain rapid growth while facilitating merger and acquisition activities.

TURNED AROUND CORPORATE WEB SITE TO RECAPTURE MARKET POSITION AND DIFFERENTIATE PBS AS KEY ECONOMIC PARTNER

Designed and implemented well-branded, unified, and highly personalized online experience of PBS to its customers.

Value and Results

- Leveraged best practices with major accounts and automated them to serve medium-size accounts and casual customers.
- Released first transaction-based web site six months after hire. Delivered WebFast six months ahead of schedule.
- Shifted PBS web site from static to fully dynamic with up-sell and cross-sell capabilities. Electronic shipment preparation went from 40% to 89% globally and 94% in the U.S. in three years, decreasing IT operational costs by 60% per shipment.
- PBS Global grew from 175 to 34,000 clients; WebFast grew from 425 to 2.5 million users in first year.

254 Glen Ellen Street, Denver, CO 80002 • Ph: (303) 555-1234
Fax: (303) 545-9923 • E-mail: rmmit21@aol.com

EXECUTIVE PERFORMANCE AND VALUE, *continued*

DROVE DEVELOPMENT OF MULTI-PROTOCOL GATEWAY THAT ENABLED PBS TO CAPTURE MARKET SHARE WHILE SAVING MILLIONS

Was challenged to provide secure, cost-effective, and faster integration solutions for high- and low-end customer segments that replicated the same levels of service. These highly customized solutions were not being offered by the competition.

Value and Results

- Architected an agile solution to fit the global IT strategy, leveraging existing assets and introducing new technologies.
- Reduced utilization of Virtual Area Networks by 105% in first 21 months, saving $4.4 million annually.
- Cut integration time from 60 days to 72 hours, handling multiple formats. Replicated architecture in three global regions.
- Boosted customer acquisition and retention, reduced IT operating costs 35% in year one, and improved problem resolution.

LED MIGRATION TO NEW SYSTEM THAT IMPROVED CUSTOMER RETENTION AND IGNITED NEW SALES WORLDWIDE

Facing obsolete legacy systems for PBS Global Logistics Solution, identified and deployed new concepts, technologies, and protocols to better manage volumes and complexities of new global business requirements, including issues for top 200 clients.

Value and Results

- Established repeatable workflows that allowed better management of initial POCs, optimized resource allocation, focused on early risk identification and mitigation, and delivered a realistic program scope, i.e., time and money.
- Delivered first iteration 11% under budget by first deadline, allowing top 25 clients access to new information services integrated with CRM and SCM systems; formed the base of the component-based architecture defined in IT strategy.
- Turned around key client retention and increased sales 54% along with 22% reduction in IT costs in first four months.

STREAMLINED GLOBAL BILLING, REPORTING, AND INFORMATION-SHARING PROCESSES WITH NEW TECHNOLOGY SOLUTIONS

Led inception of a $550 million project to reduce billing costs worldwide by 35%, consolidating and migrating legacy systems to a fully J2EE-compliant architecture. Focused on no service interruptions and new features to support current business needs.

Value and Results

- Delivered overall cost and schedule estimates including staffing needs, competency gaps, ROI, and financial forecasts.
- Designed architecture to fit current and future requirements, integration with any domain, and reusable components.
- Structured overall program that delivered competitive IT products, recapture of lost income, faster billing cycles, and improved cross- and up-selling capabilities, synergizing business with IT strategy for customer acquisition and traction.

PIONEERED CRM SOLUTION THAT FACILITATED ISSUE RESOLUTION, GENERATED LOYALTY, AND ENHANCED PBS'S REPUTATION

Redesigned CRM technology to automate all functions and integrate multiple customer centers into a unified experience, aligning PBS as the uncontested service leader in the transportation industry offering personalization and issue resolution.

Value and Results

- Designed and validated candidate architecture; tested it with development of new tracking and tracing application.
- Automated tracking and tracing capabilities reduced calls 17% and handle time 33%, increased first-time resolution 40%, and saved $3.3 million per year. Web- and email-based self service further reduced calls 19% in two months.
- The Global CRM solution was later adopted and deployed in Asia and Europe, gaining credibility for U.S. IT.

RESTRUCTURED FRAGMENTED OPERATIONS ON TWO CONTINENTS AND FUSED INTO SEAMLESS NETWORK WITH MORE CAPABILITIES

Faced need to consolidate and fully integrate all PBS North and South American global and regional IS functions into one facility with a closely located network and critical system backup. Few resources were available for the 12-month life cycle.

Value and Results

- Created highly specialized project teams to manage key elements, e.g., operations, networking, help desk, product support.
- Accelerated ROI by leveraging global contracts to renegotiate existing hardware, software, telco, and service contracts.
- Facilitated knowledge transfer from key intellectual property owners to global IT resources and outsourced resources.
- Completed program in 11 months with headcount reduction of 25%, closure of eight locations, reduction in servers from 550 to 213, and a yearly cost savings of $22 million with more network capacity and development capabilities.

CAREER DEVELOPMENT

BRANDSTREAM CONSULTING, Denver, Colorado   2001 to present
Partner; Strategic Business Growth Consultant

DataPort Holdings (San Jose, CA): assisted in developing a strategic OEM partnership with a major mobility equipment manufacturer. Aligned product development and marketing efforts between the two entities ... **FusionFire** (Boston, MA): created business and marketing plans to secure seed capital—overseeing initial application prototype for a Series A—and established partnership agreements ... **Definity Wireless** (Boulder, CO): provided strategic plans to fine-tune and brand the firm's message and product marketing. Designed case studies and helped identify ROI for targeted customers.

PBS GLOBAL LOGISTICS, Hamburg, Germany / Manchester, UK   1995 to 2001
Global CTO and Director of E-Commerce Development

Recruited to create and manage web services division for PBS, a leading global express air network with annual revenues of $9.5 billion and 99,000 employees servicing 1.4 million customers in 100,000+ destinations. Promoted to Chief Technology Officer reporting to Global CIO. Delivered multimillion-dollar ROI via web and e-commerce initiatives that streamlined operations, improved productivity, increased revenues, and reduced costs. Staffed and managed architecture and development divisions representing 47 employees, 100+ contractors/consultants, and international outsourcing with annual budget of $25 million and global IT budget of $750 million. Trained and motivated staff and also formulated robust succession plans.

BIG DOG NETWORKS, Mountain View, CA   1991 to 1995
Senior Architect and Development Manager – Global Web Services

Managed 23 employees in three locations (U.S., UK, Sydney) for Big Dog, a leading provider of innovative voice and data networking products, services, and solutions for public- and private-sector organizations. Reported to SVP of Architecture and Planning. Designed, developed, and deployed e-commerce and marketing Internet applications. Directed the architecture and technical deliverables for Big Dog's worldwide corporate Intranet/Internet/Extranet. Deployed infrastructure in seven replicated hubs to support virtually all functions of the organization and 19,000 users. Lead architect for SAP R3 Phase 2 deployment and web integration. Designed integration plan to optimize assets and reduce costs in acquisition of XCell Data.

SUNLIGHT TRADING SOLUTIONS, Houston, TX   1989 to 1991
Network Principal Architect

Sunlight Trading Solutions provides business and operational consultancy, technical services, and research and development expertise to the energy industry worldwide. Managed WAN/LAN architecture group of 16 architects and engineers. Leveraged Internet to optimize network, streamline information flow, reduce costs, and increase productivity. Oversaw R&D prototypes.

EDUCATION AND LEADERSHIP

Columbia University, New York, NY – **BS in Economics, 1989**

Board Directorships and Advisory Roles: Plaxo Advisory Board • Logi2Web Advisory Board
Ballesta Customer Advocacy Group • Global Port Board • Advisor to GP of Syliconn Funds

MANAGEMENT EFFECTIVENESS

DEEP UNDERSTANDING OF THE BUSINESS MISSION

"I have known Robert for nearly twelve years ... watched him grow into the position of CTO of PBS ... he was the brightest, most energetic executive at PBS as well as one of the most progressive and successful when it came to measurable results ... others value him as a great communicator and a poised leader."
— *Sawyer Cahill, Chairman & CEO, Logi2Web*

CONCEPTUAL, CREATIVE YET PRAGMATIC

" ... a terrific CTO, out-of-the-box thinker and strategist. He can conceptualize the most complex environments, visualize a solution, and has the know-how to bridge the 'now' and the future mission. He truly owns the business blueprint."
— *Noah Lehman , CTO, Align Wireless*

TECHNOLOGY PROFILE

Presentations

Presented for *Information Week*; *CIO Magazine*; *JAVA One*
Keynote speaker for **Plaxo**; **SUN**; **Global Fuel Index**

Technology Summary

Operating Systems:

Windows (NT, 2000, 2003, XP) • SOLARIS • HP UX • OS/390 • AS/400

Software:

IBM Rational Rose XDE Modeler • AllFusion ERwin DataModeler • IBM Rational ClearCase • IBM Rational RequisitePro
MS Project • Visio • ACT! • Photoshop CS • Illustrator CS • MAYA 5 • MS Office (Word, Excel, PowerPoint, Access)

Enterprise Software:

JD Edwards • PeopleSoft • BAAN • SAP • Oracle Financials • I2 • Manugistics • EXE • Tetra CS/3 • Yantra
Epiphany • Sieble • Business Objects • Plaxo WLI • Vitria • WebMethods • Tibco • IBM MQ Series
Informatica ETL • Tuxedo TPM

Firewall: CheckPoint
Languages: C • Perl • Java • JavaScript • VB
Authoring Tools: Macromedia Dreamweaver • Macromedia Studio • MS FrontPage
Environments: J2EE • .Net • CORBA • DCOM
Internet Applications: ATG • Vignette • PBS WebLogic • PBS WLI • IBM WebSphere

Vendor Relationships

"Robert's ability to think boldly and his willingness to consider different approaches to solving problems made it both rewarding and productive to be one of his vendors … he acts as a change agent working with his corporate management team to assure that both tactical and strategic goals are met."
— *Louis Bittleson, Global Sales Director, InSight Logistics Software*

Technology Case Study

Chief Technology Officer: PBS Global Logistics

Challenge: Develop a global IT strategy as a response to the Business Development Strategy, 2003–2005

Solution: Using business tactical plans, IT industry trends and available technologies, company IT legacy and assets, as well as competitive analysis, developed "IT Strategy—Platform 21," a 250+ page document that provided strategic and technical direction for execution across the global organization.

Organizational Impact: Combined results from this initiative now serve as the guideline for all development and operational projects across the organization. The repeatable processes defined in these documents—along with existing PBS IT assets— were critical factors in the Hamburg parent company decision to utilize these assets and services to manage partner integration, as well as accelerate integration for new merger and acquisition partners, e.g., Deutsche Logistics, Avetrans, and GlobEx.

The strategy launched a roadmap that converted IT from a product-driven organization to a service-driven one, delivering products in a consistent, predictable, and measurable framework. It also drove a profound change from a relationship model to a process model—where intellectual property is no longer accessible only through the good will and personal relationships between parties, but is centralized and open to all, managed by repeatable processes.

Complete Career Portfolio Available at Interview

Worldwide Commercial Consultants
Solutions for Multinational Business

Jennifer R. Brown, JD, MBA
President

58 Washington Street
Bayville, New Jersey 09529
jbrown@email.net

Office: (765) 208-3290
Mobile: (765) 208-0397
Fax: (765) 208-2094

Expert advisors on complex international and domestic contracting activities, creating flexible, systems-led solutions and applying structured best practices to maximize opportunities and manage risks of new market initiatives.

- Global Markets – International & Domestic
- Manufacturing Project & Product Applications
- Software / Intellectual Property
- Complex Transactions – Drafting & Negotiating
- Systems Development & Automation

- Risk Analysis & Management
- International Public Procurement
- International Finance & Transport Solutions
- Import/Export Regulatory Compliance
- Standardization & Process Improvement

CAPABILITIES AND VALUE OFFERED

COMMERCIAL INFRASTRUCTURE

➤ **Improving and streamlining performance of functional organizations.** WCC helps align responsibilities and accountability of managers, enabling improved efficiency, responsiveness, and transparent governance.

➤ **Implementing risk management techniques that enhance commercial relationships and profitability.** WCC enables more informed decisions and competitive differentiation by identifying, assessing, quantifying, and mitigating commercial risk through automation and standardization.

➤ **Establishing standards and controls for an increasingly complex global business environment.** WCC creates and standardizes form agreements, checklists, and playbooks and helps clients develop procedural guidance for negotiating or escalating non-standard terms.

PRE-CONTRACT

➤ **Navigating unfamiliar regulations and methods of contracting for expansion into new markets.** WCC helps target new prospects, address risk and mitigation strategies, and develop commercial infrastructure to drive outsourcing, offshoring, and growth into emerging markets.

➤ **Minimizing performance and transparency risks in procurement from suppliers.** WCC helps qualify preferred suppliers and assures proper distribution of responsibilities and rewards.

➤ **Structuring multi-party relationships that promote capture strategies and diminish risk.** WCC brings a buyers' and sellers' perspective to develop unified commercial strategies and sound proposals.

POST-AWARD

➤ **Optimizing financial and operational performance by managing relationships in distant markets.** WCC acts as an intermediary to build and manage relationships with global suppliers, freight forwarders, banks, regulatory authorities, and customers.

➤ **Developing and executing strategies to resolve commercial disputes amicably.** WCC helps clients to perform accurate assessment of parties' positions and to resolve differences while avoiding costly litigation.

SPECIAL PROJECTS

➤ **Supporting successful acquisitions and formation of joint ventures.** WCC provides due diligence support and post-closing transition management to help clients drive growth, establish alliances, and expand into new markets.

➤ **Fostering adoption of best practices to support implementation of new enterprise systems.** WCC helps clients achieve desired improvements by facilitating all aspects of such undertakings.

Jennifer R. Brown

(765) 208-3290
jbrown@email.net

58 Washington Street
Bayville, NJ 09529

CONTRACTS AND PROCUREMENT EXECUTIVE

Building value and enabling complex global transactions through expertise in implementing commercial contracting best practices and introducing creative, systems-led solutions to business needs.

Corporate leader of global commercial management functions offering more than 20 years of contracting and procurement experience delivering responsive support to close and manage transactions according to best-practice commercial standards. Proven ability to identify opportunities and lead corporate initiatives involving application of best-practice risk management techniques to complex transactions. Passion for creating and implementing automated and standardized solutions that facilitate achievement of strategic objectives in an increasingly complex, regulated, and competitive business environment.

Multifaceted experience in:

- International & Domestic Markets
- Commercial & Government Clients
- Manufacturing Project & Product Applications
- Commercial & Custom Intellectual Property

- Complex & Multi-Party Transactions
- Multilateral Financing
- International Payment & Transport Methods
- Export of Sensitive Technologies—FOCI

MBA (Contract Management) and JD (Contract Law) degrees.

PROFESSIONAL EXPERIENCE

VICE PRESIDENT, CONTRACTS AND PROCUREMENT
XYZ Solutions ▪ 2001 to 2004

Built and led commercial functions globally for a newly formed Fralcot/Barkley joint venture specializing in systems for nuclear and conventional power plants as well as jet engine performance monitoring in commercial and military applications.

Devised and implemented company policies, accounting for local law considerations in worldwide locations. Developed standards and systems for contract review and approval, letters of credit (LOCs), export compliance, anti-corruption, and Foreign Ownership and Control (FOCI). Negotiated agreements and service-level commitments with senior managers, delineating services delivered by functional organizations.

- **Created and staffed commercial functions worldwide,** building teams in U.S. headquarters and in UK, French, and Czech subsidiaries.
- **Enabled UK subsidiary to perform projects involving export of sensitive U.S. technology** by reconciling U.S. and UK export and security laws. Qualified company for EU-funded projects in Russia and Eastern Europe.
- **Saved costs of employing in-house counsel** by engaging and managing outside counsel to support commercial and dispute-management activities, including assessment of negotiation objectives and alternatives to litigation.
- **Expedited payment and supported project bonding requirements** by developing and forming multi-tiered banking interfaces.
- **Performed and supported commercial due diligence of company acquisitions** in France and Scotland and supported evaluation of prospective domestic acquisitions.

DIRECTOR, CONTRACTS, PROCUREMENT AND IMPORT/EXPORT
International Laboratories ▪ 1999 to 2001

Recruited to rebuild commercial functions, lead adoption of best practices, and turn around troubled satellite communications product and services groups, playing a key role in establishment and launch of a revolutionary new line of business. Replaced majority of staff and overhauled commercial infrastructure to support new business needs.

- **Facilitated global distribution of products** through identification and development of quality channels.

…Continued…

- **Devised methods for conducting international transactions,** including creative solutions to facilitate business and ensure payment from customers in less developed countries.
- **Established manufacturing outsourcing capability,** coordinating supply and demand forecasting for an evolving and highly complex product.
- **Spearheaded initiative to select and implement new factory management system;** achieved implementation and integration with outsourced manufacturer on a tight schedule.
- **Developed export compliance program** to ensure 100% compliance with Technical Assistance Agreements (TAAs) and federal regulations for export of highly classified technology.

DIRECTOR, CONTRACTS
Worldwide Network Systems ▪ *1992 to 1999*

Managed commercial activities worldwide for a $50 million telecommunication product business. Advanced business objectives with sales-oriented agreements incorporating financing and bundled purchase incentives. Supported deployment of a $200 million cellular network for in-flight telephones.

- **Built distribution channels throughout Russia** and assembled a team to capture business using multilateral and private financing.
- **Enabled performance of a $50 million contract with an Iranian customer** by obtaining export reclassification of product. Worked with banks to secure payment in advance of the imposition of U.S. sanctions against Iran.
- **Improved delivery and payment performance** by developing and fostering preferred freight forwarder and banking relationships.

ATTORNEY AT LAW
Bayou, Charles & Kahn ▪ *1990 to 1992*

Negotiated contracts and conducted procurements up to $100 million on behalf of foreign governments for their purchases in the U.S. Advised on contracting methods and resolved multimillion-dollar disputes without litigation. Developed client relationships with governments of Taiwan and Australia. Increased billings to more than $600,000 annually.

MANAGER, SUBCONTRACTS AND MATERIAL
MTR International, Inc. ▪ *1989 to 1990*

Directed subcontract and proposal functions for systems integration and professional services businesses. Managed hardware and software acquisitions (for the EDGAR system) for a $52 million win at the Securities and Exchange Commission.

MANAGER OF PROCUREMENT
Dopson Corporation ▪ *1984 to 1989*

Supported contracts and multimillion-dollar proposals. Initiated purchase and lease subcontracts for $300 million in telecommunications and computing products for the Automated Patent System.

SUBCONTRACTS ADMINISTRATOR
Phoenix Computer Corporation ▪ *1980 to 1984*

Promoted through progressive positions involving contracting for sonar systems. Collaborated on team that developed the first military personal computer.

EDUCATION

Juris Doctor (J.D.) – *Plymouth University*
Master of Business Administration (M.B.A.) – *Washington State University*
Bachelor of Business Administration (B.B.A.) – *University of Michigan*

Member of New Jersey Bar

JONATHAN DIAZ

(H) 916-623-1857 • (W) 916-623-2405 • (M) 916-589-2154
2115 Castle Ct. • Randall Island, CA 91598
jt@emnow.com

EXECUTIVE PROFILE

Highly accomplished and dedicated Quality Consulting professional with a proven track record of effectively managing all aspects of operations and integrating successful concepts to increase value/quality, streamline operations, reduce costs, and boost profits. Visionary leader with key success in launching and managing creative programs for business development.

Solid background in systems analysis and process improvement with extensive exposure to a broad range of entities including Fortune 500 companies and government agencies as well as diverse companies in the healthcare, manufacturing, and real estate industries. Polished communicator and instructor/presenter with excellent negotiation and problem-solving skills. Thrive in a fast-paced, intensely competitive environment while remaining calm and focused.

PROFESSIONAL EXPERIENCE

TODAY'S TECHNOLOGY RESOURCES, INC.—Sacramento, CA   1999 to 2005
Fast-track progression through the following positions:

VP of Operations and Information Technology (2002 to 2005)

Promoted to lead operations and IT efforts for an innovative start-up company launching a unique approach to the medical billing process for healthcare providers in 26 major markets nationwide. Served on a seven-member management team for an organization with 125 employees located both locally and nationwide. Supervised, trained, and mentored three direct reports including a Director of Operations, Director of IT, and a Director of HR. Oversaw all aspects of the organization, excluding accounting and sales/marketing functions. Concurrently developed systems for processing claims and led negotiations with clearinghouses regarding electronic claims forwarding.

- Negotiated a contract with a major outside healthcare vendor to provide a re-pricing software engine, data center, and communications services in addition to core technology.
- Re-worked a critical strategic partnership agreement as an alternative to Electronic Data Systems (EDS); integrated 17 vague agreements into one master agreement with multiple statements of work.
- Successfully negotiated with Bank of America for its data imaging services, and negotiated with a company seeking overseas outsourcing for digital data capture and processing.
- Re-engineered a complex pricing process to quickly secure payment for doctors without inconveniencing patients. Performed extensive data analysis and redesigned parameters to get the best results from claims flowing through the system.
- Led healthcare compliance efforts in developing policies, procedures, and training to meet complex federal Health Insurance Portability and Accountability Act (HIPAA) regulations involving privacy, security, and electronic data interchange of protected health information.
- Extensively trained and critiqued the sales force, presenting the "Tactics of Innovation" strategies to successfully promote a radical new idea within the industry/market. Facilitated ongoing training meetings and offered valuable feedback, resulting in significantly more effective sales presentations.

Director of Operations (1999 to 2002)

Managed all aspects of operations for a computer services consulting/recruiting firm serving both national and international markets. Supervised six direct reports. Created and managed budget for payroll and hardware acquisition. Developed business/strategic partnerships and managed international contractual agreements. Recruited international computer specialists and managed logistics to relocate, house, transport, and place candidates. Interacted with governmental agencies to secure visas.

- Instrumental in leading the organization to accomplish $4.4 million in revenues from a previously negative cash flow, while doubling the number of employees.
- Pioneered an integrated data management system to accurately and efficiently manage all projects, financial information, contracts, assignments, and personnel on a national level.

87

RESOURCE UNLIMITED—Roseville, CA   1995 to 1999
Director/Manager and Quality Consultant

Spearheaded and managed a consulting firm, working with a broad client base ranging from top-level and Fortune 500 companies to healthcare organizations, state environmental agencies, defense contractors, manufacturing firms, and automotive suppliers, improving organizational management through quality principles. Served clients such as QUAKER OATS and WILLAMETTE INDUSTRIES in identifying critical issues, improving quality/productivity/performance, and increasing profits. Provided statistical analysis services for a company developing electronic components.

- Played a key role in developing a major commercial real estate broker's winning proposal for a prestigious State of California commercial property management and acquisition contract; all bids were evaluated against the Malcolm Baldrige National Quality Award standards.

MADISON STATE COLLEGE—Sacramento, CA   1993 to 1999
Adjunct Professor

Taught four core courses in Total Quality Management (TQM).

- Consistently received top scores on instructor performance evaluations.
- Concurrently conducted training seminars in Essential Process Analysis for the Sacramento County Department of General Services; played a key role in successfully improving their services.
- Designed, coordinated, and taught an Internet class.

MILITARY EXPERIENCE

US AIRFORCE LOGISTICS CENTER, STOCKTON AFB

Senior Quality Advisor/TOTAL QUALITY OFFICE—Sacramento, CA: Served as advisor to the Commander and senior executive staff on achieving higher quality, lower costs, and more efficient service. Facilitated training for senior management in the use of the Malcolm Baldrige National Quality Award criteria for organizational self-assessment, advising in quality gap analysis and identifying opportunities to streamline processes.

Commander/Director of Operations: Promoted to lead daily operations in managing $16 million in equipment. Concurrently managed a $100,000 budget.

- Cited as "Vanguard of Quality" for entire operational support airlift fleet throughout the U.S.; revised administrative procedures, eliminating major potential problems; and served as part of a logistics process improvement team that effectively reduced engine replacement time from more than 24 hours to less than 9 hours while maintaining high safety standards.

Wing Executive Officer/Assistant Operations Officer: Directed operations involving 200+ personnel and 16 aircraft throughout Europe and the Mediterranean.

- Maintained a perfect safety record, 100% operational reliability, and 97% maintenance reliability.

Manager/International Command, Control, and Communications Projects: Oversaw all aspects of the development of a military Mission Control Center for a $29 million Search and Rescue Satellite-Aided Tracing (SARSAT) program in conjunction with an international technological, scientific and humanitarian effort. Traveled extensively, interacting with numerous international organizations.

EDUCATION & PROFESSIONAL CERTIFICATION

MS in Systems Management, AIR FORCE INSTITUTE OF TECHNOLOGY—Janesville, MD
BS in Computer Science, UNITED STATES AIR FORCE ACADEMY—Colorado Springs, CO
Certificate in Total Quality Management, MADISON STATE COLLEGE—Sacramento, CA

JONATHAN DIAZ

(H) 916-623-1857 • (W) 916-623-2405 • (M) 916-589-2154
2115 Castle Ct. • Randall Island, CA 91598
jt@emnow.com

TRAINING ADDENDUM

Degrees and Certificates	**Master of Science, Systems Management** AF INSTITUTE, SCHOOL OF ENGINEERING, WRIGHT-PATTERSON AFB	Dayton, OH
	Bachelor of Science, Computer Science USAF ACADEMY	Colorado Springs, CO
	Certificate, Total Quality Management AMERICAN RIVER COLLEGE	Sacramento, CA
	Certified Quality Manager (CQM) AMERICAN SOCIETY FOR QUALITY	1997 to 2000
Quality Training	**Baldrige Award Self-Assessment Training for Service Industries** AMERICAN SOCIETY FOR QUALITY, DR. MARTIN STANKARD	Wright-Patterson AFB, OH
	ISO 9000 Assessor / Lead Assessor Training #A2174 NEVILLE-CLARKE INC., MARIE FIELDS	Sunnyvale, CA
	Understanding Industrial Experimentation STATISTICAL PROCESS CONTROLS, INC, DR. DONALD J. WHEELER	Knoxville, TN
	Metrics for Managers US AIR FORCE	McClellan AFB, CA
	Statistical Process Control for Short Production Runs CHAD CULLEN, INTERNATIONAL QUALITY INSTITUTE	Sacramento, CA
	The Seven Management and Planning Tools DR. MICHAEL COWLEY, GOAL/QPC	Sacramento, CA
	Quality, Productivity, and Competitive Position DR. W. EDWARDS DEMING	Sacramento, CA
	The Joy of Work: Optimizing Organizational Quality DR. KOSAKU YOSHIDA	Sacramento, CA
	Joel Barker's Strategic Exploration Tools & Methods CHARLES HAYWOOD, CONSTELLATION PERFORMANCE GROUP	Atlanta, GA
	Systems Thinking DR. HERBERT WONG, QUANTUM SOLUTIONS	Boca Raton, FL
Facilitation and Leadership	**Quality Improvement Facilitator** ORGANIZATIONAL DYNAMICS, INC.	Stockton AFB, CA
	Games, Etc: How to Improve Learning, Performance, and Productivity SIVASAILAM THIAGARAJAN, WORKSHOPS BY THIAGI	San Francisco CA
	Direct Attention Thinking Tools DR. EDWARD DE BONO	Schaumburg, IL
	Leadership: Bringing Out the Greatness in You QUANTUM SOLUTIONS AND DR. PETER KOESTENBAUM	Los Angeles, CA
	Lateral Thinking Skills, Certified Instructor DR. EDWARD DE BONO	Boca Raton, FL
	Six Thinking Hats Method, Certified Instructor DR. EDWARD DE BONO	Chicago, IL
	Myers-Briggs Type Indicator Qualifying Workshop OTTO KROEGER ASSOCIATES OTTO KROEGER/JANET THEUSEN	San Francisco, CA
	Kirton Adaption-Innovation Inventory DR. MICHAEL J. KIRTON	Sacramento, CA
Writing and Data Presentation	**Presenting Data and Information** EDWARD TUFTE	Palo Alto, CA
	Developing Procedures, Policies, & Documentation INFORMATION MAPPING, INC.	San Francisco, CA

BLAIRE S. WEYLAND

SENIOR MARKETING EXECUTIVE ● CORPORATE IDENTITY DEVELOPMENT ● BRANDING CAMPAIGNS

Resilient, analytical senior marketing leader with deep experience rebuilding sales and marketing cultures for companies involved in international trade and brokerage, global logistics, supply chain, and import/export management. Deliver an entrepreneurial, "think-tank" focus on corporate identity development, new-market research, and channel design, as well as expansion of new product and service line extensions. Execute and lead robust customer communications and service programs in response to impact of environmental, e-commerce, and global regulatory changes and trends on the bottom line.

STRATEGIC MARKETING EFFECTIVENESS:

▶ Wrote monthly e-tips "Branding Your CRM Advantage" to move sales concepts from transactional to solution-based.

▶ Catalyzed turnaround of company in crisis with new marketing strategies that generated revenue from existing resources.

▶ Marshaled all available resources, leveraged competencies, and allocated limited funds in ways that harvested maximum

▶ Seized market share from rivals by augmenting services and positioning early market entries for bold revenue growth.

AREAS OF EXPERTISE

COMPETITIVE INTELLIGENCE ● PRODUCT DIFFERENTIATION ● BUSINESS ANALYSIS & FORECASTING ● STRATEGIC PLANNING
MULTI-CHANNEL MARKETING ● TEAM BUILDING & MOTIVATION ● INTERNATIONAL TRADE ● MARKET OPPORTUNITY ANALYSIS
Regulatory & U.S. Customs Compliance ● P&L Oversight ● Due Diligence ● Global Logistics ● Project Management
Customer Relationship Management ● Startups ● Venture Sourcing ● Seminar Content ● Online Sales & Lead Generation
Anticipative Marketing ● Interactive Web Site Design ● Contract Negotiation & Administration ● Corporate Communications
Performance Measurement/ROI ● Internet Marketing ● International Distribution Channels ● Key Account Maintenance
E-Training ● Advertising/PR ● Product Development ● Customer Surveys ● Process Improvements ● Substitution Solutions

EXECUTIVE PERFORMANCE HIGHLIGHTS

CREATED A MARKETING FUNCTION WITH THINK-TANK DYNAMISM THAT CHANGED THE SALES CULTURE AND SPURRED REVENUES

Reversed a shrinking revenue stream and deteriorating market share for Marene—an established niche-market broker—by creating first marketing department in firm's 50-year history. Challenged by urgent timeline, zero budget, and little direction.

Value and Results

- Conducted Customer Perceived Value (CPV) research, Market Opportunity Analysis (MOA), and other targeted analyses, e.g., cost-benefit, lost business, and market alternatives, to create a market-centric business environment company-wide.
- Executed local Integrated Customer Relationship Management Programs that branded company strengths and added real-time value with minimal investment and lag time. Incorporated hybrid customer contact strategy with a 15-day cycle.
- Educated senior and branch management teams on customer lifetime value vs. transactional profitability.
- Developed firm's market portfolio: Logistics Chain Risk Assessment Services, Global Trade Competitive Market Advantages, and Export Due Diligences. Identified the digital marketplace and established market channel programs.

REFINED SALES MANAGEMENT SYSTEMS AND TOOLS THAT SOLD MULTIPLE KEY CLIENTS REVENUE-GENERATING ADD-ON SERVICES

Redirected Marene's sales strategy, management, and training to focus on solution-centric, long-term approach to profitability.

Value and Results

- Wrote sales management manual and performed business intelligence exercise to define and understand selling strategies and core competencies of regional, national, and international competitors.
- Conceived and wrote a leading-edge corporate total service solution RFP presentation and booklet that increased sales teams' grasp of product profit margins. Implemented a lead-generation and new business development tracking system.
- Established sales-support team to increase time on the road for company sales reps and created an online sales management and tracking system to reduce redundant sales calls and expenses. Set up account mapping with a "Top 40 Customer Profile Sheet," designed monthly lost-business and lost-sales logs, and wrote the Marene Sales Strategy Guide.

1210 Sugarland Drive, Houston, TX 77001 ● Phone: (713) 595-4111
Fax: (713) 391-5432 ● E-mail: bweyland1@houston.1.net

EXECUTIVE PERFORMANCE HIGHLIGHTS, *continued*

AUTHORED BUSINESS INTELLIGENCE STRATEGY THAT DELIVERED REVENUE ENHANCEMENTS FOR MATURITY STAGE COMPANY

Defended market share against threat of lost business from large national brokers' competing e-services and increased RLFs.

Value and Results
- Used "Market Detour" to enter the easiest, cheapest markets to broaden customer base and improve revenue streams.
- Entered new geographic markets, developed product line extensions, and leapfrogged to new technologies to supplant existing products for purchase order, inventory, and supply chain management. Led product differentiation strategies, oversaw sales promotions on trade deals, defined new user segmentation, and positioned company for new corporate image campaign.

TURNED AROUND MARENE'S IMAGE WITH A COHESIVE BRANDING CAMPAIGN TO RECAPTURE EARLY-STAGE SERVICE CYCLE

Persuaded executive management team to expand offerings for the first time in 43+ years. Built consistent family brand with local attributes across 17 branches, addressing issues of decentralized ownership, unique operational priorities, and business goals.

Value and Results
- Developed individual branch and corporate business plans to maximize existing tangible and intangible resources.
- Built product lines with broad appeal to importers/exporters, including risk management/maritime liability assessment services, global supply chain data, PO management, and web database integration services (see addendum for complete list).
- Educated and unified stakeholders on importance of new company image and internal capabilities such as ICRM programs.
- Launched a "call-ready selling site" to execute online customer forms, solution-specific E-zines, and 24x7 support.

CEMENTED STRONGER CUSTOMER RELATIONSHIPS TO GAIN SUSTAINABLE, LONG-TERM COMPETITIVE MARKET ADVANTAGES

Directing international trade, sales, and marketing efforts for Marene, sought disciplined, unified marketing platform to retrieve lost business. Defined improved customer dialogue and customized interactions as inducements for cross- and up-selling opportunities.

Value and Results
- Developed integrated customer relationship management practices to permeate all marketing efforts.
- Redesigned web site as enhanced service and information tool, augmenting direct, targeted involvement with client base.
- Designed interactive profile to identify interests, legal business formation, and projected areas of growth.
- Built quality e-tips and news and information e-alert services via a permission-based marketing strategy.

ENSURED A QUALITY U.S. CUSTOMS AUDIT AND VALIDATION WITH POTENTIAL FOR FUTURE JOINT MARKETING DEVELOPMENTS

Recruited to lead company through post-9/11 U.S. Customs-Trade Partnership Against Terrorism (C-TPAT) certification and validation audit. United multiple departments with opposite goals, quickly achieving C-TPAT Security Audit Validation status.

Value and Results
- Compiled C-TPAT manual. Assessed security programs of corporate and 17 branch offices. Documented SOPs.
- Set up mailings to importers, sea and air carriers, warehouses, container freight stations, and trucking companies, communicating applicable security recommendations. Developed "interest/more information" response vehicle.
- Currently implementing monthly C-TPAT Breakfast Club Teleforum and online monthly chat topics for customers.

APPLIED RAZOR-SHARP ANALYTICS TO DETERMINE OPTIMAL FOREIGN MARKET ENTRIES

Led Marene into emerging markets worldwide through analytical approach to deciding where to allocate limited international marketing dollars among 17 branches, 23 countries, and 10 primary service groups.

Value and Results
- Delivered snapshot of current opportunities including U.S. port-of-entry tax and financial incentives, distribution and operational advantages, costs, competitor metrics, and company profitability potential vs. adequacy of resources.
- Pinpointed growth prospects for each branch and potential service group and performed analysis of foreign supplier network data, country data, and exports by industry.
- Identified highest ROI for foreign market efforts. Enhanced results by allocating resources in extremely short time.

CAREER DEVELOPMENT

THE MARENE COMPANY, INC., Houston, TX   2003 to present
Director of International Trade, Marketing and Sales   www.mareneco.com

Recruited to design and implement turnaround strategy to support new marketing concept and culture for the largest privately held U.S. Customs brokerage and international freight forwarder in southeastern U.S. with 17 branches and $350 million in annual net revenue. Generate push marketing strategy across international, integrated channels of distribution. Lead cross-divisional teams that develop, execute, and assess strategic integrated marketing programs to enhance new corporate image. Outline and execute marketing and advertising plans. Identify, prioritize, and target undeveloped customer segments. Established corporate communications, branding, client relationship, key account maintenance, and public relations programs.

IMPORT KNOWLEDGE MANAGEMENT SYSTEM, LLC, Savannah, GA   2000 to 2003
Owner / Software Developer / Designer

Started the first minority-owned company to be accepted into E-Space, Georgia's high-tech business incubator. Conducted market research; wrote and presented business plan for angel funding. Developed and copyrighted IKMS, a proprietary global regulatory alert system and risk management tool. Designed industry-specific applications that could be used either to solve individual companies' own regulatory compliance problems or as new profit center with ongoing license and software-purchase revenues. Startup funded through grant from Georgia Science & Technology Council and E-Space. Closed company due to marketplace shifts and lack of adequate funding to build the Alpha model for commercialization justification.

GLOBAL TRADEX, INC., Baltimore, MD   2000
Import Regulatory and U.S. Customs Compliance Consultant   www.globtradex.com

Evaluated regulatory compliance/control programs within companies in six states to identify business opportunities for leading U.S. Customs broker and freight forwarder with worldwide agent network and annual revenues of $280 million. Launched new business development strategy, including new account acquisition and customer retention initiatives, with focus on providing clients with solutions to global trade and market barriers as well as customs compliance issues. Generated $375,000 in new customs compliance consulting business after presenting the first formal, structured International Trade and Customs educational seminar in Metro-DC area. Advised clients on planning, scheduling, budgeting, and regulatory compliance.

LOGISTICS INTERNATIONAL, Baltimore, MD   1993 to 2000
Senior Import Broker / Shift Coordinator / Agent / Account Representative   www.dhl.com

Licensed U.S. Customs broker responsible for all European freight inbound to domestic hub totaling 39% of daily import volumes for freight carrier with sales of $527 million. Troubleshot and resolved problems surrounding clearance of critical, time-sensitive shipments. Developed import marketing service guidelines. Reduced overtime by 75% without compromising quality by reorganizing clearance processes. Fostered excellent relationships with government agencies. Designated broker for Reebok, Hewlett-Packard, Lockheed Martin, Lands' End, AT&T, GIS, and Motorola. Created, wrote, and presented course materials on company policies and procedures, and OSHA, DOT, and FAA regulations. Ranked #1 formal entry writer out of 35; achieved 300% average hourly production with excellent accuracy. Played key role in achieving ISO 9000 certification. Managed territory generating $426,000 a month.

EDUCATION AND LEADERSHIP

George Washington University, Washington, D.C. • **MBA, 2004**
Major: International Business and Global Marketing • **GPA 3.9**

Georgia Institute of Technology, Atlanta, GA • **Bachelor of Business Administration**
Major: Marketing • **Minor:** Finance • **Who's Who in American Colleges**

Continuing Education: Export Shipping & Documentation • Facilities Engineering • Export Letters of Credit and Drafts Fundamentals of Importing • NAFTA • Duty Drawback • Marketing and Operations of Foreign Trade Zones (FTZ) Quota/Visa Requirements and Marking Issues Related to Textiles • Port Administration and Information Technology Footwear • General Order • Container Examination Stations (CES) • Advanced Displays and Telecommunications Devices

Certification: Licensed U.S. Customhouse Broker

1210 Sugarland Drive, Houston, TX 77001 • Phone: (713) 595-4111
Fax: (713) 391-5432 • E-mail: bweyland1@houston.1.net

MARKETING PROFILE

Publications

- ▸ Sales Strategy Guidebook, Marene
- ▸ C-TPAT Certification Manual, Marene
- ▸ Designated Trainer Workbook, LI
- ▸ Public Relations Media Plan for DC-8 Kick Off, LI
- ▸ Write monthly: "Branding Your CRM Advantage"
- ▸ Value Proposition Demonstrator Publication (Case Examples)
- ▸ 2004 Quarterly Newsletter Series "Employee Press Room"
- ▸ 12 month Brand Audit with Opportunity Report Card

E-zine: "Reviewing Your Zone Flexibility . . . Claim Your Marketing Advantage"
E-zine: "Asset Saver Alert . . . Assessing Cargo Insurance Clauses"
E-zine: "Secretly Securing Your Future . . . C-TPAT e-tips"
E-zine: "Don't Let The Bottom Drop Out . . . P.O. Information Management Hints"

Marketing Tools and Methodologies

Designed Forms:
- ▸ Customer New Web Site Functionality Surveys
- ▸ Market Expectation and Performance Evaluation Surveys
- ▸ Customer Risk Savvy Awareness Surveys
- ▸ Business Sales Lead Tracking Worksheet
- ▸ Marketing Math, Sales Cost and Account Profitability
- ▸ Monthly Lost Business and Lost Sales Log
- ▸ Generic, Customizable Corporate Request for Proposal Format
- ▸ Daily Log Lead Qualification Sheet
- ▸ Sales Call Departmental Action Follow-Up Sheet
- ▸ Country Data Sheet Search Request
- ▸ Account Mapping

Built Product Lines:
- ▸ Risk Management and Maritime Liability Assessment Services
- ▸ Global Supply Chain Information
- ▸ Purchase Order Management Systems
- ▸ Web Database Integration Services
- ▸ Foreign Trade Zone Operators
- ▸ AOG Service Providers
- ▸ C-TPAT Destination Management Facilitators
- ▸ Export Sales and Channel Marketing Evaluation Services
- ▸ International Freight Networking Capabilities
- ▸ 24 Hour International Trade Support Library Network with Gistnet
- ▸ In development: Export Due Diligence

1210 Sugarland Drive, Houston, TX 77001 • Phone: (713) 595-4111
Fax: (713) 391-5432 • E-mail: bweyland1@houston1.net

Expert in building and leading profitable businesses and regional sales/marketing organizations for a global Fortune 200 company and joint venture.

Dynamic general management career includes all core functions: manufacturing, engineering, sales, marketing, product, P&L, finance, human resources, purchasing, customer service, and technical services. Analytical, problem-solving and negotiation strengths combine to identify and manage strategic issues, resulting in the profitable growth of both developing and established business groups. Organizational, team-building, and leadership talents are evident in the ability to develop, mentor, and manage staffs to peak performance.

CAREER MILESTONES

- Revitalized and restored profitability at a non-performing business through aggressive strategies: improving manufacturing efficiency, diversifying product line, and creating new pricing structure.

- Key contributor in maintaining company's #1 ranking in worldwide market share despite entry of 3 new domestic competitors that increased product capacity 75%.

- Led region to rank #1 in sales performance, exceeding volume, new business, and account targets by 28% (from $175 million to $225 million) over prior year.

- Spearheaded division's integration into the region and trained field sales representatives on 3 additional lines, providing skill development to achieve performance goals.

- Instrumental in negotiating contracts and creating price escalation mechanism for 2 major long-term agreements valued above $150 million.

- Led cross-functional team in identifying 5 viable product derivatives providing an estimated $15 million in profit improvement.

- Negotiated 80% of existing customer base under long-term agreements generating $32 million in annual sales, thereby maintaining leading edge over 3 new competitors.

- Delivered 90% increase in international sales revenue through lead generation and sales force development. Enhanced brand recognition and global identity through a creative ad campaign.

- Led development of vital logistics programs saving $1.2 million annually by maximizing 3-plant, 17-terminal domestic network while minimizing freight and storage costs.

- Innovated system to project and monitor product demand by customer segments, allowing for more targeted long-term demand forecasting and capital expansion planning.

PROFESSIONAL EXPERIENCE

SANDSTONE CORPORATION • Philadelphia, PA • 1980 to present
Fast-track advancement through sales, marketing, and division management positions at a $4 billion company and joint venture.

Division Business Manager, Philadelphia, PA (1997 to present)

- Senior manager with full P&L responsibility for $166 million business, including 5 domestic production facilities. Provided strategic planning and leadership to 2 product lines. Manage inventories and other resources to maximize manufacturing and distribution facilities. Structure and manage major sales contracts. Direct plant expansion, cost reduction initiatives, and vertical product integration for performance and income enhancement. Lead activities for site and technology selection for major plant expansion efforts.

4998 Sullivan Avenue • Philadelphia, PA 09778 • 668.944.2288

Business Manager – Tarpey Products Company, Albany, NY (1994 to 1997)

- Selected from among 5 candidates for newly created key position managing $45 million joint venture. P&L accountability included development and execution of effective worldwide marketing strategies, plans, and initiatives to strengthen market presence and address impending market entry of 3 domestic competitors, increasing U.S. product capacity by 75%. Spearheaded development and launch of 2 successful new products. Managed logistics, customer service, regional managers, and field sales staff. Provided management expertise to sales groups through active participation in customer presentations and contract negotiations.

Regional Sales Manager, Columbus, OH (1991 to 1994)

- High-profile position managing $225 million regional sales organization comprising Northeastern U.S. and Canada. Diverse scope of responsibilities included sales/product training, annual sales planning, key account management, forecasting, budgeting, and pricing strategies. Negotiated and managed key customer contracts totaling $50 million to $60 million annually. Effectively allocated product during peak demand periods without loss of a single account. Developed and advanced the careers of 5 sales professionals.

Marketing Manager, Houston, TX (1989 to 1991)

- Directed all marketing programs for 3 major product lines; developed marketing plans, prepared financial and product forecasts, held domestic pricing authority, and oversaw contract implementation for purchasing. Focal point with sales, customer service, technical service, market research, and legal services to achieve business objectives. Chosen as one of 4 on management team to evaluate product line that was subsequently sold for $15 million. Successfully maintained entire customer base despite crisis situation during peak demand period. Trained, developed, and motivated new sales personnel to achieve top performance.

Manager of Energy Affairs, Kansas City, KS (1988 to 1989)

- Selected for management position in recognition of expertise and proven ability to cultivate effective relationships. Managed all aspects of energy affairs with 3 utility companies, representing $250 million annually. Developed long-term energy forecasts for existing/potential facilities, participated in rate case hearings, attended political functions, and remained current on environmental/deregulation impact and related issues.

Sales Representative, Kansas City, KS (1984 to 1988)

- Joined company as Chemical Engineer and recruited from plant to manage regional territory with accountability for commodity/industrial product line. Developed existing/new accounts and negotiated sales contracts, growing territory from $2.7 million to $12 million in annual sales. Winner of 1986 President's Award for individual superior sales performance and in 1987 for outstanding contributions to region's growth.

EDUCATIONAL BACKGROUND

Executive MBA Program • Syracuse University • Syracuse, NY
Bachelor of Science in Chemical Engineering • Boston University • Boston, MA

Professional Development Seminars
Leadership Development, Finance, Sales, Marketing

4998 Sullivan Avenue • Philadelphia, PA 09778 • 668.944.2288

Recognized as an accomplished management executive, Ms. Thomas has established a successful career directing major business groups and regional sales and marketing organizations. She has been a significant contributor to company growth and profitability through expertise in strategic planning, general management, sales, marketing, product development, profit improvement, and staff development/management. Experienced in managing nearly every core functional area in a manufacturing environment, she is highly regarded for her business acumen, technical expertise, relationship management strengths, and consistent performance achievements benefiting the bottom line.

Recruited while in college, Ms. Thomas launched her career as a Chemical Engineer with Sandstone Corporation, a $4 billion Fortune 200 company. From that position, she progressed rapidly through a series of management roles to her most recent assignment as Business Manager with P&L accountability for a $166 million division that included five domestic production facilities. An adept negotiator, she was instrumental in securing agreements and creating price escalation mechanisms for two major long-term contracts valued at more than $150 million. She also led a cross-functional team in identifying five viable product derivatives generating $15 million in profit improvement and directed the development of key logistics programs that realized more than $1.2 million in annual savings.

In 1994, she was chosen from among five candidates for a newly created position as Business Manager of $45 million business in a joint venture between Sandstone Corporation and Rowman Company, Inc. An effective strategic planner and marketer, she successfully retained the company's #1 ranking in global market share despite three new competitors that entered the market—representing a 75% increase in product capacity. She ensured the company's competitive advantage by securing 80% of the existing customer base under long-term contracts producing $32 million in annual sales revenue. In addition, Ms. Thomas delivered a 90% increase in international business and initiated a creative ad campaign that strengthened brand recognition and global identity. During her three-year tenure in this position, she also launched two successful new product lines and restored profitability to a nonperforming business.

Her prior experience from 1991 to 1994 as Regional Sales Manager of a $225 million sales organization spanning the Northeastern U.S. and Canada markets was no less impressive. Here, she led the region to achieve #1 ranking out of seven in sales performance. Her region exceeded volume, new business, and account targets by 28% over the prior year, growing from $175 million to $225 million. Recognized as an excellent team leader and staff motivator, she developed and managed the sales staff to achieve top performance. Rising to the challenge, she even integrated a new division into the region and provided the necessary training on three additional product lines to equip her sales staff to accomplish all business objectives.

Ms. Thomas's capabilities were equally evident in her previous position as Marketing Manager when she was promoted in 1989 to plan, execute, and direct programs for three major product lines. During her three years in this position, she effectively managed a crisis situation during peak demand while retaining 100% of the customer base. Appointed to a management team of four, she demonstrated her analytical strengths in providing an exit recommendation for a nonperforming product line that resulted in a $15 million sale for the company.

Prior to the marketing management position, Ms. Thomas had been promoted in 1988 to manage energy affairs—representing $250 million annually—with three utility companies. In this capacity, she excelled through her technical expertise and ability to cultivate strong business/political relationships. She kept abreast of environmental/deregulation issues and developed long-term energy forecasts critical for existing and potential company facilities.

Previously, she was recruited from her first full-time position as plant Chemical Engineer and given full autonomy to manage a regional sales territory for an industrial/commodity product line. While in this position from 1984 to 1988, she drove annual sales from $2.7 million to $12 million through the development and management of new as well as existing accounts. She earned two corporate awards for superior sales performance and contributions to the region's growth.

Ms. Thomas holds a B.S. in Chemical Engineering from Boston University and attends professional development programs/seminars to remain current in today's dynamic business climate.

4998 Sullivan Avenue • Philadelphia, PA 09778 • 668.944.2288

CHAPTER 9

Writing Achievement Summaries

Naturally, your significant achievements will be featured prominently in your resume. Yet there might be times when it will be beneficial for you to provide additional details of some of those achievements, or to present just your achievements without the additional information that is included in your resume. In these instances, a separate achievement addendum can be a powerful tool.

How will you use these documents? Consider the case of a marketing executive who has a concise two-page resume highlighting nearly 15 years of career achievements. To provide greater insights into how she tackles marketing challenges, she used a one-page addendum to expand on several of her key achievements and shared this during the interview and as a follow-up communication. She could easily edit or add to the addendum depending on the specific circumstances and challenges of the job for which she was interviewing. You can see her documents in Example 2 of this chapter.

Or imagine that you are similar to the global sales and marketing executive in this chapter who started his career with Hewlett Packard and contributed to several of their global successes during 17 years in progressive sales and marketing positions. As you can see in the first example that follows, this individual created a separate achievement summary to briefly highlight just the success stories of his blue-chip career. He sent this document to recruiters and to his network contacts, sharing his full resume as a follow-up.

Use the following guidelines and examples as you prepare your achievement summary:

1. Keep it brief

A one-page addendum is inviting to readers and should provide ample space for your key achievements. If you have more to say than will fit on one page, consider creating two or more distinct pages, each grouping together similar challenges and successes under a headline that is helpful to the reader. For example:

- Strategic Leadership Initiatives
- Marketing Successes
- Sales Performance

2. Be specific

Because you are sharing only selected information in your addendum, you can provide additional details that would be too weighty if included in your complete resume. Be sure to include details related to the context or challenge as well as specifics about what you did. And, to be meaningful, your achievement summary needs to include numbers and other hard results.

Examples

The following achievement addenda are high-impact documents. One is a true summary of achievements, pulled from a detailed two-page resume, while the other two examples provide expanded information about achievements that are stated only briefly in the resume.

EXAMPLE 1: Resume and Achievement Summary: Hillary James Ingraham
(pages 100-102)
(Writer – Arnold Boldt)
Hillary's stellar career at Hewlett Packard is a focal point of his achievement summary. You may recall his Career Marketing Plan from Chapter 1; you can now see how his resume and his achievement summary both support his career plan and relate to his target positions.

EXAMPLE 2: Resume and Achievement Addendum: Flor San Miguel (pages 103-105)
(Writer – Louise Kursmark)
In this document Flor follows the CAR (Challenge-Action-Result) format to provide a logical flow of information for telling her success stories. First the situation is explained, then strategies and actions are detailed, and finally there is strong focus on bottom-line results.

EXAMPLE 3: Resume and Achievement Addendum: Suzanne Perry (pages 106-109)
(Writer – Phyllis Shabad)
The addendum that accompanies this three-page resume is an explication of Suzanne's significant achievements as a consultant. She used the addendum when interviewing for consulting positions or as documentation for her product strategy, marketing, and management skills.

HILLARY JAMES INGRAHAM

36 Whitehall, Bloomfield, New York 14469
585-657-2491 (Office) / 585-737-7899 (Cell)
hjamesingraham@frontiernet.net

GLOBAL SALES AND MARKETING EXECUTIVE

Accomplished General Manager / Senior Sales and Marketing Executive with 20-plus years of demonstrated success providing leadership in setting strategic vision and implementing initiatives to achieve revenue, profitability, and market-share objectives across numerous programs and product lines. Proven track record as a take-charge leader who embraces challenging assignments and achieves business objectives. Excellent ability to hire/develop talent and build high-performing teams that deliver exceptional business results.

PROFESSIONAL EXPERIENCE

HJ INGRAHAM & ASSOCIATES, Bloomfield, New York   June 2003–Present
A professional sales and marketing consulting organization, specializing in channel strategy by the development of "go-to-market" sales and marketing programs that are enabled by vertical and segmentation implementation.

TechPrint UNLIMITED, Buffalo, New York   Jan. 2001–June 2003
A leading manufacturer of line matrix, thermal & fanfold laser printers & network management software.

Senior Vice President of Sales & Marketing—Worldwide
Accountable for global sales and marketing generating $230 million in annual revenues, with 50% from domestic markets and 50% from EMEA and Asia. Direct line accountability for 150 employees, worldwide. Managed global marketing functions, including Internet marketing, public relations, and product marketing.

- Successfully managed worldwide relationships with strategic partners, including OEMs and VARs, as well as direct sales channels and professional services.
- Achieved 5% market share increase for line matrix printers while industry declined by 15%.
- Increased sales of high-end thermal printers by 44%, year-over-year, gaining significant market share.
- Focusing on key segments, grew yearly run rate 70% ($10.5 million to $18 million) for thermal printers.
- Shareholder value of the company increased by 49% during 2002.
- Maintained stable position in a declining market, gaining market share and sustaining revenues.

HEWLETT-PACKARD CORPORATION   1973–2000

Vice President—e-Marketing, San Jose, CA (1999–Dec. 2000)
Developed and implemented marketing, branding, advertising, and segmentation strategies globally to drive aggressive revenue growth in both online and offline sales of equipment, services, supplies, and software.

- Launched global partner site for a complex partner environment using a common system with customized web interfaces that enabled 30% revenue growth for partners in 2002.
- Led team that integrated online marketing programs with other channels to drive customers to the web, telesales, and direct sales representatives.
- Grew web-touched revenues from approximately $1 million in 1999 to $50+ million in 2000 and $500 million in 2001, a 500-fold increase in just two years.
- Developed all online content and managed outside creative partners.
- Established web-marketing messages that increased click-through rates on key programs to 5–15 times the industry average.
- Managed development and implementation of extranet/trading hub strategy to expand revenues while decreasing cost to service major accounts by 50% in 2001.

100

HEWLETT-PACKARD (continued)

Vice President / General Manager—Certified Pre-Owned Business Unit, San Jose, CA (1998)
P&L accountability for $250 million business units. Established strategic alliances and vertical market strategies and developed alternative sales channels for remanufactured office imaging equipment.

- Focused strategies on new market segments and increased market share from 7% to 15%. Grew revenues from $100 million to $250 million, with a major focus on annuities.
- Grew the marketing and sales group from two people to a team of 50 in the first two months.
- Managed delivery of services and set up manufacturing lines in Mexico and two U.S. locations, with accountability for integrated supply chain operations.

Vice President / General Manager—High-End Printer Products, San Jose, CA (1997)
P&L responsibility for this worldwide business unit generating $3 billion in revenues and $800 million in profits. Managed product development, product marketing, integrated supply chain, and customer service operations. Direct accountability for 150 employees, with strong dotted-line responsibility for manufacturing operations.

- Reversed 1995/1996 under-plan performance by focusing strategy on new segments and high-margin products.
- Implemented marketing initiatives by segments, resulting in a 30% growth in outsourcing service revenues.
- Delivered pre-tax profits that accounted for 40% of Hewlett-Packard's total corporate profits.

VP of Marketing—Office Document Products Business Group, Western U.S. (1996–1997)
Created sales and marketing strategies for product introductions, pricing, sales coverage, and training that led to revenue growth exceeding 20%. Accountable for $1.4 billion in annual revenues. Direct responsibility for 100 of the company's top sales specialists.

- Implemented segmentation strategies, enabling a 65% growth in outsourcing and services business.
- Managed marketing and sales initiatives that led to success in winning outsourcing contracts with state governments and Fortune 500 clients.
- Built model that was used to develop telesales units that now account for revenues above $850 million.

General Manager, Professional Services Market, San Jose, CA (1994–1995)
Developed product offerings that gave Hewlett-Packard a competitive advantage in the legal, accounting, and professional consulting market segments. This business generated $500 million in revenues from the North American market. Reversed a four-year decline in revenues and market share.

- Implemented marketing programs that led to 150% increase in outsourcing and service business.
- Increased market share by 9%, while maintaining revenues in a declining market segment.
- Instituted direct mail and customer seminars that increased awareness and led to business growth.

Sr. Marketing and Executive Sales Management Assignments, Southern CA / Rochester, NY (1980–1993)
Held various field and staff assignments with accountability for marketing, program management, and senior sales management positions.

- Accountable for $200 million in revenues and 150 member sales organization. Exceptional results in revenue/profit growth, outsourcing, expense management, and customer satisfaction.
- Managed worldwide direct and indirect channel strategy development for the first of Hewlett-Packard's new line of digital systems with the capacity to scan, print, copy, and fax.
- Developed software that enabled set of high-end printing products to work in the DEC environment, and achieved 200% of plan ($200 million) and year-over-year growth of 40%.
- Identified new business opportunities, leading product-marketing managers in introducing new software that complemented high-end printing systems and delivered $50 million revenue and 50% rise in profitability.

EDUCATION

Bachelor of Science, Business Administration, 1979
Rochester Institute of Technology, Rochester, New York

Hillary James Ingraham

Achievement Highlights

As Senior Vice President of Sales and Marketing for TechPrint Unlimited, a leading manufacturer of high-volume thermal and laser printers:

- Increased market share in an industry that was declining 15-20% per year by capturing market share from the competition through focusing on segments in key vertical markets.

- Achieved an 85% increase in yearly run rate ($18.5M vs. $10M) for a product line priced higher than the industry leader's, through creative channel marketing programs and a successful segmentation focus.

- Maintained a stable position in a declining market, which increased shareholder value by 58%.

In progressive marketing, sales, and general management roles during 20 years with Hewlett-Packard:

- Worked with under-performing business units to develop out-of-the-box strategies that enabled over-achievement of business goals. Developed a well-established track record of reversing downward trends and revitalizing business units.

- Focused on market segmentation and new channels of distribution to grow revenues by 150% ($250M vs. $100M) in one year as Vice President / General Manager of the Certified Pre-Owned Business Unit.

- Developed and launched a global partner website that enabled a 40% revenue growth for partners, as Vice President of e-Marketing.

- Increased revenues related to "web touches" from $1M to $500M in just two years, with the majority of this new business enhancing partners' revenues.

- Focused all marketing initiatives on key segments to enable 30% growth in outsourcing business. This $3 billion business met its sales objectives for the first time in three years during tenure as Vice President / General Manager of High-End Printer Products.

- Enabled 65% growth in outsourcing and services business revenue, as Vice President of Marketing, Office Products—Business Unit/Western U.S. (a $2.2 billion business).

- Pioneered segmentation strategies and built a telesales model originally implemented with 10 telesales representatives. This program was rolled out to more than 600 telesales reps, accounting for more than $800M in company revenues.

- Developed the channel strategy for Hewlett-Packard's and the industry's first line of digital multi-function printers.

- Developed software and segmentation strategies in a Product Manager role within the DEC environment that led to $250M incremental revenue from an unscheduled program.

Flor San Miguel

513-249-8786 • 513-604-3943 • fsan@cinci.rr.com
7943 Village Circle Drive, Cincinnati, OH 45241

Strategic Marketing Executive

Marketing strategist, innovator, and tactical leader of enterprise-wide initiatives that build brand value and result in sustainable, profitable growth.

Driver and champion of transformational programs—able to gain executive sponsorship, build internal support at all levels, and create cross-functional project teams that deliver exceptional results. Expert in aligning strategy with organizational vision/goals and interpreting the voice of the customer through enhanced customer insight and knowledge management.

Proven professional with a strong record of results in diverse industries—financial services, healthcare/insurance, professional services, and packaged goods—both business-to-business and consumer.

Areas of Expertise

- Strategic Planning
- Consulting
- Market Research
- Product Development
- Market Segmentation
- Branding
- Advertising
- Direct Marketing
- CRM
- Customer Satisfaction
- Project Management
- Strategic Alliances

Career Highlights

- **Smythe Associates:** Delivered a branding and communications redesign that established progressive image and positioned firm for accelerated expansion in strategic market segments.
- **Pioneer Health Services:** Transitioned business division from risk-avoidance to risk-management strategy, introducing new product portfolios that drove sales up 50% and market share 40% in just 2 years.
- **Fifth Third Bank, Procter & Gamble:** Improved sales, profitability, and market share through creative marketing and new product initiatives focused on strategic goals and the bottom line.

Professional Experience

SMYTHE ASSOCIATES, Cincinnati, OH *($50 million revenue, top-35 accounting and consulting firm)*, 2002–2005
VICE PRESIDENT, DIRECTOR OF MARKETING

Transformed marketing strategy for traditional services organization, creating a more dynamic, market-driven firm targeting business for sustainable growth. Established, staffed, and directed 8-person marketing and communications team during rapid growth, merger activity, and diversification. Supported 15 offices, 6 lines of business, and 5 affiliate companies.

- **Revitalized corporate branding and communications** and created a cohesive, integrated image supported by tag line, website, newsletter, and all corporate communications.
  - New website awarded "National Top 5" ranking for regional firms by Professional Services Monitor.
  - Newsletter became a powerful lead generator, averaging 5 leads per issue on featured services.
  - Tag line became litmus test for communications, proposals, client reports, staff evaluations, and hiring profiles.
  - Firm was positioned as a major regional force on par with national employers in its industry, attracting both experienced recruits and new college grads.

- **Ignited stalled business development** through strategy to improve lead development and consultative selling skills of partners and managers.
  - Produced more than $60K in ongoing new annuity and project revenue in just 3 months, realizing a 300% ROI.
  - Program won the top national award from the Association of Accounting Marketing.

- **Initiated, developed, and sold partners on a major $350K CRM initiative** that captured immediate $15K savings in marketing mailing costs, created benchmarks for marketing performance, and established targets for growth.

PIONEER HEALTH SERVICES, Covington, KY *($100MM start-up division of $2B insurance and healthcare services company)*, 1998–2002
CHIEF MARKETING OFFICER

Drove shift in business and marketing strategy from risk-avoidance to risk-management, transforming division and ultimately impacting the entire marketplace. Built a 20-person organization, comprising marketing, telemarketing, R&D, communications, and legal compliance, to create and implement total marketing program for newly merged $100MM division.

- **Revamped product portfolios to improve market position and profitability.**
  - Surpassed aggressive first-year goals for sales and profits by 50%.
  - Increased market share 4 points in 2 years.
  - Doubled broker channel business to 30% in most profitable customer segment.
  - Achieved 15% ROI for direct-response advertising.
  - Reclaimed market dominance, growing share from 45% to 50% in 3 years.
  - Increased share of most profitable customer segment to 60%.

- **Defined service excellence, created powerful management tools, drove up scores and drove down costs.**
  - Improved customer satisfaction on all key measures from upper 80s to low/mid 90s.
  - Lowered unit costs 14% over 3 years even though staff increased.
  - Created a practical management tool that was used to define strategies and improvement initiatives.

FIFTH THIRD BANK, Cincinnati, OH, 1996–1998
ASSISTANT VICE PRESIDENT 1997–1998 • **PRODUCT MANAGER** 1996–1997

Brought on board to manage $43MM transaction account portfolio. Held P&L responsibility; managed channel and product development, advertising, promotions, and sales training; supervised 4-member team. Promoted after 6 months.

- Improved product profitability 10% through a new pricing strategy while remaining competitive.
- Reversed declining market-share trend in only 9 months by returning to traditional benefits-based lifestyle advertising.

PROCTER & GAMBLE, Cincinnati, OH, 1993–1998
ASSISTANT BRAND MANAGER—PAMPERS 1995–1998 • **BRAND ASSISTANT—TIDE** 1993–1995

Advanced rapidly through classic marketing roles with one of the world's most successful consumer goods companies. Managed consumer and trade advertising, promotion, packaging, product development, and test-market activities.

Education / Professional Development / Affiliations

MBA, Xavier University, Cincinnati, OH
BS, Political Science and Business; The Ohio State University, Columbus, OH

American Marketing Association • Association of Accounting Marketing

Marketing Leadership Initiatives: Smythe Associates

- **Revitalized branding and communications.**

  Communications programs were outdated, content-deficient, and failed to communicate firm's value proposition or differentiators. Brand was unclear and visual identity chaotic.

  Created project objectives: *simplicity—clarity—identity—image.* Built internal coalition of support and launched a comprehensive overhaul beginning with interviews with key stakeholders.

  Implemented new promise line and directed redesign of entire visual identity. Led road show to introduce new identity in all 15 offices. Accelerated timetable to 7 months to coincide with 30th anniversary celebration.

  Bottom Line:

  - New website awarded "National Top 5" ranking for regional firms by Professional Services Monitor.
  - Newsletter became a powerful lead generator, averaging 5 leads per issue on featured services.
  - Tag line became litmus test for communications, proposals, client reports, staff evaluations, and hiring profiles.
  - New image helped facilitate merger that resulted in successful expansion into New Jersey and the addition of critical expertise and leadership resources.
  - Firm was positioned as a major regional force on par with national employers in its industry, attracting both experienced recruits and new college grads.

- **Ignited business development.**

  Growth had stalled in mature markets and awareness was low in regions targeted for expansion. Business development was unfocused and partners/managers (primary drivers of new business) lacked confidence in consultative selling.

  Designed strategy to improve lead development and consultative selling skills of partners and managers. Set aggressive goal to earn 100% ROI on campaign cost within 12 months.

  Bottom Line:

  - Produced more than $60K in ongoing new annuity and project revenue in just 3 months, realizing a 300% ROI.
  - Added 150 new self-identified "interested" prospects to database in a single test market.
  - Program won the top national award from the Association of Accounting Marketing.

- **Drove successful customer relationship management (CRM) initiative.**

  Information systems for the firm's most valuable assets (clients, prospects, referral sources, alumni, staff capabilities and experience) were outdated, fragmented, unreliable, and unconnected to the financial system. There was no ability to track a client's total value to the firm or identify cross-sell opportunities.

  The impact was wasted money, poor response times, duplication of efforts, and missed opportunities.

  Initiated, developed, and sold partners on a major $350K CRM initiative (software, hardware, implementation, training, and ongoing database management). Established project goals and benchmarks. Created internal champions by recruiting an Advisory Committee of influential partners and staff. Selected vendors. Recruited and coached project manager and cross-functional project team.

  Bottom Line:

  - Captured immediate savings of $15K on production and mailing costs; return rate dropped from 10% to less than 2%.
  - Enhanced reputation as trusted source of timely knowledge to clients.
  - Gained ability to evaluate profitability by client, line of business, service, and geography, creating benchmarks for marketing performance and targets for growth.

SUZANNE J. PERRY
Corporate Strategist and Business Growth Accelerator

SENIOR OPERATIONS EXECUTIVE • DOMESTIC / INTERNATIONAL BUSINESS DEVELOPMENT

Improved targeted research and grew revenues 333% over 2.5 years

Developed a clear, concise market position and differentiation strategy focused on business applications of technology, encompassing an enterprise-wide research agenda and quality control process. Multi-tiered pricing and research product offered customized service solutions to clients, distinguishing firm's branding and image against competitors.

Reduced unit costs for a manufacturing firm by 50%

Turned around cost and pricing disadvantages for a consumer products company by negotiating a contract with an offshore firm. Initiative catapulted divisional profitability by becoming highest in profits as a percentage of sales—critical to product success.

Recruited as top-school MBA talent to shape strategic and tactical plans for BGS FG

Helped structure and manage a pioneering strategic consulting practice that integrated subject matter experts into the planning process earlier, giving the firm fresh access to C-level/Boardroom decision-makers and building its blue-chip reputation for IT planning.

Designed robust Internet strategies to cut costs and secure customer traction

Advised JPMorgan Chase, HSBC, and Bank of New York on new product category development and B2C Internet solutions to originate financial services products. Efficient, scalable customer-direct features stimulated operational cost cutting and profit margins.

AREAS OF EXPERTISE

FINANCE & OPERATIONS LEADERSHIP • TURNAROUND MANAGEMENT • IT PLANNING & STRATEGY DEVELOPMENT

Start-Ups / New Ventures • Venture Funding • M&A • Strategic Alliances / Joint Ventures • Global Business Platforms
Organizational Infrastructure • Business Process Redesign • Contract & License Negotiations • Deal Structuring • Consulting
Product Branding & Positioning • Research • Competitive / Trend Analysis • New Product Launches • Channel Strategies
CRM Tools • P&L Management • Investor / Vendor Relations • Retail Banking & Lending • B2B Internet Strategies

EXECUTIVE BUSINESS PERFORMANCE

DEVISED A PIVOTAL MARKET-BRANDING BLUEPRINT THAT ACCELERATED ANNUAL EARNINGS BY UP TO 75%

Directing the Global Consumer Banking Group for Paradigm, developed an enterprise-wide, cohesive research agenda and "Data Bible," quality control process, and press relations campaign to compete with new, larger market entrants.

Strategic and Commercial Successes:

- Spurred annual revenues in a mature firm, enabling a lucrative sell-off to Reuters, the first news and financial information service with a large, computerized network. Paradigm's success attracted 21 suitors, including four large competitors.
- Conceived and drove a concerted market position and branding strategy, building considerable influence within the company that opened opportunities for attracting better research talent, investors, and offerings to clients.
- Led the proposed acquisition of 4 firms and 5 joint ventures, redistributing products in Latin America, Europe, and Asia.
- Excelled in advisory role to both proprietary clients and clients of other services on banking trends, assessment of business models, pre-release evaluation of new products, validation of new corporate strategies, and other specific issues.

BUILT A TECHNOLOGY-PLANNING AND IMPLENTATION PLATFORM TO SELL MORE SERVICES AND FORTIFY REVENUES

Turned around BGS's risk-averse project deployments that contributed to lost business and lower-level sales relationships.

Strategic and Commercial Successes:

- Pioneering the practice approach for FG US, helped launch a critical strategic consulting initiative that contributed to a healthy 200% increase in firm revenues in 4 years—from just over $750 million to $2.19 billion.
- Created subject matter practices, e.g., mortgage, credit card, risk, consumer lending, core banking, etc., that not only forced sales people to own a client relationship but also to sell more than just commoditized technology and IT solutions.
- More potent sales model that incorporated tactical solutions poised BGS to be named to "America's 400 Best Big Companies" for five consecutive years on the *Forbes* list. Firm also garnered wide recognition from finance giants.
- Played key role in generating $21 million in billable projects in first year of banking practice, exceeding goal by 53%.

5455 Michigan Avenue, Chicago, IL 60601 • Phone: 312-257-4505 • Cell: 646-222-2889 • E-mail: sjperry@optonline.net

EXECUTIVE BUSINESS PERFORMANCE, *continued*

STRUCTURED HIGH-VALUE, TRANSACTIONAL INTERNET STRATEGIES TO CUT COSTS AND AMPLIFY BUSINESS VOLUME

Developed solid, integrated web vehicles for 4 major financial services clients in an unproven, early-stage channel. Addressed issues of fusing new strategies with operations, preserving the low-cost Internet promise while averting potential alienation of brokers.

Strategic and Commercial Successes:

- Envisaged a new product strategy and created 6 distinct product groups to align with JPMCB's different market segments. Created web tools for brokers with unique, customer-direct features, e.g., download of paperwork, planning tools and online applications that incorporated the $5 million to $20 million loan range.
- Redesigned CHSF's commercial mortgage lending process to fit seamlessly with the web-based delivery infrastructure, retail sales, and backend processing systems and personnel. Sleeker retail support environment enabled sales teams to use the web in concert with their clients—not just as a pure sales tool—and continue offering clients affordable pricing.
- Generated agile web plans for finance firms at a time when most were ill-conceived, unprofitable, and poorly executed.

LEVERAGED COMMERCIALLY FOCUSED INSIGHT TO NEGOTIATE CRITICAL CONTRACTS FOR A START-UP

As Top Fund's President and CEO, was charged by the Board to lead and complete development of a suite of technology tools, data, and analytics targeted to the financial services market for customer relationship management/retention of loan customers.

Strategic and Commercial Successes:

- Led a key refinement in firm's technology growth plans to develop two new product lines—one sold to existing clients and the other completed with a joint venture partner—to reach a new, untapped market with lucrative revenue potential.
- Negotiated multi-vendor contract to secure critical service data sources; drove application for a proprietary process patent that secured significant market advantages and served as a barrier to competitors.
- Engineered beta testing of process and technology with a major U.S. bank and generated results reporting.
- Deftly navigated the sales and negotiations process with our first 4 clients: a top-5 U.S. bank, a top-20 insurance and financial services firm, and a top-10 U.S. lender.

CAPTURED NEW BUSINESS AND REVENUE SOURCES, DRAFTING CONTRACT-WINNING RESPONSES WORTH $7 MILLION

As a Director of FG Europe, developed a business pipeline that expanded the practice in 10 months and led BGS in growth.

Strategic and Commercial Successes:

- Mitigated risk by paving the way for acquisition of 15 new clients worth $45 million over 4 years, and helped win 5 European contracts valued at $3 million annually from an unofficial partnering initiative with firms like Gartner & Co.
- Devised reorganization strategies for two large international banks (France, UK) with project outcomes delivering 10.5% improvement to the bottom line for the 2nd largest French bank and 9.4% cost savings for the major UK bank.
- Serving as subject matter expert, e.g., banking, securities risk management, lending, collections, and customer-facing e-services, oversaw multiple projects in the UK, Italy, Denmark, and France that contributed to 55% growth.

DEFTLY EXPLOITED OPPORTUNITIES FOR PRODUCTS IN A DOWN MARKET, EXPANDING MARKET REACH AND SEGMENTATION

Facing a $2.5 billion debt resulting from one of the largest loan loss reserve write-offs in history, a regional two-year decline in revenues of $575+ million, and the potential of massive layoffs and office closures, helped Bancorp turn around its lending business in Maryland. Conducted a strategic analysis of markets, trends, and competitor challenges, developing an aggressive business plan and new model for a correspondent and broker-lending program to expand entry into new markets.

Strategic and Commercial Successes:

- Entered new geographic markets and market segments that boosted nearly $77 million in added sales revenue annually by year three, achieving 55% over goal. Concurrently, saved nearly 40% of Maryland positions slated for elimination.
- Established a direct presence in the region by developing a lending suite of products in collaboration with several contract partners, able to resell Bancorp financial products into their respective retail markets.
- Lending program helped recover most of the lost revenue due to the state's economic slump, and the model—with some modifications—became the template for a national expansion of a new wholesale lending division.
- Secured a 35% higher profitability rate per full-time employee as compared to the rest of the group.

CAREER DEVELOPMENT HIGHLIGHTS

TOP FUND PARTNERS, INC. – Chicago, IL   2001 to present
President and CEO

Leading a diverse staff, grew revenues from zero at inception to current annualized revenues of $8 million within 6 months of launch. Managed operations, technology development, and strategic business planning. Originated and developed products, identified and mined new markets and distribution channels, and negotiated contracts with clients, data providers, potential resellers, and joint venture partners. Negotiated a joint venture, new market entry of our lending suite and CRM tools, deftly structuring partnership contributions, revenue splits, and contracting/licensing agreements worth $18 million–$20 million annually in total gross revenues for both firms combined. Provide overall leadership for Midwest market development.

PERRY & ASSOCIATES – New York, NY   2000 to 2001
Executive Director; Principal   *(please see addendum for detailed project information)*

Founded and led a strategic management and IT consulting firm focused on financial services companies, winning 13 contracts in the early stages of the practice. Offered domestic clients expertise in planning, organizational development, IT strategy, and business process redesign. Client base grew to represent small-market, multimillion-dollar U.S. technology firms to global $12 billion technology firms, as well as clients among the top 40 U.S., Asian, and European banks.

PARADIGM CONSULTING, INC. – Philadelphia, PA   1997 to 2000
Director, Global Consumer Banking Group

Shepherding the consumer-banking group to a lead-market position, grew the practice to acquire both small and large clients in 25 countries. Personally attracted stellar clients, e.g., Morgan Stanley, Bank of Japan, Wachovia, Chase, Bank of Ireland, Barclays, Bank Leumi, and others, to become the top research firm in the financial services industry. Overseeing several direct employees and a budget of $10 million, did extensive work with domestic, Asian, and European clients, presenting to national and international audiences and user groups and driving significant business growth.

BRITISH GLOBAL SYSTEMS, INC. – Boston, MA, and London, UK   1993 to 1997
Director, Finance Group (FG): Europe – Global Financial Management Practice, 1995 – 1997
Managing Director, Finance Group (FG): U.S. – Consumer Banking Practice, 1993 – 1995

Brought in by FG's President, held responsibility for multiple projects simultaneously, both managing project and financial lifecycle and participating in some as subject matter expert as well. Managed up to 85 consultants, including various project managers, and oversaw a $2.8 million operating overhead budget. Performed financial analysis and due diligence on 3 potential acquisitions with aggregate value of $110 million, and won and developed 5 multimillion-dollar client proposals. Selected to play a key role as a senior steering committee member. Oversaw 7 project budgets simultaneously, with total project budgets equaling $45 million–$50 million annually. Managed timelines, needs, staffing challenges, and client conflicts.

CHS FINANCIAL CORPORATION OF GEORGIA – Atlanta, GA   1991 to 1993
Senior Vice President, Sales and Operations

Recruited by the EVP and CEO to build and oversee a network in Texas, Oklahoma, and Kansas, created 3 full-service branch operations and a network of 45 third-party brokers, dealers, lenders, and correspondents. Oversaw P&L, budgeting and management of loan origination, processing, decisioning/underwriting, closing, sales, relationship management, affinity operations, investor relations, and regional product creation. Identified and negotiated key distribution relationships that secured 65% of $55 million in sales generated. Branding message and product positioning secured $10.2 million in income.

BANCORP, INC. – Baltimore, MD   1989 to 1991
First Vice President, Correspondent Lending, Mid-Atlantic Region

Led strategic planning, start-up, and operations for the region that became Bancorp's national model for wholesale lending. Used process redesign to achieve 75% improvement in loan processing time within 4 months. Selected by President to serve on a 5-member council, designing and executing CRM strategies that resulted in 33% increase in customer satisfaction.

EDUCATION

University of Pennsylvania – The Wharton School – Philadelphia, PA • **MBA,** 1989
Majors: Finance; Operations Management

Cornell University – Ithaca, NY • **BS in Business Administration,** 1987, **magna cum laude**
Major: Finance • Minor: Economics

5455 Michigan Avenue, Chicago, IL 60601 • **Phone: 312-257-4505** • **Cell: 646-222-2889** • **E-mail:** sjperry@optonline.net

STRATEGIC LEADERSHIP SUCCESSES

International Consulting Assignment

Secured a nine-month consulting assignment with Silicon Fen Software, a $250 million UK-based software firm and global provider of IT solutions, services, and hosted applications to financial services, manufacturing and consumer products clients. Was retained by the CEO to examine several commercial software product lines for recommendations on product positioning and branding. Analyzed two new product businesses via a business-case methodology, estimating demand and market size and following up with a decision, approach and structure for the offering. In addition, helped create the marketing and business plans for multiple products that involved cross-market launches.

Outcomes:
- Two products initially introduced in the UK were selected for U.S. market entry.
- One U.S.-developed product was targeted for European and Asian market entries.

Product and Investment Challenges

One of Silicon Fen's software products was languishing at the time, without a new sale in a 21-month period. The firm was constrained by a slow decision process on capital investments due to senior management's penchant for outside opinion as the driver of investment and product strategy. Another product was hampered by stalled growth despite resources allocated to it. Five products in all—representing a $77 million investment—were preventing this firm from accelerating earnings. Assessed products as well as the management and development structure of three product groups, also testing customer feedback and the marketing and sales processes.

Consulting Recommendations:
- Recommended development enhancement for the first product that included strategy and cost estimates.
- Identified benefit of moving core development of the new product to Russia that included a plan for managing the remote development and design of criteria.
- Advocated a partnership agreement on the second product to create new, blended software and outsourcing of the product to extend product appeal to a broader audience.
- Urged a dramatic overhaul of the management team on the third product and enhancement of the product set and no new product in the group.

Outcomes:
- Offshore product enhancement was paid for jointly by a lead client.
- Product sales increased with first six sales in the U.S., with more sales in 12 months following the overhaul than in the prior five years combined.
- Silicon Fen was able to shed an unprofitable division within 11 months and save significant resources on another product's development.
- Concurrently, drastically overhauled an outdated product at only 10% of the cost that would have been incurred in the UK.
- Earnings improved by 34% and low performers were turned around or eliminated—important to a public firm's bottom line.
- Greatly improved prospects allowed the firm to be acquired by Oxford Technology Group at a 63% premium over market value.

CHAPTER 10

Writing Executive Branding Statements

From the very beginning of this book we have discussed the importance of defining and communicating your executive brand—your unique value. It is critical for you to understand your brand so that you can speak with confidence about what you can do, what you have done, and how you achieve results. Digging deep to identify your brand is a valuable exercise that will yield rich nuggets of distinguishing information that you can use in your resume and all of your career marketing documents.

Follow these guidelines when developing your personal branding statement.

1. Tell "how" as well as "what"

Your brand must say something that is unique to you, and thus it's not enough to declare that you "build revenues" or "manage multibillion-dollar companies." Many other well-qualified executives can claim the same achievements. Instead, think about how you accomplished them and use that information to personalize your brand statement. For example, "Drive rapid revenue growth by seizing emerging opportunities in undervalued markets" or "Create culture of innovation and shared mission that unites employees of multibillion-dollar companies toward clearly defined goals." These insights are unique and valuable.

2. Back it up

We can all come up with lofty and powerful brand statements, and you might be tempted to slap one down on your documents. But be careful. Your brand must be authentic—it must represent what you're really all about—and it must be supported by your specific actions and accomplishments. So before adopting a brand slogan, take the time to identify several specific examples of each trait and accomplishment that you are promoting as your brand.

3. Distill big, broad thoughts to concise statements

No one comes up with a true brand statement just by thinking about one-liners. Before those magical few words come together, you will want to spend some time thinking deeply about the traits, achievements, actions, and ideas that together comprise your brand. Take lots of notes, try to identify trends, and "try on" a variety of synonyms before deciding on the precise language for your brand.

Examples

In the following examples you will see brief language that has been distilled from deep thoughts and extensive notes. These examples will help you see how a brand statement can add power to your resume and other career marketing materials and distinguish you from other well-qualified candidates.

EXAMPLE 1: Senior Executive, Financial Services
(Writer – Deborah Wile Dib)

> **■ Branding Statement:**
> A visionary and ethical rainmaker, I propel triple-digit advances in growth and revenue through the conception and building of new businesses and new products. When I build a business I do what I say and I do it the right way—without micromanaging—to deliver spectacular results and winning teams.
>
> Most effective in a core leadership role (VP or above) in a growing, forward thinking financial services firm, I am focused on creating or revitalizing internal groups, building and managing client relationships, and training/mentoring teams to outperform the competition.

This expansive brand description clearly communicates what this executive does, how he does it, where he is most effective, and his distinctive personal attributes.

EXAMPLE 2: Senior Executive, Sales & Marketing, Technology Products & Services
(Writer – Louise Kursmark)

> **■ Branding Statement:**
> Ignite Revenue ■ Drive Change & Growth ■ Build Dynamic Organizations

This three-part branding statement appeared on this executive's resume, just below his headline/title. The image conveyed is of an aggressive leader who propels rapid growth—certainly not a warm-and-fuzzy caretaker of existing business.

EXAMPLE 3: Chief Technology Officer
(Writer – Louise Kursmark)

> **■ Branding Statement:**
> Marshaling technology resources to support business priorities and enable the achievement of extraordinary goals

Used as a resume tag-line, this branding statement was created for a technology executive who had, indeed, achieved extraordinary goals. Remember, you must back up the images and impressions included in your branding statement; otherwise you lose credibility and the statement loses meaning.

EXAMPLE 4: Senior Finance Executive
(Writer – Deborah Wile Dib)

> ■ **Branding Statement:**
> Visionary, gifted with the drive and skills needed for high-level strategic and tactical implementation that drives revenue. Have "made the impossible possible" for a number of Wall Street's leading financial firms.

If you look at the complete package of materials for Syed Ramjeet on pages 183-191, you will see how this brand statement serves as the foundation for content, organization, and focus of each document in his career marketing portfolio.

CHAPTER 11

Writing Executive Job Proposals

It might surprise you to learn just how many jobs are created or refined to match the skills and fit of a good candidate. During the course of your search, if you follow the networking and referral strategy we recommend most strongly, you will end up meeting with lots of people who don't have a job to offer or whose open positions don't take full advantage of your skills and expertise. Smart executives will recognize your value and will want to bring you on board. And more often than you think, as the discussions continue over the course of several weeks or even months, it becomes clear to the hiring executive that the best solution is to create a new job or alter the existing position.

In other cases, you might meet with someone who is filling a position that you are very interested in but that, on the surface, doesn't seem like an ideal match. Yet during your discussions you are able to bridge the gaps and position yourself as a strong though perhaps nontraditional candidate. A good example of this might be a corporate executive deciding to pursue a leadership role with a nonprofit organization.

In both of these cases, your existing resume and other career marketing materials might not be enough or might not be precisely on point with regard to the current opportunity. Instead, a job proposal could be the best vehicle for communicating not only your relevant skills, but your passion for the position and the organization and your deep connection to the needs and challenges of the job.

Keep these important points in mind as you prepare your job proposal:

1. Each job proposal is unique

A job proposal is entirely customized to a specific opportunity, and it is essential to show a precise match between each aspect of the position and your skills and qualifications, especially if your background is in a different role or different industry.

2. Your job proposal justifies the choice to hire you

A job proposal and customized resume (see item #4 below) will help the executive who is championing your cause make a compelling case for hiring you. Without this documentation, it might be difficult for your champion to persuade other decision-makers that you are the right person for the job or that you deserve higher-level responsibilities or greater compensation than currently envisioned for the role.

3. Show that you understand the position and the organization

When preparing your job proposal, focus on the key challenges of the position, the organization's mission and priorities, and your areas of perceived strength as defined during your discussions with the hiring executive. It might be that some of your most significant achievements will not be mentioned, while others of lesser importance will be prominently featured. Your goal is to create a document that immediately resonates with the leadership of the organization, whose reaction should be, "This person knows what our organization is all about, believes in our mission, understands our challenges, and has both the experience and the passion to move this organization forward."

4. Custom-edit a resume to match the job proposal

If your job-proposal position is substantially different from the targets you envisioned when preparing your resume (the case of the corporate executive switching to the nonprofit sector is a good example), go back to your resume and create a different version that matches up with the new position. You can remove certain items, rearrange others, add new facts, and expand on certain achievements and activities to change the flavor of your resume while still presenting your strongest qualifications. When you submit the new resume along with your job proposal, it will show a clear correlation between what you have done and what you want to do in your new role.

Examples

The two job proposals that follow are distinctly different, but each one is closely tuned to the specifics of the position and the unique value that each candidate offers.

EXAMPLE 1: CEO Job Proposal: Sarah Gaylord (page 115)
(Writer – Christine Edick)
Each item in this CEO proposal supports a key challenge or opportunity of the particular position. You can see how Sarah has tailored her most relevant experiences and qualifications to the company's mission and strategic goals, and has provided a few select examples of how she will achieve them.

EXAMPLE 2: Chamber of Commerce Executive Director Job Proposal: James Wallis
(page 116)
(Writer – Louise Kursmark)
This corporate executive neatly ties his business experience to the needs of the Chamber of Commerce Executive Director position he is seeking. Beyond business expertise, he relates his passion for the community and its multiple cultures as strong selling points.

SARAH GAYLORD

The Ideal CEO for Samson Industries

Global Perspective
Out-of-the-Box Thinker
Embraces Change
Leadership Skills
Analytical
Flexible
Team Builder
Entrepreneurial
Strength in Sales
Empowering Manager
Strong Decision Maker
Excellent Business Acumen

- **Action-driven executive** able to evangelize company vision of "global leader in manufacturing parts and equipment for highly specialized and experimental medical technologies and procedures."

- **Leader by example,** promoting teamwork and information sharing with the goal of strengthening operations and individual performance—critical performance goals to achieve $10 million revenues by year-end 2007.

- **Transformational change leader,** strategically turning around and refocusing corporate direction, creating a unified vision and mission—revitalized Elger Industries to grow from 10% to 80% market share in its niche.

- **Pioneer** in strategic alliances, business partnerships, and networks, with exposure to multiple frameworks for C-level discussions—essential to meet goals of global sales and international production. Exceptional gains achieved through key alliances with investment bankers, venture capitalists, and private investors.

- **Sales expert**—proactively implemented creative selling techniques, presenting value-based selling to top management down, closing complex sales, maintaining business plan goals, achieving and exceeding sales targets.

- **Market visionary,** adept at understanding industry trends and building forward-looking, profitable strategic business relationships—to help the organization remain at the forefront of medical technology advances and seize emerging opportunities.

- **Team builder**—achieve corporate objectives and individual goals by building high performance teams that are motivated with strong complementary skill sets inspiring passion for excellence with a "make it happen" attitude.

- **Bridge builder**—overcome corporate and cultural adversity, with understanding of culture differences and related cross-cultural issues.

sgaylord@gmail.com • 2940 Bay Hill Street, San Francisco, CA 94105 • Mobile 415-745-0930

JAMES T. WALLIS

39 Cripple Creek Road
Ridgefield, CT 06877

203-781-5600 day
203-249-8117 eve
jwallis@yahoo.com

VALUE OFFERED TO THE McALLEN CHAMBER OF COMMERCE

OPERATIONAL LEADERSHIP EXPERTISE

❑ **Performance improvement.** During my career in progressive leadership roles with TAP Services, twice I took over struggling organizations and created top performers—efficient operations, productive staffs, and clear-cut operational procedures that enabled the organization to run like a well-oiled machine. Even the best-run organizations benefit from process improvements that enhance productivity and efficiency. I am an expert in analyzing operations, finding opportunities to improve, then putting in place the essential systems and processes.
Value: Free CEO time for strategic initiatives. Improve staff morale and focus. Cut costs.

❑ **Staff recruitment, selection, development, and retention.** The most valuable resources of any organization are its people. With deep experience selecting and managing sales, marketing, administrative, and management staff, I recognize both the tangible skills and the intangible qualities that make the best employees. As a manager, I promote the success of each employee by setting clear expectations, finding opportunities for staff to stretch their capabilities, and creating a culture of excellence with a shared sense of mission and goals.
Value: Maximize contributions of each staff member. Strengthen member services. Boost image and reputation of the Chamber. Reduce costs of attrition and recruitment.

❑ **Business management.** My experience building and leading multimillion-dollar organizations has given me deep capabilities in all areas of operations, administration, and human resources. With both strategic and hands-on tactical skills, I am an effective executive who delegates appropriately. Perhaps most importantly, I have a passion for solving operational problems and leading tight, well-run organizations.
Value: Appropriately manage essential and time-consuming business operational issues with strict attention to budget parameters and cost controls.

BUSINESS DEVELOPMENT

❑ **Business-building skills.** In the cutthroat competitive world of financial services, I have been a consistent top performer both personally and while leading a sales team. I know how to generate revenue through targeted sales and marketing, and I can effectively sell intangible services to a diverse client base.
Value: Strengthen the Chamber's business-development team. Promote its identified strategic objectives. Increase membership. Add value to primary role of operations leadership.

KNOWLEDGE OF AND PASSION FOR THE COMMUNITY

❑ **Board liaison.** As an experienced board member of nonprofit organizations, I can lead in outreach to the business community. My successful business background adds credibility and establishes strong peer-to-peer relationships.
Value: Enhance the contributions of the Chamber's board of directors. Build and promote board-training programs as a member benefit.

❑ **Multicultural business experience.** I have been active and successful in multiple markets with strong Hispanic presence—South Florida, California, and Texas. I understand and appreciate the Mexican culture and communicate effectively with individuals of every background.
Value: Enhance relationships with individual members and community groups. Within McAllen and state/nationwide, promote positive value and benefits of multiple cultures.

❑ **Choosing McAllen.** My family and I have chosen to return to McAllen. We feel at home, enjoy its "small big town" atmosphere, and feel privileged to live in its unique culture. Personally and professionally, my years in McAllen were among the happiest and most satisfying of my life. I'm eager to again contribute to the city and its people.
Value: Genuine fervor and enthusiasm that can't be bought.

CHAPTER 12

Writing Special Reports

In sharp contrast to every other document you will prepare during your job search, a Special Report is not about you! Instead, it is an interesting, helpful, educational presentation of some facet of your expertise and wisdom, written to benefit your readers. You are probably wondering why you should write a report like this and how in the world it can help you land your next job. In fact, Special Reports are one of the most unusual and out-of-the-box ideas you can use during your search.

In a nutshell, you can use a Special Report to:

- Communicate your market value.
- Help readers understand how they can benefit from your knowledge.
- Differentiate yourself from other candidates.
- Position yourself as an expert with valuable intelligence, *not* as a job seeker.

A well-crafted Special Report has much more impact on potential employers than the typical resume. Here's why:

- It focuses on the reader's needs and interests.
- It positions you in an entirely different way than your resume—as an expert who understands the reader's needs and is generously sharing some time-tested solutions.
- It gives you credibility because it is not accompanied by your resume, cover letter, or any other reference to the fact that you are looking for a job.
- It shares information that will help your readers save time, save money, improve efficiency, reduce waste, or otherwise achieve bottom-line benefits.

Consider these guidelines for creating and using a Special Report for your executive job search campaign.

1. **It's not rocket science**

   You do not have to share groundbreaking news or reveal high-value proprietary information in your Special Report. You simply have to provide some common-sense, time-tested, proven ways for your readers to benefit.

2. **Tap into your expertise**

   What do you know and how can it benefit others? Your experience gives you the background to provide tips and techniques that can mean the difference between success and failure. Be sure that your Special Report positions you appropriately for your current career goals and your executive brand.

3. **Create a catchy title and format**

   A title and format such as the "Top Ten Tips for Increasing Sales in Developing African Nations" will help you structure your report, keep the content to a manageable length, and pique your reader's interest. Be sure the title of your report communicates some benefit to the reader.

4. **Include interesting information**

   Here is some more advice from Christine Edick, a career coach who helped her client prepare the Special Report that is included as a sample later in this chapter. "Search your experience for the simple principles that make your job or business successful. Remember, they don't need to be earth-shattering revelations; basics are fine." Create a list of four to 12 items and flesh these out to create the heart of your Special Report.

5. **Give yourself credit**

   Be sure you are identifying yourself as the author and providing full contact information on each page of the report. A separate brief bio page can appear at the end of the report; this can be a mini-resume that summarizes your professional history and expertise.

6. **Don't be proprietary**

   Don't make the mistake of copyrighting your Special Report, limiting distribution, or restricting reproduction. The point is to get it in as many hands as possible so that more and more people will become aware of you, impressed by your knowledge, and aware of what you might be able to do for them.

7. **Present it appropriately**

   Standard business-page size, bound into an inexpensive but classy-looking folder, is an ideal presentation for your Special Report. Don't worry about length of the report so much as content, organization, and readability.

When you have created your Special Report, send it out to anyone whom you think would benefit or is in an influential position in your target companies or industries. Use it as a follow-up with people you meet at professional conferences or meetings. Share it with your own circle of contacts. The purpose is to position yourself as a credible expert who has a wealth of valuable information . . . and is willing to share it.

Remember, don't send your resume with the report. But do be prepared to send your resume in response to phone calls and other communications that arise from people reading the report and contacting you to discuss an idea or ask you some questions. At that point, they'll be very receptive and already influenced in your favor.

EXAMPLE: Special Report: Johnny Hiro (pages 120-126)
(Writer – Christine Edick)
Titled "Four Simple Ways to Improve Your Software Development Process and Make Your Users Happy," this Special Report relates common-sense strategies to do exactly what the title says. Notice the "About the Author" page that closes out the report and relates key achievements as well as a brief career history. After writing the Special Report as a tool to help him obtain a higher-paying job with greater responsibility, Johnny shared it with his manager, who was so impressed that he awarded Johnny a raise and a promotion. Not only that, he has asked other company employees to prepare similar Special Reports to help the company gain a competitive edge with clients and prospects.

4 Simple Ways to
Improve Your Software
Development Process
And
Make Your Users Happy

By Johnny Hiro
October 2005

Introduction

Software development is tricky business. One second too long in your program and you can **lose your user's patience**. One penny too short in your accounting software and you can **lose your user's confidence**.

Improving your **software development process** can prevent these mishaps.

From my academic experience in computer science and my experience as a software developer specializing in collaboration tools, I have identified 4 simple ways to **improve your software development process** and **make your users happy**.

Principle 1: Really Gather Users' Requirements

Perhaps one of the most embarrassing things that can happen to an application team is to deploy a product that their users do not want. Oftentimes, developers jump the gun and create what they believe is the perfect solution to their users' problems. This almost always guarantees that their users will send back this solution for revision over and over again.

Gathering requirements is one of the most basic principles in software development; yet, we don't do enough of it. Here are a few key elements that will help you get to the bottom of your users' requirements:

- **Let your users do the talking**
  Host requirement workshops! Be an apprentice! Watch your users at work! Listen to your users and let them speak freely! Only by listening to your users will you improve your chances of developing a solution that will make them happy.

- **Draw diagrams**
  Most people understand diagrams better than words. Draw diagrams for your users, then have them draw you diagrams. Diagramming not only clarifies difficult problems, but it also increases user participation in your development process.

- **Document as much information as possible**
  There is no such thing as too much documentation; even documenting seemingly irrelevant information may someday surface as solutions to your problems.

- **Review requirements with users at all stages of development**
  Requirements will always change, and we will always miss those "hidden" requirements. Continually review requirements with your users to ensure that you provide them with the best product possible. Your users will also be less likely surprised by any missing functionality and more likely pleased with the delivered product.

Question: Have you ever deployed software that didn't meet your users' needs?

Principle 2: Work As a Team

You can't expect to develop exceptional software if your team doesn't work together. Creating software requires teamwork. Learn to harness the power of your team by the following tips:

- **Use collaboration tools**
Utilize available **source control** tools. This type of tool not only provides a central database for your source code, but it also improves team collaboration and increases productivity.

  Use a **team calendar.** Want everyone to know important release dates? A team calendar will help ensure all your team members receive the same message. You can use it to store deadlines, vacation days, etc.

  Use a **centralized repository** for documents, designs, test cases, meeting notes, etc. It is often difficult to share accurate information between team members; keeping information in a central repository ensures all your team members receive the same message.

- **Follow coding standards**
Following coding standards will allow your developers to easily understand each other's code, improve code maintainability, and also increase efficiency and productivity.

- **Share information among team members**
Train everyone in your team about the key functions in your software; don't allow developers to focus only on their area of work. Cross-train your team members and continually update them on new application  functions or requirements. This will not only allow work to be dispersed equally among team members, but it will also ensure consistent responses to questions asked from members of your team.

 Question: Can you easily disperse work among your team members?

Principle 3: Really Test Your Software

What's worse than having your application crash during a demo? Testing an application is tricky business; follow the tips below to not only improve your testing, but to also gain your users' confidence:

- **Create your test conditions from your users' cases and ensure each test condition is linked to a requirement and each requirement is linked to a test condition**
  This will guarantee that you are able to test all of your users' requirements. This will definitely reduce the number of "missed testing conditions," thereby decreasing application downtime.

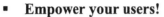

- **Empower your users!**
  Work with them to create and clarify test conditions.

  - **Define and organize your test cases**
    Unclear and disorganized test conditions will only create confusion and slow progress. Organize your test conditions in a logical manner that both developers and users understand.

  - **Provide a central test and defects repository and share it with the users**
    This will not only reduce miscommunication between your users and developers, but it will also allow your users to view your testing progress and also review current defects.

- **Prioritize your testing**
  Test the most critical and widely used parts of your application first. This will ensure that if you run short on time, you will have at least tested your users' most-used functions.

- **Test your application on your users' machine**
  You may have tested your application in your own controlled environment, but does it work on your users' machine?

 Question: Who finds errors in your application, you or your users?

Principle 4:   Learn From Your Mistakes

Nothing is worse than your users losing confidence in your software. Making the same mistakes twice is a surefire way to accomplish this. Decrease your chances of repeating past mistakes by following these simple tips:

- **Keep an organized "Lessons Learned" log**
Log the date and time the problem occurred, the description of the problem, the people involved with the problem, and the steps taken to resolve the problem.

  It is best to keep this log in a database where it can be shared with your teammates.

- **Review lessons learned at each stage in development**
This will remind you and your developers of problem areas and will greatly reduce your chances of repeating the same mistakes twice.

- **Share your "Lessons Learned" with your users**
This will not only show your users that you are proactive in improving your process, but it will also allow you to gather feedback from your users.

 Question: Do you unknowingly repeat past mistakes?

Page 5 of 6

About the Author

Johnny Hiro is a software developer in the financial industry. He currently develops applications for portfolio accountants, project managers, and other programmers.

In his previous position, he provided support for a 600+ user time-and-attendance reporting system and developed several collaboration tools for project managers and training teams.

Over the years, he has
➤ **saved** a company at least **$30,000** by providing accurate database reports to executives in a timely manner.
➤ **improved** customer service, **increased** class throughput, and **saved** a company at least **$45,000** per year by developing a multi-user, company-wide class enrollment database.
➤ **saved** a company approximately **1 million dollars** by discovering and informing executives of a hidden database consistency error.

You may contact the author at:

Address   : 100 E. Anywhere Ave. #30
                  City, CO 90000
Home   : 000-000-0000
Cell   : 000-000-0000
Email   : johnnyhiro@aol.com

Please feel free to copy and distribute this special report as often as you wish; please include this author information when you do.

CHAPTER 13

Writing Reference Dossiers

Your professional references are among your most powerful assets. Have you considered what they can do for you during your career transition? Of course, when contacted by potential employers they will gladly endorse you by saying positive things about their experiences with you and impressions of you. But beyond (and outside) that box, consider these additional ways your references can help you:

- They can serve as key links in your network, connecting you to influential decision-makers and actively fostering your job search.
- As mentors and advisors on your Executive Success Team, they can be a critical factor in the success of your job search. (See Chapter 4 for more information on forming your executive success community.)
- Your references can provide written testimonials that you can excerpt for your resume, cover letters, or more completely in a Reference Dossier, as discussed further in this chapter.
- Your references can help you paint the picture of yourself that you want your audience to perceive.

Don't rely on your references to understand precisely how you want to be perceived or how they can best help you. Let them know! They will appreciate the guidance and do their best to support you, provided what you are asking them to say about you is congruent with their experiences. You can't—and shouldn't—attempt to put words in their mouth or pressure them to give anything other than their honest evaluation of who you are, your strengths, and your weaknesses. But when you let them know what will be most valuable for them to say about a specific opportunity or your career in general, you help them give you the support and assistance that will be most valuable.

What is so valuable about your references is that they provide third-party endorsement of you and your strengths and capabilities. This reinforces and lends credibility to everything you have communicated in your resume, cover letter, additional profiles or addenda, and interviews. To make the most of these endorsements, consider creating a Reference Dossier that is much more than simply a list of the people who will serve as your references.

Key points about your Reference Dossier:

1. **Use reference endorsements to support your brand**

   Whether publishing an excerpt of a written reference or just describing what your references will say about you, focus your message on your core attributes—those that make up your executive brand and support your current career targets. Even if references commented positively about other attributes, don't muddy up the waters by including these in your dossier.

2. **Choose the most advantageous format**

   If your references have written glowing comments about you, showcase these comments as excerpts in your dossier. If, on the other hand, your references prefer to speak rather than write about you, consider the creative idea shown in the second example, and project what they *will* say when called.

3. **Have references represent a broad cross-section of your career**

   A good variety of references will allow potential employers to see many facets of who you are and learn how you are viewed by the different people with whom you interact. Consider tapping these sources for a broad slate of references:

   - Your direct managers
   - Executives from other areas of the company
   - Fellow members of a board, committee, or taskforce
   - Subordinates
   - Project team members
   - Competitors
   - Strategic partners
   - Vendors
   - Mentors
   - Community leaders

4. **Your references must know you well**

   No matter how tempted you might be to include a high-profile business leader, politician, or other notable, don't do so unless that individual knows you well and can speak positively and intelligently about your core attributes. A vague reference will connote "name dropping" and can actually harm rather than help your career.

Examples

The following two examples show creative ways to make the endorsements of others an integral part of your career marketing materials.

EXAMPLE 1: Reference Dossier: Emily Simon (page 130)

(Writer – Phyllis Shabad)

Using the actual words of several executives and professionals at Emily's current company, this one-page document offers powerful first-person endorsements that clearly sustain Emily's brand as a dynamic leader in her field of corporate legal affairs.

EXAMPLE 2: Reference Dossier: John Brach (pages 131-135)

(Writer – Gayle Howard)

John's dossier very cleverly projects what references *will* say about him. It conveys to the hiring authority a clear and broad understanding of who the references are, their relationship to John, and the areas of his performance on which they are qualified to speak. If you use this format, it is absolutely imperative that your references talk about you just as you say they will; otherwise you will lose credibility and appear to be egotistical.

EMILY SIMON

REFERENCE DOSSIER

HIGH-QUALITY INTELLECTUAL INPUT COUPLED WITH ENTREPRENEURSHIP AND INITIATIVE

"… Emily is an excellent communicator who can articulate complex legal issues in a succinct, user-friendly fashion … she has a strong grasp of the underlying commercial issues. Some key examples of initiative and achievement have been the identification of potential legal/regulatory loopholes in Boom's *Dynamite* launch, influencing future competitive launches in the category … a lucid articulation of the legal pros and cons of launching into this category with the Boom brand … and the excellent case she developed by personally driving the R&D and quality control departments for preventing a recall of Boom Spot-Lifter that would have cost us millions of dollars. Emily has also been a key player in trying to improve the performance and effectiveness of the regulatory group … and streamline the document management and approval process in a number of areas. There are many other examples where Emily 'leads from the front' and provides invaluable support to the North American business."

— S. Rowan, Executive Vice President for North America, Boom Industries, Inc.

TRUSTED BUSINESS PARTNER DRIVING RESULTS THROUGH BETTER CONSUMER COMMUNICATION, RISK MANAGEMENT, AND POLICY DEVELOPMENT

"… Emily implemented a Legal Advertising Review System, which ensured clear and consistent development of claim support protocols, as well as providing timely review on a large volume of labels, advertising and consumer communications … The process was instrumental in enabling speed-to-market on innovation. Emily also played a key role in ensuring competitiveness for the launch of the new Boom Lift-Off product, working with R&D to develop claim support protocol and new consumer-relevant claims … result was a very competitive advertisement that drove success in the marketplace. The implementation of Emily's idea for in-house business/legal training has been a central ingredient in our approach to risk management … ensuring that our employees understand our policies and appropriate business conduct on a range of issues … I often hear people refer to it in difficult situations. Emily paved the way forward for local governance in each marketplace … which will have a positive, long-range impact on the business."

— J. Smythe, VP of Global Product Development, Boom Industries, Inc.

THOROUGH COMMERCIAL OUTLOOK RESPECTED BY THE COMPETITION

"… She has always demonstrated several critical skills, the first of which is her ability to work quickly and efficiently … Emily generates a significant quantity of high-quality, actionable work product … has moved the company to quick resolution … brings a thoroughly commercial outlook to any issue … is clearly respected by the competition. We worked on an important conflict with Colgate-Palmolive involving trademark registrations … Emily was a very effective negotiator … we achieved a mutually acceptable settlement that saved both companies a great deal of money in legal costs. Emily also led negotiations with BritGroup—a diversified UK company—involving potentially hostile trademark disputes around the launch of an important new product for Boom. She deftly managed the expectations of all parties, ensuring that neither party lost face in the negotiations, and the launch proceeded unencumbered."

— R.M. Woodruff, Global Trademarks Director, Boom Industries, Inc.

ROLE MODEL WHO ELEVATED LEGAL/REGULATORY FUNCTION TO TRUSTED BUSINESS PARTNER

"As a manager, she was open, trustworthy and empowering … she stretched her team and encouraged us to develop into areas that we had previously felt to be beyond our reach. Emily was an excellent role model for commercial leadership … at her very best when discussing new projects with marketers … her energy and interest in any project were highly infectious and her contributions and leadership helped ensure that the legal function was seen as a key partner as opposed to a hurdle to be overcome."

— T. Powers, Trademark Attorney, Boom Industries, Inc.

2945 Silvercreek Circle, Cincinnati, OH 45241 ● Mobile Worldwide: 513-200-3210 ● E-mail: emsimon@gmail.com

CONFIDENTIAL

REFERENCE DOSSIER

CANDIDATE: JOHN BRACH

REFERENCE: MR. RICK JACKSON

CHIEF EXECUTIVE OFFICER
MANUFACTURER'S INSURANCE COMPANY

RELATIONSHIP

Immediate Supervisor, ITTP (2 years)

QUALIFIED TO SPEAK ON

Mr. Jackson will testify to the candidate's talents in terms of innovation, resourcefulness, leadership, and marketing prowess. Additionally, Mr. Jackson can speak with authority on the subject of John Brach's financial acumen and strengths in managing budgets to achieve corporate goals during his engagement as General Manager of Marketing and E-commerce at the ITTP.

EXPECTED RESPONSES

It is expected that Mr. Jackson will give positive responses to cost-saving initiatives driven by John Brach. Mr. Jackson can be invited to speak of the candidate's restructuring of the Marketing Division that successfully integrated two insurance company operations post-merger. Mr. Jackson would describe John Brach's attitude as excellent and characterize him as an individual who "makes things happen."

In response to questions designed to highlight professional limitations, his anticipated response would be the candidate's tendency to assume a workload "above and beyond" his designated role.

He will confirm that John Brach left the company on a positive note for a career advancement opportunity.

CHARACTER AND PROFESSIONAL TRAITS

Mr. Jackson is anticipated to substantiate assertions that John Brach's efforts changed the company culture within the ITTP for the better, and that he had worked very hard on his interpersonal skills—developing strong working relationships throughout the organization.

REFERENCE: MR. STAN BROWN

CHIEF EXECUTIVE OFFICER
WALL ADMINISTRATION

RELATIONSHIP

Colleague/Peer at the Society of CPAs. Former Director.

QUALIFIED TO SPEAK ON

Mr. Brown will testify to the candidate's talents in marketing and financial management and his observations of John Brach's operational style and relationship with others.

EXPECTED RESPONSES

It is expected that Mr. Brown will speak glowingly of the candidate's marketing abilities, having previously acknowledged the candidate as "One of the best marketers" he has known. Mr. Brown will reiterate that the candidate demonstrated innovation in marketing and a passionate focus, and that he would not hesitate to rehire given the opportunity. Mr. Brown can also speak from first-hand observation of the candidate's willingness to take direction and work cooperatively with others.

He will confirm that John Brach performed above expectations in brand building for the SCPA, taking the designation to a higher level and meeting all significant timelines.

CHARACTER AND PROFESSIONAL TRAITS

Mr. Brown is anticipated to confirm that John Brach fostered strong and positive relationships both up and down the ladder and that he demonstrated a positive attitude to his work and his staff.

REFERENCE: MR. KEVIN STEVENS

CHIEF EXECUTIVE OFFICER
REVENUE SOLUTIONS MANAGEMENT

RELATIONSHIP

Mr. Stevens has acted as a professional mentor for more than seven years. He maintained board-level relationships with the ITTP.

QUALIFIED TO SPEAK ON

Mr. Stevens is qualified to speak of the candidate's performance and professional growth over several years. He can speak with authority on John Brach's talents as a marketer, has first-hand knowledge of the successful "Hey You!" ITTP campaign, and his capacity to turn around business profitability.

EXPECTED RESPONSES

It is expected that Mr. Stevens will confirm John Brach's consistent performances in changing workplace culture through innovation in all positions the candidate has held over the past seven years.

He will respond positively to the candidate's abilities in fostering good working relationships despite the challenges inherent in strategically implementing significant organizational change.

It is anticipated that Mr. Stevens will corroborate the success of the "Hey You!" ITTP campaign, further substantiating claims that the program was both cost-effective and profitable. He will also confirm that John Brach was instrumental in turning around the financial position of the AMI in the face of severe financial difficulty.

CHARACTER AND PROFESSIONAL TRAITS

Mr. Stevens will testify that John Brach has, since he has known him, taken his work and his professional reputation very seriously and that he has a very good marketing mind that integrates workable theory with a practical approach towards complex marketing problems.

REFERENCE: MR. PETER FARR

BOARD MEMBER
ITTP

RELATIONSHIP

As a board member of the ITTP, Mr. Farr has first-hand knowledge of John Brach's performance at the highest level.

QUALIFIED TO SPEAK ON

Mr. Farr can speak with conviction of the candidate's talents in brand strategy and development, board presentations, and superior grasp of complex and strategic market solutions.

EXPECTED RESPONSES

Mr. Farr is anticipated to refer to John Brach's executive presentations to the board, believing them to be concise, articulate, logically sound, and strategically appropriate. He will also speak of the board's satisfaction and surprise at the marketing exposure the candidate accomplished on a limited budget.

Mr. Farr will confirm that the candidate left the ITTP on good terms to pursue career advancement.

CHARACTER AND PROFESSIONAL TRAITS

Mr. Farr will describe John Brach's attitude as being professional and dynamic. He will speak of the candidate's reputation for developing rapport with staff at all levels.

CHAPTER 14

Writing Executive Cover Letters

A powerful executive cover letter is an essential—and critical—element of your job search campaign. In fact, you will be writing many such letters, because you will need to include some kind of cover message with every resume that you send out. While it's true that each cover letter should be customized to the specific individual, opportunity, and company, that doesn't mean that you must start from scratch each time you write one. In all likelihood, much of the information can remain the same from one letter to the next, although you will want to review each letter and edit as appropriate to be sure you are communicating effectively to the specific audience for each letter.

Your cover letter introduces your resume and is an important positioning piece in which you must quickly communicate "who you are" as it relates to the needs of your reader. Some of your cover letters might be simple one- or two-sentence email messages, while others will be a full page or longer, printed to match your resume, and mailed to a decision-maker. This diversity makes it a challenge to create a "formula" for writing cover letters, but use these guidelines to be sure your letters are well received and effective.

1. Know your audience

It is always preferable to write to a specific individual. Not only is this most favorable to the reader, it allows you to personalize and customize the content most appropriately. Even if you can't find out the name of a specific individual (for instance, if you're responding to a blind job posting), think about who the person is (is s/he a recruiter, a business owner, the head of HR?) and use the appropriate tone and language to connect with that audience.

2. Tell them why you're writing

It is important to let your readers know immediately why you are writing—this is simply good business etiquette, so be sure this important information appears toward the beginning of your cover letter. In the case of an email, use the subject line to communicate why you are writing.

3. Zero in on their needs

Although you are writing about yourself, it's advantageous for you to communicate the benefits your reader will receive from speaking with you. Can you solve problems for them? Help them achieve organizational goals? Meet their current challenges? Help them grow and prosper? Present your experience and track record as solutions to the reader's problems, and you will capture their interest.

4. Hit the highlights

We recommend that you keep your cover letters to one page, as a general rule. An email cover letter should be even shorter—a few paragraphs at most. You don't need to give your readers a complete synopsis of your career; all you need to do is provide enough of the highlights to entice them to read your resume and/or call you for an interview.

5. Ask for the next step

Your goal is to extend your written communication to a personal meeting, either face-to-face or by telephone. Be sure you ask for this meeting in the close of your cover letter. And just as you would follow up with any business correspondence, follow up your cover letter with a phone call, if possible, a few days after you send it. Your job search is a number-one priority for you (not for your reader), so it's up to you to press for the next step in a proactive, yet appropriate, manner.

Examples

The three cover letters that follow all adhere to the five guidelines above. Yet, you'll notice how much they differ in content, tone, and style. Your letters can be a unique expression of you, your career, and your current goals while still following the traditional and expected format for business communications.

EXAMPLE 1: Cover Letter: Karl Kent (page 138)
(Writer – Don Orlando)
Karl worked with his career coach to identify companies that were a good fit for his expertise, and in the process they found a company in California that was thinking about moving to Karl's part of the country. This cover letter was written specifically for that company and earned a return phone call within three days of mailing.

EXAMPLE 2: Cover Letter: Sarah Wilson (page 139)
(Writers – Michelle Dumas and Dan Dorotik)
This letter helped Sarah gain an opportunity for a meeting to discuss brand-building strategies, and she was eventually offered a VP position to launch a new brand for the company. Notice how closely her bullet points connect to her area of interest and expertise.

EXAMPLE 3: Cover Letter: Beale James (page 140)
(Writer – Helen Oliff)
Leveraging his expertise in import/export/international trade along with his high-profile background as a Presidential appointee, Beale still manages to focus his letter on what's important to the employer and how he can provide value.

Sarah Wilson

2 Robinson Lane ▪ Phoenix, AZ 83009
swilson@email.net

Home: (602) 291-0596

Cell: (602) 291-2209

July 19, 2005

John Q. Phelan, Executive Vice President
Copeland Products, Inc.
2317 Central Parkway
Phoenix, AZ 85007

Dear Mr. Phelan:

In the current economic climate, launching and building small and start-up companies and brands are interesting challenges. To do so requires high levels of dedication from the participants, flexibility in reacting to constantly changing market demands, and the willingness to "wear many hats" in the effort to meet and exceed goals. It is this level of performance and dedication that I would bring to your organization based on my experience as an integral player in driving 10-fold growth, to $400 million, for the Omni brand over the past nine years.

Because I have progressed through sales, operations, and general management leadership positions in start-up, growth, and turnaround situations within the consumer packaged goods industry, I have developed a deep understanding of the importance each plays in the overall success of an organization. What I offer, in turn, is the ability to meet your organization's needs in a wide range of objectives, as illustrated by my previous accomplishments:

- **1999–Present, Regional Sales & Operations Manager**—Introduced unknown brand and captured 75%+ market share.
- **1998–1999, Area Sales & Operations Manager**—Opened new facility that led to a 40% sales increase in 12 months.
- **1997–1998, Area Business Manager**—Achieved 100% employee retention in an industry with high turnover rates.
- **1994–1997, Route Sales Representative**—Designed area's 1st express route, generating 100%+ territory expansion.

Although I am proud of my past achievements, I maintain a forward-thinking approach and am most interested today in what I can do for you and your organization. Perhaps a personal interview would allow us the opportunity to discuss in detail your current needs and the strategies I can contribute towards their fulfillment.

Thank you for taking the time out of your schedule to review and consider my candidacy. May we meet in the near future to discuss your goals and how I might help you meet them? I would be pleased to make myself available at your convenience.

Sincerely,

Sarah Wilson

Sarah Wilson

Enclosure

Sarah Wilson

2 Robinson Lane ▪ Phoenix, AZ 83009

swilson@email.net

Home: (602) 291-0596   Cell: (602) 291-2209

July 19, 2005

John Q. Phelan, Executive Vice President
Copeland Products, Inc.
2317 Central Parkway
Phoenix, AZ 85007

Dear Mr. Phelan:

In the current economic climate, launching and building small and start-up companies and brands are interesting challenges. To do so requires high levels of dedication from the participants, flexibility in reacting to constantly changing market demands, and the willingness to "wear many hats" in the effort to meet and exceed goals. It is this level of performance and dedication that I would bring to your organization based on my experience as an integral player in driving 10-fold growth, to $400 million, for the Omni brand over the past nine years.

Because I have progressed through sales, operations, and general management leadership positions in start-up, growth, and turnaround situations within the consumer packaged goods industry, I have developed a deep understanding of the importance each plays in the overall success of an organization. What I offer, in turn, is the ability to meet your organization's needs in a wide range of objectives, as illustrated by my previous accomplishments:

- **1999–Present, Regional Sales & Operations Manager**—Introduced unknown brand and captured 75%+ market share.
- **1998–1999, Area Sales & Operations Manager**—Opened new facility that led to a 40% sales increase in 12 months.
- **1997–1998, Area Business Manager**—Achieved 100% employee retention in an industry with high turnover rates.
- **1994–1997, Route Sales Representative**—Designed area's 1st express route, generating 100%+ territory expansion.

Although I am proud of my past achievements, I maintain a forward-thinking approach and am most interested today in what I can do for you and your organization. Perhaps a personal interview would allow us the opportunity to discuss in detail your current needs and the strategies I can contribute towards their fulfillment.

Thank you for taking the time out of your schedule to review and consider my candidacy. May we meet in the near future to discuss your goals and how I might help you meet them? I would be pleased to make myself available at your convenience.

Sincerely,

Sarah Wilson

Sarah Wilson

Enclosure

Beale James

2307 Freetown Court
Reston, VA 20191

BJames@comcast.net

Home: 703-264-1171
Cell: 703-995-0706

Senior Executive, International Business
Import/Export ~ Business Development ~ Business Management

May 1, 2005

Patricia Montserrat
President
I-Products, Inc.
7819 Commerce Parkway
Reston, VA 20195

Dear Ms. Montserrat:

Is your organization looking for a seasoned international business consultant? Someone with direct experience in trade contracts and import/export markets, who can help you manage and leverage your staff and key relationship? I am such a person.

I am also a Presidential appointee with White House experience and other Executive Branch appointments. In fact, my career experience is equally split between the two—making a nice mix for any company that really wants to break out of the red tape and break into international markets.

My value to a potential employer or customer is:

> ➤ International business development experience
> ➤ Import/export and trade contract expertise
> ➤ Export promotions experience for small to mid-sized businesses
> ➤ Strong track record for business and fiscal management
> ➤ Exceptional results in personnel motivation and management
> ➤ Global network of high-ranking government and industry officials

My vast experience with helping small to mid-sized businesses enter profitable export markets spans many industries in many countries—healthcare, energy, technology, and manufacturing.

I am seeking opportunities to perform senior-level import/export and trade functions and international business development and consulting. I will contact you within the next week to discuss your needs and your organizational goals and how I might help you achieve them.

Sincerely,

Beale James

Beale James

Enclosure: Résumé

CHAPTER 15

Writing Thank-You Letters

Powerful, executive-level thank-you letters are more than a mere formality and a sign of good manners. Not just a quick *"Thanks for the interview ... can't wait to hear from you"* message, thank-you letters can have tremendous value in moving your candidacy forward and positioning you above the competition. Although much of what you include in your thank-you letter may have already been communicated during your interview, there is nothing more effective than the written word to etch those thoughts into your interviewer's mind.

You can use your thank-you letters to:

1. Reiterate your expertise as it relates to a company's specific challenges

During the interview, you have learned about the company's specific needs, issues, and/or challenges as well as performance expectations for the new executive. Use your thank-you letter to demonstrate how you can meet those needs, master those challenges, and exceed those expectations.

Example: You've interviewed as CFO for a distressed company in need of immediate action if it is to survive. They need a candidate with proven success in fast-track turnarounds and revitalizations. Consider presenting your experience in a format such as:

- In 2000, led the turnaround and return to profitability of a $75 million apparel manufacturer, rebuilt customer credibility, and launched a new pipeline of marketing and development activity.
- Between 1998 and 2000, restored profitability to a $200 million consumer products manufacturer who had multimillion-dollar losses for the past six years. Today, the company boasts profits of more than 18% annually (4% over industry average).
- In 1997, consulted with a Fortune 50 company to create a strategic turnaround program for all 290 of its production facilities worldwide. To date, the company has implemented two of my programs and generated cost savings in excess of $100 million.

2. **Directly relate your core professional competencies and successes to the company's needs**

> If, during an interview, company representatives communicated their ideal qualifications for a candidate, use your thank-you letter to outline how you meet and/or exceed each of those qualifications.

> *Example*: You've interviewed as EVP of Technology and Product Development with a high-tech venture, and the company has clearly communicated its four essential candidate qualifications. Let them "see" immediately that you have those four qualifications with a letter format and structure like this:

> > **New Product Development**
> > Include a two- to three-sentence paragraph with a strong overview of your total experience in new product development, then add a list of three to five bullet points highlighting specific projects, achievements, operations, etc.
> >
> > **Technology Commercialization**
> > Write two to three sentences that give a capsule view of your total experience in technology commercialization, followed by three to five bullet points highlighting specific projects, achievements, operations, etc.
> >
> > **Team Building and Leadership**
> > Again, start with a brief paragraph that summarizes your experience in team building and leadership, and then add three to five relevant examples in a bullet-point list.
> >
> > **Global Business Development**
> > Summarize your total relevant experience in a concise paragraph followed by a short list of your top achievements, projects, and initiatives related to global business development.

3. **Overcome objections**

> Specific objections to your appropriateness as a candidate might have been raised during the interview. Use your thank-you letter to respond to, and overcome, these concerns. Communicate that it's not an obstacle but, rather, an opportunity, and that you're fully prepared to meet the challenge.

> *Example*: You're interviewing as CEO for a well-established company in the Midwest. Although you're extremely well qualified, they're concerned that you've never lived in the area and have no network of local contacts. Eliminate their concerns by explaining that your network of professional contacts is nationwide and, in fact, you know John Doe of the XXX Company, have a long-standing relationship with an economic development director in the area, etc. These contacts will serve to further expand the company's already established network.

Length of Your Thank-You Letter

How long should your thank-you letter be? Of course, as with anything else in job search, there is no definitive answer, but one to two pages is the norm, depending on the amount of information you want to communicate.

Remind yourself that you already have the company's interest or you would not have been interviewing, and use your thank-you letter as a tool to communicate valuable information. Remember, the entire process of job search is marketing and merchandising your product — YOU. There is no reason why writing thank-you letters should be any different than any other of your job search activities!

Examples

Thank-you letters are unique because they must reflect a specific interview. Thus you will notice how different each of the following letters is, in content, tone, and style, and how in each letter the "voice" of the candidate comes through.

EXAMPLE 1: Thank-You Letter: Kathy Miller (page 144)
(Writer – Louise Kursmark)
Written by an aggressive sales leader, this letter pulls no punches about what she can deliver. It is confident, assertive, and energetic — just like the candidate herself.

EXAMPLE 2: Thank-You Letter: Dana McGuire (page 145)
(Writer – Louise Kursmark)
After reiterating enthusiasm and specific strengths for the position, in the third paragraph of this letter is a powerful example of overcoming an objection that was uncovered in the interview. Note how it then closes on an upbeat, confident note.

EXAMPLE 3: Thank-You Letter: William Cary (pages 146-147)
(Writer – Wendy Enelow)
Each of the bold headlines is a specific match for the challenges that were discussed during the interview, and each bullet point below the headline is compelling evidence of relevant experience and success in meeting those precise challenges.

KATHY MILLER

2943 Hillside Street, Unit 2-B ▪ Oakland, California 94624 ▪ 510-245-7450 ▪ kathymiller@verizon.net

October 30, 2005

Steve Rostakoff
Western Regional Manager
NuTraders Network
9090 Mile High Drive
Denver, CO 80209

Dear Steve:

NuTraders has an exciting future, and I would like to help the Institutional Services division skyrocket to a market-dominant position in the West.

NuTraders's new offerings put the company in a short-term position of market advantage. To seize this advantage requires a "hit the ground running" sales approach. As we discussed, my experience with Schwab closely parallels your new Western Sales Manager position. I know the market... I know the key players... I know the industry and the products... and I have the experience and track record to deliver both immediate revenue results and sustainable long-term growth.

With the right person at the helm, the first-year goal of $100 million in sales is easily reachable. I believe I am that person. I hope you agree.

As you requested, I am attaching a list of professional references, and I will follow up with you early next week to see if you have any additional questions. Thank you for sharing so much time and information with me this week; I am inspired by your enthusiasm and eager to play a part in building a strong Western Region for NuTraders.

Sincerely,

Kathy Miller

Kathy Miller

enclosure

DANA McGUIRE

203-484-7190   184 George Street, East Haven, CT 06512   dmac@hotmail.com

October 30, 2005

Ellen P. Rogers
President and CEO
Packright, Inc.
252 South Causeway
New Haven, CT 06523

Dear Ms. Rogers:

Thank you for sharing so much of your time with me on Thursday. I remain enthused about the Customer Service Director position and confident that my strengths, skills, and style are a good fit for your needs and the culture at Packright.

I am a firm believer in building relationships to build business. In particular, we discussed improving relationships within the Customer Service department; building trust between Customer Service and Sales; and boosting account retention through relationship-based customer service. My ability to deliver on these key priorities will benefit Packright, your employees, and your customers.

While it is true that my direct staff-management experience is limited, I feel well equipped to take on this challenge because of two key qualifications: one, my recent business education, including exploration of leadership style and ethical management approaches; and two, my proven ability to get results through persuasion, influence, and leadership by example rather than direct control. I think you'll agree that these are important abilities in a leader, and that specific management techniques can be built from a foundation of management knowledge, strong interpersonal skills, and a clear understanding of the mission of the organization.

I am excited about bringing fresh ideas to your Customer Service operation. Given the opportunity, I guarantee I will not only meet but exceed your expectations.

Sincerely,

Dana McGuire

Dana McGuire

WILLIAM CARY
120 Port Street, Lawrence, KS 66046
785-382-8937
willcary@aol.com

January 14, 2006

Steven Donovan
President
PYD Technologies
1209 Robert Trent Street
Los Angeles, CA 90045

Dear Steve:

First of all, thank you. I really enjoyed our conversation yesterday and am truly impressed with the tremendous success you have brought to PYD. There are but a handful of companies like yours that have experienced such aggressive growth and can predict strong and sustained profitability over the years to come.

I would like to be a part of the PYD team—in whatever capacity you feel most appropriate and of most value. I realize, of course, that you already have an HR Director who has successfully managed the function throughout the course of the company's development. It is NOT my intention to compete with Leslie Ralson, but rather to complement her efforts in bringing renewed HR leadership to PYD.

Let me take a few minutes to highlight what I consider to be my most significant assets:

I have met the challenges of accelerated recruitment:

- In 2002, I launched a recruitment initiative to replace 50% of the total workforce in a 900-person organization. This was accomplished within just six months and was the key driver in that company's successful repositioning.

- In 1995, when hired as the first-ever HR executive for a growth company, I created the entire recruitment selection and placement function. Over the next two years, I hired more than 50 employees to staff all core operating departments.

- Between 1991 and 1995, I spearheaded the recruitment and selection of technical, professional, and management personnel. This was a massive effort during which time I interviewed more than 300 prospective candidates throughout the U.S. and Europe.

I have met the challenges of employee retention:

- During my employment with Helms Financial, we were staffing at an unprecedented rate. Inherent in this situation is the need to initiate programs to ensure staff retention over long periods of time. The faster an organization grows, the more critical this focus must become. Costs associated with recruitment can be significant and must be controlled. Following implementation of a market-based research study at Helms, I was able to reduce turnover 35%, saving more than $350,000 in annual operating costs.

I have met the challenges associated with international HR leadership:

- Throughout my tenure with Laxton Data, I led the company's international employment and employee relations functions. This was a tremendous experience that provided me with excellent qualifications in domestic and expatriate recruitment, compensation, benefits, and relocation. Further, I demonstrated my proficiency in managing cross-cultural business relationships spanning the globe.

I have met the challenges of growth and organizational change:

- Each of the organizations in which I have been employed has faced unique operating and leadership challenges. These situations have been diverse and included high-growth ventures, turnarounds, and internal reorganizations. Each has focused on improved performance and accelerated market/profit growth. To meet these challenges, I have created innovative, market-driven organizational structures integrating pioneering methodologies for competency-based recruitment and performance management.

- Most recently, I orchestrated the workforce integration of two acquisitions into core business operations. This required a comprehensive analysis of staffing requirements, evaluation of the skills and competencies of the acquired employees, and accurate placement throughout the company. The integration was successful and all personnel are now fully acclimated and at peak performance.

I hope that the above information demonstrates the value I bring to PYD—today and in the future. You will also find that my abilities to lead and motivate are strong and have always been the foundation for my personal success.

I look forward to speaking with you and scheduling an appointment to meet with Mr. Baldwin. Again, thank you for your time, your interest, and your support.

Sincerely,

William Cary

William Cary

CHAPTER 16

Writing and Publishing Web Portfolios

The Internet has made it simpler than ever to manage an effective job search. Think how fast, easy, and inexpensive it is for you to email a resume, contact someone in your network, gain access to published openings, and research your target companies and industries! The Internet also makes it possible for you to produce and publish a comprehensive portfolio showcasing your executive career and capabilities. Such a portfolio can help you during your job search and beyond, as you manage your career and your professional brand.

Consider these benefits:

1. **Centralized site for your most critical career information**

   By storing all of your career successes and accomplishments, positions and promotions, key project summaries, education and training details, performance evaluations and testimonials, community leadership affiliations, and more on your own website, you can easily maintain a comprehensive, ongoing record of your career. And because the portfolio is stored online rather than in a file cabinet at home or at work, important information won't get lost.

2. **Powerful tool for ongoing career management**

   Your web portfolio will assist you in managing your career long after you have completed your latest transition. You can use it to present yourself as a candidate for internal projects or key initiatives; as a promotional link from articles you write for online or print publication; during performance review sessions; and to assist your coaches and mentors in understanding you, your capabilities, your strengths, and your passions. The possibilities are unlimited.

3. **Means to control and manage your online brand image**

   More and more, business people are turning to the web to find out about people they are doing business with. Whether evaluating a potential job candidate, a strategic partner, a selling or buying relationship, or a possible Board member, individuals can quickly "Google" your name to see what is being said about you. Go ahead and try it—where does your name appear? What are the most common "hits"? In a shrinking electronic world and global economy, it is critically important that you position yourself as you wish to be perceived in the market. While you can't control what others say about you, by creating a web portfolio you can influence your image so that it is congruent with your brand and is among the first things that web surfers find out about you.

4. Tactic to establish a cutting-edge image

As of the writing of this book, web portfolios as an executive career tool are growing in popularity but are still on the leading edge of technology and career management. If you wish to position yourself on that leading edge, then a web portfolio is a must! Web portfolios also allow ample opportunity to demonstrate creativity and to prove, in multiple ways, the skills, capabilities, and potential you offer to a company.

Your web portfolio should be as unique as you are. What can you include to showcase your one-of-a-kind career successes and attributes? Consider these ideas . . . and then let your imagination run wild, as you make your web portfolio a reflection of who you are, your personal/professional style, and your professional brand.

- Career success stories, expanded from the accomplishments on your resume
- Vision or philosophy of management, leadership, technology advances, or other critical facet of your career brand
- Endorsements and testimonials
- Graphics, photographs, and other visual illustrations of some of your work
- Photographs of yourself
- Audio and/or video—perhaps a welcome message, testimonials, or a recording of one of your presentations
- A PowerPoint-style slide show of one of your executive presentations
- Summaries and links to news articles in which you are featured or mentioned
- A listing of professional distinctions, perhaps with links to the awarding organizations
- Your biography
- An interview format in which you can provide insights to current issues related to your field of expertise
- Pertinent quotes—quick statements that reveal your thoughts on key issues
- Link to PDF and MS Word versions of your resume that can be viewed, downloaded, and printed
- A blog to share ongoing thoughts and ideas related to your profession, your industry, and your job search
- A contact page that encourages visitors to get in touch with you via multiple methods

Planning and Developing Your Portfolio

To foster your job search and ongoing career management, it is a must for your web portfolio to be polished and professional. There are four critical components to consider during the planning and development stages:

1. **Strategy:** Clear understanding of what you are trying to convey and a general perspective on how you will do so
2. **Content:** The specific elements that you will include in your portfolio
3. **Writing:** Carefully crafted pieces for each of your strategic content areas
4. **Design:** Distinctive, professional appearance along with easy navigation; all in all, your design must support your brand and your strategy for the site

Examples

It is essential that you be closely involved with the development of your portfolio, but don't feel that you must plan, write, design, and manage the entire project by yourself. The sample portfolios in this chapter were created by each individual through collaboration with strategists, writers, designers, and web technology experts. These professionals can assist you with any or all components of the project and help ensure that your web portfolio portrays the appropriate professional image and brand congruity so it will support, rather than damage, your job search.

EXAMPLE 1: Web Portfolio: Heather Henricks (pages 151-155)
(Writer – Kirsten Dixson)
Through its design, photographs, and content, Heather's web portfolio shows her vibrant personality as well as her significant career achievements. Notice the branding statement ("Leading Web users to new frontiers") that appears in large red type on her home page. Everything in the portfolio supports this brand.

EXAMPLE 2: Web Portfolio: Derek Newsom (pages 156-161)
(Writers – Louise Kursmark and Louise Fletcher; Flash Design – Lucky Marble Solutions Corp.)
Offering both traditional, fast-loading HTML and slower but jazzier Flash animation, this web portfolio is designed to provide essential career-related information while also building Derek's reputation as a creative and dynamic executive who goes "above and beyond" in new technology ideas.

EXAMPLE 3: Web Portfolio: Andy Waterman (pages 162-168)
(Writer – Deborah Wile Dib; Site Design – Kirsten Dixson)
This well-designed portfolio leads off with a powerful branding statement and an audio-streamed welcome message so that you can hear Andy's own voice. The site is rich with examples, details, and supporting documentation relating to his successful career in new media.

ame

oout Heather

rengths

reer Highlights

sume

ntact

About Heather

Recognized for her **passionate advocacy for the Web end-user**, Heather Henricks is a champion in converging business, team and customer objectives when managing web design, infrastructure, usability and marketing projects. In her seven-year tenure at Microsoft, Heather has gained incredible experience in working on large-scale, high-profile initiatives, resulting in a reputation described by managers and colleagues as a **razor-sharp intellect, contagious optimism and a refreshing "tell it like it is" style**.

Heather's strengths lie in effectively translating consumer research in a way that resonates with internal stakeholders. The end results are **effective web design, infrastructure and, ultimately, web products that are useful to consumers**. For the past year and a half, Heather has been working as the Worldwide Online Marketing Manager for the Microsoft Partner Program website on the www.microsoft.com network. She is responsible for driving and building the virtual relationship with Microsoft's small, medium and enterprise partners through the Microsoft Partner Portal website. This includes **developing comprehensive worldwide online marketing strategies for acquiring, converting and developing partners**, as well as planning and executing marketing campaigns and promotional strategies worldwide.

While working in a strategic web strategy and business development role for the MSN.com Channels team, Heather **owned the vision and content development of two top grossing web channels** - MSN Dating & Personals and MSN Careers. She also led the research and discovery process that ultimately supported the development of a teens-oriented destination on the MSN.com network.

Instrumental in building these major Web portals for MSN (teens, health, careers, etc.), Heather has worked with many diverse product groups within the organization and **faced challenges unique to the second largest Web portal on the internet, MSN.com**. This experience has exposed her to sophisticated technologies and taught Heather to think about design, web infrastructure and content in a way that accounts for, and serves, all competing interests.

She began her successful career as the International Organized Play Development Manager at Wizards of the Coast, Inc. in Seattle, Washington. Her international perspective and experience in marketing games resulted in her **recruitment by Microsoft's MSN Gaming Zone**.

Heather's ability to articulate a clear strategic vision and rally the strong support of people and teams, while under a high degree of scrutiny, has been key to her success. Her approach to project management has always been to **uncover**

I just have to tell you once again how super cool your presentation was on Wednesday! Way to go! Thank goodness someone else has a sense of humor and enjoys having a good time at work. Very glad to have you on the

151

Heather Henricks

Home

About Heather

Strengths

• Career Highlights

Resume

Contact

Career Highlights

Web Design
* Managed full redesign of MSN Careers (2003) on the MSN.com network, including information architecture and usability studies, to design wire framing and editorial strategy. Details...

Market Research
* Led six-month project discovery that would drive support for the release of a teen-oriented web destination on the MSN.com network and provide data analysis for strategic planning and feature prioritization. Details...

Online Marketing
* Designed and implemented a more effective internal online marketing process for the Microsoft Partner website in replace of a process that was unsuccessful in quickly responding to urgent market needs. Details...

Web Usability
* Assigned by Vice President of the Worldwide Partner Group to oversee the usability and information architecture efforts for the release of the Microsoft Partner Program online account management tool. Details...

Heather Henricks · Seattle, WA · Email

Portfolio site by Brandego

152

Leading Web users to new frontiers.

Heather manages high visibility web design, web usability and web marketing projects for companies and organizations who share her enthusiasm for innovative, leading-edge information technology.

Heather is much more than simply tech-savvy; she is vigilant about incorporating and balancing the needs of the business with the needs of the customer into everything that she does.

For the past seven years, Heather has held increasingly responsible web marketing positions within Microsoft while acting in diverse roles such as Web Product Manager, MSN Channel Manager and Worldwide Online Marketing Manager. Currently, she is accountable for managing and growing the virtual relationship with Microsoft's small, medium and enterprise business partners through the Microsoft Partner Portal on the Microsoft.com network.

Heather's energy and conviction are also evident in her passion for adventure and endurance sports and her commitment to volunteering within her local community.

Learn more about how Heather pushes the limits.

Heather Henricks · Seattle, WA · Email

153

Home

About Heather

Strengths

Career Highlights

● Resume

Contact

Resume

Summary of Qualifications

- Manager of Web design, usability, information architecture and online marketing projects with 11 years' experience in multiple online proficiencies and a seven-year tenure with Microsoft Corporation.

- Skilled at balancing needs of external business partners with those of online audiences to implement compelling online communications that deliver measurable business results.

- Experience and success working with diverse, cross-functional teams.

- Proven ability to think strategically while executing projects to meet objectives in a fast-paced, high-performance climate.

Web Design	Online Marketing	Information Architecture
Content Management	Web Usability	Focus Groups
Marketing Communications	Partner Relationships	Strategic Planning
Project Management	Team Leadership	Oral & Written Communication

Professional Experience

Microsoft Corporation, Redmond WA   1998-Present

Worldwide Online Marketing Manager, Microsoft Partner Program (2004-Present)
Accountable for worldwide online marketing management of the Microsoft Partner Portal on the www.microsoft.com platform. Responsible for driving and building the virtual relationship with Microsoft's small, medium and enterprise partners through the Microsoft Partner Portal website. Create and improve online marketing campaigns and manage marketing budget. Work closely with editorial, product planning and production teams to integrate marketing strategies into the current site and future site releases.

- Increased online reach with program partners and potential partners by recruiting, engaging and retaining

> **"I really think you've made a good hire in Heather. FYI."**

154

me

out Heather

rengths

reer Highlights

sume

ntact

Strengths

Customer Insight and Leadership

Applies in-depth understanding of customers' business challenges, practices, needs and requirements to strategy planning, development of product/services offerings and marketing initiatives. Implements customer feedback in product/service features and marketing programs. Uses aggregate customer data to redefine, validate or establish new customer segments and profiles for offerings. Integrates customer segmentation strategy with product/service/ program planning. Analyzes customer profiles and business environments to identify priority customer issues or opportunities. Identifies and recommends priority development initiatives across the customer value creation chain, based on trends in customers' businesses.

Integrated Marketing Planning and Delivery

Works with colleagues across the organization to plan and execute coordinated and synergistic marketing initiatives. Proactively qualifies sales leads (e.g., identifies decision makers, determines budget, parameters, pinpoints client needs, etc.). Translates global marketing plans into marketing initiatives for own business, including defining budgets, metrics, and timelines. Establishes cross-group team charters, articulates shared goals, and outlines a common agenda to reinforce integrated marketing and sales efforts. Reengineers work processes and systems to ensure they support/reinforce integrated sales and marketing efforts. Identifies potent new ways to quantify marketing value (e.g., conducts comparative analyses across integrated efforts over time).

Building Partnerships and Ecosystems

Builds the market for technologies through innovative and complementary partnerships. Creates or extends the partner ecosystem for a particular product or initiative. Engages partners in ways to develop more value for both parties in the relationship. Manages multiple, complex partnerships successfully across adjacent businesses. Ensures optimal partner engagement model and team processes.

Interpersonal Skills

Develops and maintains good working relationships with others. Is aware, diplomatic, and tactful in dealing with people from diverse backgrounds. Creates an organizational climate that supports respect for all individuals and delivers clear feedback to those who fail to support that spirit. Demonstrates keen insight into others, accurately predicting how others will think and behave across a variety of different situations. Consistently builds highly effective interpersonal relationships in business partnering situations.

Another channel redesign... this time from the Greeting Cards Channel. The redesign drives to deliver better network integration, improved user experience and stronger Media Metrix & eShop performance. This design really makes the cards the hero and

155

DEREK T. NEWSOM
SENIOR EXECUTIVE: COMPUTERS & CONSUMER ELECTRONICS

| Profile | Highlights | Interview | Testimonials | Resume | Biography | Contact |

BIOGRAPHY

Download a copy of this Bio in <u>MS Word</u> *or* <u>PDF</u>

Derek Newsom is a versatile senior executive with over 10 years of international business experience in the world of high-technology products.

Most recently he served as Executive Vice President and President/CEO of Medion USA, Inc., a wholly owned subsidiary of Medion AG with annual revenues over $3B, and a leading global provider of computing and consumer electronic products, solutions and services for the retail channel market in Europe, Asia, and the US. Newsom launched the subsidiary in 2001 and led its successful entry into the North American market.

Under his leadership, Medion USA generated more than $10M in first-year revenues and rapidly accelerated to $50M in its second year. Medion developed relationships and expanded its product presence with several major retailers such as Best Buy, Costco, CompUSA, Aldi, and Amazon, to name a few. In addition to launching Medion's high-quality PCs in the US market, Newsom most notably introduced the first successful desktop system (in November 2001) and notebook computer system (in July 2002) ever to be sold in a supermarket in the history of the United States. His business and product experience encompasses the full spectrum of innovative consumer electronics and computing products, which include PCs, notebooks, PDAs, computer peripherals, plasma and LCD TVs, DVD players/recorders, audio systems, digital still and video cameras, convergence products, and navigation hardware.

Prior to joining Medion, Newsom spent six years at Hewlett-Packard Company, where he held a number of leadership positions. Beginning at HP's corporate headquarters in California, he was quickly recruited to join the start-up computer division in 1996. Newsom helped lead HP's entry into the consumer market for home computing products; during his tenure, HP solidified the top market position in the retail channel. Newsom is also known for managing and leading the first successful introduction of HP home computers into the Japanese and German retail markets. He is a skilled negotiator who was responsible for negotiating HP partner contracts valued over $1B.

Newsom holds a Master's degree in Business Administration, a Master of Science degree in Engineering Management, and a Bachelor's degree in Mechanical Engineering.

156

DEREK T. NEWSOM
SENIOR EXECUTIVE: COMPUTERS & CONSUMER ELECTRONICS

HIGHLIGHTS

Built Medion AG's US business from zero to $50 million in less than 3 years...
Recruited to create mission, business plans, supply chain, brand strategies and corporate policies for US start-up division of Medion AG, $3 billion European computer and consumer electronics company.

- Launched first PC within 6 months by quickly establishing the necessary service and support infrastructure in the US.
- Successfully positioned unknown brand in the crowded US market – developed "German engineering" messaging that resonated with consumers, and marketing campaigns and product strategies that worked for retailers.
- Established critical US strategic supporting relationships with market leaders such as Intel, nVidia, and Microsoft.
- Penetrated new alternative retail channel and developed channel-specific marketing approach that generated an average of $25 million per year.

Grew HP's profit margin by $65 million and boosted divisional revenues 300% ...
Identified and managed opportunities to reduce pricing by outsourcing design, technology and production in North America, Asia, and Europe. Advocated for the change despite intense internal resistance. Shifted the cost of poor quality from HP to the vendors.

- Facilitated the shift by negotiating partner contracts worth more than $1 billion.
- Drove 300% revenue increase by breaking the $499 and $599 price point for the first time in the company's history.
- Grew company's Asia and Europe business in similar manner by working closely with HP's regional heads of management, and rapidly implementing and expanding the new supply and market model into those regions.
- Division ultimately moved nearly all of its business to this new model.

Spearheaded successful launch of HP's home computers into Japan and Germany...
Managed all aspects of one of the biggest launches in the company's history and delivered within a very short timeframe.

- Established supply chain, service and support – qualified and sourced vendors and partners and led all negotiations.
- Consulted on ground-breaking partnership with Vivendi Universal.
- Launched entire line from start to finish in 6 months.
- Managed all product technology program implementation and pricing negotiations.

INTERVIEW

What are your key strengths?

I bring real energy, vision and excitement to any position. I lead with integrity, empower and energize my employees, and create a culture of shared mission and core values.

My broad-based business experience has enabled me to consistently deliver positive results - I have an extensive knowledge of managing international operations, administration, engineering, R&D, outsourced manufacturing, marketing, and sales and so I'm able to find the right solution to most business problems.

Finally, I am extremely proud of my international expertise. Cross-cultural awareness and communication skills are increasingly important in this global economy, which is demonstrated by my leadership of the successful HP product launches in both Germany and Japan.

Tell us a little about your management style.

First, I believe a manager must create an environment that allows others to excel - I support and empower my staff, I train them and I always give credit where credit is due.

Second, I'm a firm believer in effective planning. Technology changes rapidly and - while you can never avoid risk altogether - you can minimize it through careful planning and effective ongoing project/program management.

I have developed a strong business and management philosophy which guides everything that I do. To learn more, you are welcome to review a brief PowerPoint presentation.

What are your most important values?

My commitments are "golden." When I was asked to spearhead HP's entry into Japan, I was given an extremely short timeframe to complete the launch. I worked nights and weekends for 6 months to make sure I met the deadline. Bottom line: if it can be done, I'll get it done.

I also feel very strongly about the fact that people are any company's most important asset. Many managers say this, but they don't all live by the principle in their day-to-day life. I know that I am not able to do it all alone, hence I hire, train and support the very best people I can find.

Lastly, I believe that it is important to be very realistic when it comes to setting the right expectations to the Executive Management team or company's Board of Directors whether it be regarding the business potential, projected growth, revenues, and P&L. This discretionary realism also applies to large scale projects/programs when managing and balancing scope, schedule and resources in order to meet a set deadline.

Have you ever made a mistake that changed the way you do things?

Absolutely! I encourage my teams not to be afraid of making a mistake, but I also emphasize that making the same mistake twice is unacceptable.

What was the best piece of business advice you ever received?

Two actually and they're related. The first was: "Keep things simple"

The second relates to technology: Be careful not to implement technology that restricts the business - only implement systems that improve efficiency, productivity and flexibility.

What are your professional goals?

I don't have a specific title in mind - titles are just not that important - but I do love the challenge of building a best-in-class, global technology organization. I'm excited about creating and/or implementing a business plan that drives revenue

158

DEREK T. NEWSOM
SENIOR EXECUTIVE: COMPUTERS & CONSUMER ELECTRONICS

| Profile | Highlights | Interview | Testimonials | Resume | Biography | Contact |

PROFILE

When one of Europe's leading computer and consumer electronics companies decided to enter the US market, they turned to Derek Newsom, a versatile executive with a proven track record of successful product launches worldwide. They made the right choice - within 6 months, the company had launched its first product and within 2 years they had surpassed all expectations, netting annual revenues of $50 million.

Prior to joining Medion AG, Derek helped lead Hewlett-Packard to a #1 US market share in home computers and introduced HP home PCs into Japan and Germany.

No matter what the challenge, Derek meets it head-on. He is truly a corporate "triathlete," skilled across all areas of executive management - strategy, global operations, product development and engineering, manufacturing and distribution, sales and marketing. Former co-workers, employees and managers all know Derek as an accomplished executive who:

- Creates vision, values and shared goals to inspire employees to extraordinary achievement
- Drives rapid revenue growth and market expansion using a lean operations model
- Devises successful product strategies in a global sourcing and marketing environment

To learn more, review Derek's resume, or contact him directly.

 Listen to Derek's Welcome Message.

159

DEREK T. NEWSOM
SENIOR EXECUTIVE: COMPUTERS & CONSUMER ELECTRONICS

| Profile | Highlights | Interview | Testimonials | Resume | Biography | Contact |

RESUME

Download a full copy Derek's resume in MS Word or PDF

MEDION USA, INC., Chicago, IL 2001-Present
Subsidiary/US division of Medion AG, a $3B publicly traded European company that is the #1 ranking volume producer of PCs in Europe and owns 11% Western Europe market share for computer systems and consumer electronics.

Executive Vice President, 2004-Present

Took on new assignment, working directly with top executive officers (CEO and CFO) of Medion AG to devise expansion strategies for US business. Identify and evaluate acquisition candidates (3 to date) and lend expertise to global sourcing challenges.

- Led 5-month due-diligence investigation into US-based company with recognized brand, well-established retail distribution strategy, and existing account relationships with the nation's largest consumer retailers. Completed all steps through $200MM business valuation before stock dip placed acquisition on hold.
- Defined easy-to-implement strategy to improve Asian product sourcing for the US market.
- Assumed executive relationship management for US business of the company's #1 worldwide account. Developed partner programs to drive volume and build product expertise at the retail level.

President and CEO, 2001-2004

Built US business from the ground up to $50MM+ revenue in less than 3 years. Recruited to launch Medion into the US market. Developed US strategic business plans and mission, vision, brand strategies, and corporate policies. Created entire operational infrastructure and built sales and marketing operation to drive rapid revenue growth.

Held full P&L and management accountability for all operations, marketing, and sales for multimillion-dollar organization. Directed product strategies for computers and consumer electronics (plasma & LCD TVs, home audio/video, small kitchen appliances, personal care products). Negotiated with major Asian CE manufacturers and defined product requirements for the US market.

Served on Medion Board of Directors and co-represented Medion Group to major US and Canadian investment firms in regular yearly investment review meetings.

- Built a lean, high-performance operation, able to support $50MM revenue with only 18-25 staff.
- Launched first PC to retail distribution within 6 months of start-up.
- Generated $10MM revenue in first full year and more than $50MM revenue in year two.
- Successfully introduced multiple products in both PC and consumer electronics product categories--including the first successful desktop and notebook ever launched in a grocery retail channel.
- Grew revenue from innovative marketing channel to $35MM annually through unique packaging, marketing, and promotional strategies.
- Developed business opportunities with major US national and regional retailers such as Costco, Wal-Mart, Best Buy, Aldi, etc.
- Formed a cooperative for regional manufacturing of PC systems in Mexico and LCD TVs in Europe.

HEWLETT-PACKARD CO., Silicon Valley, CA 1995-2001
Worldwide ODM Business Manager, Home Products Division, 1999-2001

Shifted HP's ODM business to a new product supply model and, in 6 months, added $60MM incremental contribution margin and grew the business 300%. Developed business plans and strategy; managed and negotiated with outside partners to design, manufacture, deliver, and support home PCs in multiple regions worldwide. Worked with regional operation managers to effectively grow and manage their businesses in Asia, Europe, and North America under the new model. Significantly influenced HP's $4B home computing business and P&L.

160

DEREK T. NEWSOM
SENIOR EXECUTIVE: COMPUTERS & CONSUMER ELECTRONICS

TESTIMONIALS

"Derek Newsom has been a primary driving force behind our business growth in North America...We recruited Derek from Hewlett-Packard and gave him a significant challenge: build our business from the ground up, nationwide, on a fast timetable. Derek exceeded all our expectations for a start-up... Under Derek's leadership, revenues grew from zero to $10 million in the first year and more than $50 million in the second year.... We can recommend Derek without reservation as a senior executive with vision, expertise and integrity." (Read more...)
Kim Jensen, Chief Operations Officer and Member of the Board, Medion AG

"Derek is an exceptional motivator of people with sophisticated executive leadership and business management skills critical to running a business worldwide. I am confident that he will be successful and highly valued in his next role and I recommend him without reservation as a senior executive with vision, expertise and integrity." (Read more...)
Gerd Brachmann, Founder and CEO, Medion AG

"On behalf of Hewlett-Packard Company and the Home Products Division, we'd like to extend our sincere "thanks" for all the hard work and dedication it took to ship One Million HP Pavilion PCs in such a short period. You should be proud of your contribution and happy to know that we are improving the lives of over One Million People around the world."
Webb Mckinney, General Manager, Hewlett-Packard Co.

"We in Asia have been fortunate to be able to work with Derek and our experience has been very positive and memorable."
Christine Jaccard, Corporate Controller, Hewlett-Packard Asia

"Derek is one of the finest human beings a person could ever hope to meet... His work habits are extraordinary, he is remarkably industrious, completely self-reliant, an extremely effective organizer, quick to offer assistance to others, always completes his responsibilities on or ahead of schedule, and perseveres...His character is impeccable."
Thomas Cheney, Assistant Dean, Scool of Engineering, University of the Pacific

"Derek is truly a gentleman, a professional, and very easy to work with... I strongly recommend Derek to you."
Reza Pouraghabagher, Ph.D., CPIM

Bio

Andy Waterman is a true renaissance man—a successful entrepreneur with a career traversing the worlds of business, entertainment, and education—a man who can, and has, delivered innovation and multimillions-of-dollars in profit for over twenty years. Andy is known for combining a futurist's vision with talent, drive, and industry expertise to deliver seemingly impossible results in entrepreneurial or corporate environments, in multiple industries and venues, especially in the areas of entertainment and edutainment.

> "I am the "The Master Mixer," expertly blending business, entertainment, the arts, and education to create innovative new products and the next level of success—often in untapped or unimagined areas."
>
> - Andy Waterman

From his early days as a music-obsessed student and educator; to a stint in the Chicago jingle business; to years of work as a top professional in the music, sound, film, and television "studio world;" (building Andy Waterman productions and ENTEK Centers, Inc.) through his present success as a leading "Edutainment" producer with Hal Leonard and McGraw-Hill, Andy has enjoyed a rich and varied career.

Andy's clients and projects in music, television, and the arts have included such work for Henry Mancini (Victor Victoria), David Byrne (The Forest), television shows such as "Touched by an Angel" and "The Highlander," as well as Universal Studios Tour and Disney World (soundtrack producer for major theme park attractions).

As a business development, product marketing, management, and technology specialist, Andy has conceptualized, launched, and managed high-quality entertainment and edutainment products, services, technologies, and brand / product extensions. In addition, although fully immersed in the Digital Revolution, he has an ongoing respect for the legacy technology that preceded it. There's a place for both — and he knows where that is. In an aggressively competitive industry, he has achieved commercial success and created numerous sustainable revenue streams.

Accomplished in "leadership under fire" crisis management, Andy has led multiple businesses through startup, growth, crisis, M&A, and culture change while exceeding objectives for revenue, operational performance, profitability, and shareholder value. Andy has said, "Nothing is more energizing to me than to be part of an exciting business plan and see raw thinking come to life." His successes in an enormous array of business activities support that assertion.

An accomplished salesman, Andy uses thorough planning rather than "kismet" to deliver mega results. He has closed deals with numerous "marquee players"—Fortune 500 companies and national firms. Andy likes to say, "A good business plan beats acquired sales panache any day."

As a creative director, producer, and experienced expert in creative direction, media production, postproduction, soundtrack and recording direction, script development and casting, Andy has worked with many of the top talents in the industry. He has won globally recognized awards for artistry and

162

ANDY WATERMAN

Elephants, Electronics & The Strike

For the last few months I have been completely absorbed in creating and producing interactive projects to be marketed as CD-ROMs. So how excited was I to learn that the Electronic Entertainment Expo (affectionately called E-3) was coming to town? This is a world-famous expo for everyone and everything (another 3E's) connected to interactive media. So, of course, I had to be there too.

For over 20 years in LA, I've worked on the soundtracks for numerous interactive projects. Some of these projects have been released by the biggest names in the biz - Electronic Arts, Buena Vista Games (Disney), and Microsoft. And I was the soundtrack producer for the rollout of X-Box. So I understood the mindset of interactive developers and programmers.

WRONG!! I was blown away by the overt hostility between the game designers/programmers and the voice actors whose work is featured on their video games. The actors, much like Rodney Dangerfield, get NO respect from the crowd that labors over hot computers 90 hours a week to make productions deadlines. (Unlike the actors who either pre-record or show up for a few hours as the project nears completion.) And the actors, with impeccable timing, chose the E-3 venue to announce their intentions to strike the Interactive Industry for a higher basic scale and, what's worse, additional income from that dreaded concept ... Residuals.

Let's go back a few years to 1999 and 2000 - actors went on strike against producers of commercials and ad agencies. Then writers for television shows struck. As someone who has been involved with hundreds – no make that thousands - of national and regional commercials, I can definitely say that the actors strike was a disaster for our entire industry. Don't believe me? Ask any Los Angeles actor if their career is better now than it was before the strike. But I'll rant more on this topic in future blogs.

Returning to E-3 ... The mood of the game developers was definitely anti-actor. In many of the seminars I attended, I heard CEO's of major companies saying they could easily substitute voice actors with folks working at their companies. Doing this "sound track stuff" was no big deal – not compared to the high art form of the visual design and programming.

WRONG! And I'll tell you why. But first, let me tell you a little story. A guy, let's call him Bob, works for the circus. His job is to walk behind the elephants and shovel their – well, shovel their stuff. His friend berates him saying, "How can you stay at such a terrible job – you should quit." "What!" says Bob, "And give up show business!" My point is – everyone working on a project thinks

LINKS

My Brandego Portfolio

Andy Waterman Productions

Email Me

Syndicate this site (XML)

CATEGORIES

Edutainment Production

Talent

ANDY WATERMAN

Intro	Bio	Career Highlights	Distinctions	Blog	Press	Contact

Contact

"Andy is a brilliant and sensitive collaborator [and he] has an amazing awareness of the business aspects of the entertainment industry. His ability to work within budgetary limitations without sacrificing quality is better than anyone I know."

- Gordon Hunt, DGA award-winning director ("Mad About You," "Frasier," and many Hanna Barbara projects.)

Please use this form to contact Andy Waterman. Items with an asterisk (*) are required.

* First name

* Last name

Company

Address

City

State/Province   Select a State/Province

Zip/postal code

Country   Select a Country

Phone

* Email

* Message

☐ Please send me your free demo reel on DVD. In addition to the required items above, I've provided my mailing address and phone number.

(Send)

Andy Waterman · 4834 Salem Village Place, Culver City, CA 90230 · 310-559-1363

ANDY WATERMAN

Distinctions, Awards & Affiliations

Experienced expert in creative direction; media production; all aspects of postproduction, soundtrack, and recording direction; script development; and casting. Credits (49K PDF) include **work on thousands of hours of internationally broadcast television soundtracks, over 100 feature films, thousands of national and regional television and radio commercials, over 500 music albums, and 20 years as recording producer for the largest catalogue of educational children's music in the world.**

> "My recording and mixing experience with Andy Waterman and crew was superb. Andy's technical preparation and his understanding of my creative goals for each session were met dead on and with 100% success. I recorded and mixed complete seasons of my scores for HBO's comedy 'Mind of the Married Man,' and ABC's drama 'Line of Fire.' The music for the two shows was very different and Andy's involvement guaranteed me excellent results each and every time."
>
> - _Larry Groupe, Film, Television & Concert Stage Composer_

- **Three-time Grammy nominee. Emmy nominee,** including 2004 **"Best Original Score"** ABC TV's "Line of Fire" View the clip: QuickTime, Windows Media
- **CLEO Award,** for "Pura Veda," National Hispanic Coors advertising campaign, (team award), 1995.
- **Fifteen ADDY Awards** for various regional ad campaigns including, Harley-Davidson and McDonald's.
- **Two-time cover feature,** "Mix Magazine," 1990 and 1998.
- **Originator and presenter** (lectures, radio interviews) of **"Five Key Points to Managing Creative People"** - defining strategies, persuasive, motivational techniques.
- Contractor and supervisor of **language and cultural translation services for film, TV, broadcast commercials, theme park development, and edutainment projects** in: Spanish (all cultural variations), Portuguese (Brazil), Japanese, Thai, Korean, Hawaiian, Indonesian (various dialects), Russian, German, French, Mandarin Chinese, Cantonese Chinese, Norwegian, Swedish, Danish, Greek, Hebrew, and Arabic.
- Member, **CEO Club** and **TEC-The Executive Committee** (#1 global resource for small- to mid-company CEOs).

> "Andy Waterman has guided my projects for 20 years — from cartoon voices to my live one-woman show before 1500 people at the Ambassador Auditorium — his guidance, creativity, and production savvy have shaped my career. His professionalism and artistry are beyond reproach."
>
> - _BJ Ward, recording artist, performance artist, and creator of "Standup Opera."_

ANDY WATERMAN

Intro	Bio	**Career Highlights**	Distinctions	Blog	Press	Contact

Career Highlights

Download this resume in PDF format: <u>Andy Waterman Resume</u> (57K)

- Strategic Business Development & Marketing—CEO, Entek Centers, Inc. <u>Details...</u>
- Major Account Acquisition & Management—CEO, Bakery Digital Sound & Vision <u>Details...</u>
- Edutainment Production Management—Production Director, West Coast, Hal Leonard Corporation <u>Details...</u>
- Talent, Technology & Resource Management—Production Director, West Coast, Hal Leonard Corporation <u>Details...</u>

Andy Waterman · 4834 Salem Village Place, Culver City, CA 90230 · 310-559-1363

Portfolio site by Brandego

ANDY WATERMAN

Intro	Bio	Career Highlights	Distinctions	Blog	Press	Contact

Intro

Providing Focus for the Blurring Lines Between Business and Entertainment

 Listen to Andy's Welcome Message.

Andy Waterman is the guy you call when you need a creative business visionary who understands how to maximize the opportunities presented by the dissolution of technological boundaries—intellectual property is now distributed via multiple media sources... CDs are replaced by DVDs... distinctions between film and video are blurred by Hi-Def video and ultra-compact digital production tools... traditional publishing is embracing CDs, DVDs, and website inclusion.

With more than 20 years' experience managing hundreds of creative projects, Andy's award-winning creative talent, executive leadership of media and post-production companies with a world-class roster of clients and deep relationships with the Hollywood and global creative community, makes him an expert facilitator of the collaboration between the business and entertainment worlds.

Andy's unique background provides value to companies who want to leverage new media for content delivery, product launches, or communications. Whether it's a theme park or a textbook, Andy Waterman knows how to create an incredible experience. His innovative thinking, technology focus, guerilla finance techniques, ability to manage creative people to the best outcome, and dogged determination to make projects succeed despite all odds, creates an irresistible force for change and profit.

> **"When Andy Waterman works on one of our corporate projects, he's virtually bilingual - he speaks "corporate" and he translates our goals into the artistic language our media people need. He effortlessly moves between these two very different worlds with street smarts and diplomacy."**
>
> *- Monty House, former West Coast director of Jack Morton Worldwide, the world's top producer of large corporate events.*

Andy Waterman · 4834 Salem Village Place, Culver City, CA 90230 · 310-559-1363

Portfolio site by Brandego

167

ANDY WATERMAN

Intro	Bio	Career Highlights	Distinctions	Blog	**Press**	Contact

Press

May 26, 2005	Andy Waterman Produces Soundtrack *"No Vacancy"*	*32KB PDF*

Apr 4, 2005   Andy Waterman Produces CD with Broadway Legends   *36KB PDF*
Christopher Reeve Saluted in Companion Book
Listen to an audio sample from the CD:

▶ ❚❚ ■ ━━━━━━━ 00:00

Oct 8, 2004   The Producers Guild of America Presents The 3rd Annual   *37KB PDF*
Celebration of Diversity
Andy Waterman Provides Soundtrack for Film Clips

Sep 17, 2004   Music Theater International Will Bring "Roald Dahl's Willy   *34KB PDF*
Wonka" to Kennedy Center
Andy Waterman Chosen to Produce Soundtrack

Sep 15, 2004   Macmillan/McGraw-Hill "Spotlights" New Textbook   *37KB PDF*
Andy Waterman Selected to Produce Marketing Materials

Images for media

Andy Waterman (2MB TIF)

Andy Waterman · 4834 Salem Village Place, Culver City, CA 90230 · 310-559-1363

Portfolio site by Brandego

168

CHAPTER   17

Putting the Whole Package Together

Throughout this book, we have talked about a wide array of documents beyond the traditional executive resume, and we have shown you samples and explained how they were used during an executive job search. We hope you have gained the inspiration to expand your ideas and develop new materials that will more broadly, specifically, and creatively showcase your professional capabilities.

Now it's time to show you the whole package: complete portfolios of documents as used by three senior executives during a successful career transition.

Examples

As you view the following examples, notice how well each document relates to the one before it and the one that follows, and observe how effectively the brand message is communicated and supported in every piece of documentation.

EXAMPLE 1: Portfolio Package: Rosalyn Hughes (pages 171-175)
(Writer – Arnold Boldt)

- Executive resume
- Network resume
- Cover letter
- Thank-you letter

Wishing to return to her home state of Massachusetts, Rosalyn developed career marketing materials that were suitable both for her primary goal of library leadership as well as more broad-based targets in business or nonprofit management. She used both the full-length, functional-style resume and the one-page networking resume during an active campaign using her strong professional network as her primary strategy. She was ultimately offered, and accepted, the position of State Librarian.

EXAMPLE 2: Portfolio Package: Drew Thomas (pages 176-182)
(Writer – Louise Kursmark)

- Executive resume
- Network resume
- Cover letter
- Pre-interview letter
- Job proposal

Drew combined an entrepreneurial streak with strong corporate experience, and had developed quite a bit of expertise in starting and managing offshore services organizations in India. His three-page resume contains compelling evidence of his abilities and is strengthened by the quoted endorsements of his executive team members. He sent his full resume and standard cover letter to recruiters and used his one-page resume with his professional network. Also included in this portfolio is a pre-interview letter that he sent to a senior executive after initial telephone discussions and before their planned meeting. Finally, you will find his job proposal, which he wrote following the meeting to cement the ideas that had been discussed for the new organization and his role leading it. This led to the company creating the proposed position for him.

EXAMPLE 3: Portfolio Package: Syed Ramjeet (pages 183-191)
(Writer – Deborah Wile Dib)

- Executive resume
- Network resume
- Executive bio
- Leadership profile
- Cover letter

After four years spent running his own investment-management firm, Syed decided to re-enter the corporate workforce, targeting CFO positions. He developed a comprehensive portfolio of documents that portrayed his expertise, his unique background, and his exceptional personal attributes—his unique professional brand. Ultimately he accepted a leadership position with a new real-estate development business, where he was able to combine his personal investment insights with his corporate/finance/technology experience and talent for getting things done in the most challenging of circumstances.

ROSALYN A. HUGHES

608-203-3715   3672 Picadilly, Madison, Wisconsin 53711   RosaHughes@cs.com

EXECUTIVE DIRECTOR / PROGRAM DEVELOPER / PROJECT MANAGER

Not-For-Profit Cooperatives • Government-Funded Agencies • Grant-Funded Programs

Accomplished professional with 20-plus years' experience in leadership roles with not-for-profits and government-funded agencies. Exceptional ability to foster relationships with diverse constituencies, including state and municipal governments, community organizations, and the general public. Goal-oriented and results-focused, with experience managing capital projects and directing technology and facilities upgrades. Offering knowledge and expertise in:

- Establishing Strategic Vision
- Developing & Managing Budgets
- Managing Capital Projects
- Leading Public Relations Initiatives
- Speaking to Community Groups
- Dealing with Funding Sources
- Influencing Decision-Makers
- Building & Motivating Teams
- Developing & Mentoring Staff

QUALIFICATIONS

EXECUTIVE LEADERSHIP / STRATEGIC VISION:

Reported directly to Wisconsin State Librarian as Director, Public Library Development Team:
- Wrote statewide strategic plan. Managed launch and implementation of new strategy, coordinating efforts of a variety of constituencies and outside consultants to achieve state goals.
- Restructured organization, creating new programs to address needs of children and young adults.
- Serve on several professional boards with local, regional, and national constituencies.

As Executive Director of Library Cooperative of the Dells:
- Developed and administered $1.9 million budget and answered directly to Board of Trustees to fulfill organizational objectives.
- Secured $75,000 technology training grant from the State of Wisconsin, which financed new software/hardware for training centers and facilitated new training programs for members.

PROGRAM DEVELOPMENT / PROJECT MANAGEMENT:

- Championed concept and played integral role in securing and managing a $575,000 grant to build "The Wisconsin Digital Highway," a portal to the state's historical and cultural heritage materials. Coordinated collaborative effort among state and local governments, academic institutions, historical societies, and faith-based organizations.
- Managed the selection, purchase, and implementation of new statewide interlibrary loan and virtual union catalog. Developed innovative solution for funding and implementing new system, engendering collaboration and support of regional cooperatives. Directed rollout, including training for local staff statewide. Program featured in case study by GraphicsTech, the system vendor for this project.

NEGOTIATION / VENDOR RELATIONS:

- Negotiated the $1.4 million purchase of archival materials from database provider, ArcTech, which will reduce future costs for participating libraries and provide statewide access to key databases.
- Secured discounted pricing from suppliers, resulting in savings of up to 60% on online databases purchased. Also renegotiated contracts with Britannica and MidWestLib for services they provide to cooperative.
- Negotiated agreement for new office space. Interfaced with architect, attorney, landlord, and realtor.

PUBLIC RELATIONS / COMMUNITY OUTREACH:

- Pioneered Assistant Marketing Director position for Boston Public Library to manage special events, advance public relations initiatives, and promote library as a meeting venue.
- Played a key role in developing statewide marketing campaign, including developing RFP to outside marketing firms, as Chairperson of Wisconsin Library Association PR Committee.
- Speak to community groups, professional groups, and colleagues to promote library objectives.
- Represent library interests on various advisory boards statewide, regionally, and nationally.

STAFF DEVELOPMENT / MENTORING:

- Managed continuing education programs serving the needs of library staffs and trustees statewide.
- Identified potential candidates and provided one-on-one mentoring to prepare for career advancement.

171

PROFESSIONAL EXPERIENCE

WISCONSIN STATE LIBRARY; Madison, Wisconsin

Director–Public Library Development Team 2001–Present
Manage a $35 million budget, with accountability for organizing, planning, and directing Public Library Development Team, which provides consulting services and technical assistance to libraries statewide.

LIBRARY COOPERATIVE OF THE DELLS; Fond du Lac, Wisconsin

Executive Director 1998–2001
Accountable for the planning, implementation, and evaluation of regional services for 1,200 libraries in northern Wisconsin. Developed and administered $1.9 million budget and answered directly to Board of Trustees to address the needs of public, academic, scholastic, and private libraries.

NEWTON PUBLIC LIBRARY; Newton, Massachusetts

Library Director 1992–1998
Executive responsibility for management and operation of suburban library with 75 employees, annual budget over $1.8 million, and circulation exceeding 850,000 items per year.

BOSTON PUBLIC LIBRARY; Boston, Massachusetts

Manager of Interlibrary Loan Department (ILL) 1986–1992
Planned, coordinated, and managed all interlibrary loan and centralized reserves services for the Boston Area Library System, which encompassed 160 individual branches in a four-county region.

Special Librarian, Central Library 1986
Science and Technology Reference Librarian 1981–1985

PEABODY PUBLIC LIBRARY; Peabody, Massachusetts

Acting Director 1979
Adult Services Librarian 1978–1980

EDUCATION

Master of Library Science
School of Library and Information Science
Northeastern University; Boston, Massachusetts

Bachelor of Science, Biology
University of Massachusetts at Boston; Boston, Massachusetts

PROFESSIONAL / BOARD AFFILIATIONS

Secretary/Treasurer, MidWestLib Executive Board (multi-state cooperative with 750+ members)
National Advisory Board, Proquest, Inc
Chairperson, State Library Section, ASCLA
Advisory Board, National Library of Medicine—Midwest Section

ROSALYN A. HUGHES

608-203-3715   3672 Picadilly, Madison, Wisconsin 53711   RosaHughes@cs.com

PROFESSIONAL PROFILE

Accomplished professional with 20-plus years' experience in key leadership roles with not-for-profits and government-funded agencies. Exceptional ability to foster relationships with diverse constituencies and build consensus among parties with competing interests and conflicting objectives. Goal-oriented and results-focused, with experience managing capital projects, directing technology upgrades, and overseeing building renovations.

AREAS OF EXPERTISE

Establishing Strategic Vision	Leading Public Relations Initiatives	Influencing Decision-Makers
Developing & Managing Budgets	Speaking to Community Groups	Building & Motivating Teams
Managing Capital Projects	Dealing with Funding Sources	Developing & Mentoring Staff

CAREER HIGHLIGHTS

➤ Secured and managed $575,000 grant to build "The Wisconsin Digital Highway," portal to state's historical and cultural heritage materials. Coordinated collaborative effort by state and local governments, academic institutions, historical societies, and religious organizations to obtain grant and administer its implementation.

➤ Wrote statewide strategic plan for libraries in State of Wisconsin. Managed implementation of new strategy, coordinating efforts of a variety of constituencies and outside consultants to achieve state goals.

➤ Negotiated the $1.4 million purchase of archival materials from database provider, ArcTech, which will reduce future costs for participating libraries and provide statewide access to key databases.

➤ Played a key role in developing statewide marketing campaign, including developing RFP to outside marketing firms. Served as Chairperson of Wisconsin Library Association PR Committee.

➤ Developed 3-year technology plan to upgrade automation systems for suburban library. Gained cooperation of municipalities for joint leasing plan and LAN connections, resulting in substantial cost savings.

➤ Served on professional boards: Secretary/Treasurer, MidWestLib Executive Board (750-member cooperative); National Advisory Board, ProTech, Inc; Chairperson, State Library Agency Section, ASCLA; Advisory Board, National Library of Medicine—MidWestern Section.

PROFESSIONAL EXPERIENCE

WISCONSIN STATE LIBRARY; Madison, WI
Director—Library Development Bureau   2001–Present
Managed a $20 million budget; organized, planned, and directed Library Development Bureau.

LIBRARY COOPERATIVE OF THE DELLS; Fond du Lac, WI
Executive Director   1998–2001
Planned, implemented, and evaluated regional services for 1,200 public, academic, and private libraries.

NEWTON PUBLIC LIBRARY; Newton, MA
Library Director   1992–1998

BOSTON PUBLIC LIBRARY; Boston, MA
Manager of Interlibrary Loan Department (ILL)   1986–1992
Special Librarian, Central Library / Science and Technology Reference Librarian   1981–1986

EDUCATION

Master of Library Science—School of Library and Information Science, Northeastern University; Boston, MA
Bachelor of Science, Biology—University of Massachusetts at Boston; Boston, MA

TARGETED OBJECTIVES

Not-For-Profit Leadership	Project Management	Public Relations Leadership
Governmental Liaison	Staff Development & Training	High-Level Account Relations

ROSALYN A. HUGHES

608-203-3715   3672 Picadilly, Madison, Wisconsin 53711   RosaHughes@cs.com

April 25, 2005

Ms. Harriette St. Vincent
Office of Commonwealth Libraries
85 George P. Hassett Drive
Medford, Massachusetts 02155

Re: State Librarian / Commisioner of Libraries

Dear Ms. St. Vincent:

Please accept this letter, the attached résumé, and the Personal Data Sheet as an expression of my serious interest in the State Librarian position as advertised in your recent posting. As a professional librarian with 20-plus years' experience who currently holds an Associate State Librarian position in the State of Wisconsin, I believe that my demonstrated track record in policy development, planning, and administration of state/federal aid allocation is directly relevant to this important leadership role.

Among the experiences that I can bring to the Commonwealth Library system are the following:

- **Leading a team that develops statewide policy and promotes statewide library initiatives.**
- **Managing $30 million in state and federal grants used to fund a variety of library-related programs.**
- **Representing the library community on an array of advisory boards and committees to advance overall library objectives at state, regional, and local levels.**
- **Managing capital projects to enhance infrastructure, improve access to library facilities and services for the disabled, and implement the newest technology for patron and staff use.**
- **Engaging in outreach initiatives to build community awareness and engender public support for programs.**

I am confident that my management experience and knowledge of the library community will allow me to further the mission of libraries in the Commonwealth of Massachusetts. I would enjoy discussing my candidacy with you in detail either by phone or in person. Please feel free to contact me at your convenience.

Sincerely,

Rosalyn Hughes

Rosalyn A. Hughes

Enclosures

ROSALYN A. HUGHES

608-203-3715   3672 Picadilly, Madison, Wisconsin 53711   RosaHughes@cs.com

May 15, 2005

Ms. Harriette St. Vincent
Office of Commonwealth Libraries
85 George P. Hassett Drive
Medford, Massachusetts 02155

Dear Harriette:

Thank you for taking the time to meet with me on Wednesday. I genuinely enjoyed talking with you and other members of the Commonwealth Libraries Board and appreciated the opportunity to hear about your vision for the Libraries. I regret that the schedule didn't provide more time for us to further discuss your perspectives on the challenges ahead.

As you may recall, prior to accepting a position in Wisconsin, I worked for more than 20 years in various positions of increasing responsibility within Massachusetts public library systems. These included various roles in Central Library Administration as well as a department head position at BPL, managing the ILL department of the Bay State System, and Directorship of the Newton Public Library.

From these experiences, I have gained an understanding of the structure and functioning of the Commonwealth Library System. My positions as Executive Director of a regional cooperative and as Wisconsin's Director of Library Development have given me further experience in effectively addressing the varying—and sometimes seemingly competing—needs of urban, suburban, and rural libraries across the state. My recent successes in working to achieve consensus among widely divergent constituencies on a variety of highly charged issues have prepared me well for advancing the missions of the Commonwealth system in a challenging environment.

In addition, I am acutely aware of the fiscal challenges faced by the libraries and sensitive to the complexities surrounding the development of new revenue streams; I believe it is a critical yet delicate issue to explore new approaches to funding. My expertise in developing rapport and effectively interacting with stakeholders and potential supporters at all levels, as well as my broad contacts in the library community and beyond, will further enhance my effectiveness. I believe that my dynamic, strategic leadership, combined with sensitivity and heartfelt passion for providing quality public library services to all citizens, make me an ideal fit for this unique position.

I look forward to finding innovative ways to work collaboratively with you and other members of the Library Board and other key stakeholders to enhance the viability of the Commonwealth's library system and services to its citizens.

Having lived much of my childhood and attended college and graduate school in the Greater Boston area, I have a great affection for the community and would be pleased to come home.

Thank you again for such a dynamic meeting. As you suggested, I will follow up with you next week if I have not heard from you regarding the next steps.

Sincerely,

Rosalyn Hughes

Rosalyn A. Hughes

Drew Thomas

Business Development Executive

Strategic Focus ■ Relationship Management ■ Revenue & Profit Enhancement

- Lead businesses to breakthrough financial, operational, and market success.
- Build customer-centric organizations, profitable client relationships, and successful key alliances.
- Deliver results for startup, turnaround, and high-growth entities in U.S. and multinational markets.

Strategic and growth-oriented leader with broad expertise in business development, marketing, operations, and consultative solution-selling; 15-year track record of identifying and capturing new business opportunities, developing and maintaining marquee client relationships, and aligning products/services with strategic markets.

Deep expertise in outsourcing and offshore IT solutions for multiple industries (financial and professional services, high-tech, healthcare, legal). Experience negotiating multimillion-dollar deals and communicating complex value propositions to C-level executives at Fortune 1000 and high-growth mid-market companies.

Highest levels of integrity, ethics, business judgment, work ethic, and maturity.

CORE COMPETENCIES

Innovation, leadership, and drive in developing and implementing creative solutions to business challenges. Talent for identifying strategy, communicating vision, developing tactical plans, and empowering teams and individuals to reach stretch goals. Expertise includes:

- Strategic Planning / Tactical Execution / P&L
- Business Plans / M&A / Venture Capital
- Strategic Alliance & Channel Development
- Business & Technology Liaison
- Rainmaker Marketing Expertise

- Customer Acquisition, Retention, & Extension
- Customer, Vendor & Partner Relationship Management
- Deal Structuring & Contract Negotiation
- Cross-Functional Team Leadership
- Quantitative & Business Analysis

EXECUTIVE TEAM COMMENTARY

...Broad business perspective and extremely strong business acumen... The ability to architect and drive change... Action orientation with strong execution skills and drive for results... Strong influencing skills and tremendous personal energy and edge... Passion of a successful entrepreneur and the discipline of a seasoned executive... Externally competitive and internally team-oriented.

PROFESSIONAL EXPERIENCE

- **VP BUSINESS DEVELOPMENT**   **TransIT Services,** 2003–Present
                                                                                                    Naperville, IL

Created and executed successful refocus/repositioning strategy for business services outsourcing firm. Drove revenue growth, determined strategic market focus, transformed operations, identified and negotiated alliances with strategic partners. Key member of senior management team that grew company to successful acquisition.

TransIT provides infrastructure, applications, and VOIP solutions to high-growth mid-market firms in U.S. and 8 international markets. Market focus: financial services, professional services, and high-tech industry.

- Transformed business development from technology-focused to customer-centric "partner" approach.
  - IMPACT: — Doubled revenues in 1 year through aggressive focus on existing customer relationships.
    - — Identified unmet client needs and focused product/service development in these high-potential areas—new services now represent 30% of total business revenue.
    - — Increased operating margins 25% through value-based service differentiators.
    - — Developed business cases showing impressive ROI and 20%–40% cost savings for managed outsource/offshore solutions. Smoothly transitioned each client, remaining in the loop as pivotal customer liaison during transition and through operational success.

---

275 Lakeshore Drive #7C, Chicago, IL 60611   drew.thomas@gmail.com ■ 312-600-4548

- **TransIT Services,** continued

  - Sharpened marketing strategy. Zeroed in on vertical and regional financial-services industry, established niche expertise, and inked exclusive partnerships with reputable high-value providers serving core clientele.
    IMPACT: — **Achieved rapid growth in a challenging economic climate—150% in the last 18 months.**
    — **Leveraged strategic relationships to boost credibility. More than doubled length of typical outsourcing contract, securing $100MM in contractual backlog obligations—critical to long-term growth and a key asset in positioning TransIT for sale.**

  - Engaged in executive decision-making for all areas of the company.
    IMPACT: — **Eliminated complete line of business (custom applications group) and redirected $1MM operating capital toward strategic growth areas.**
    — **Aligned VC relationships with strategic direction of the company. Generated second- and third-round financing exceeding $12MM.**
    — **Participated in M&A analysis; identified potential partners and closely examined for fit with existing strengths and growth opportunities. Key member of integration team into new organization (Q4 2005).**
    — **Structured agreements for corporate services and to extend business capabilities to new markets and new regions via strategic partners such as Cisco and Dell. Negotiated contracts with sharp focus on *cost, profitability,* and *strategic business goals.***

  - Streamlined operations and built a solid operational infrastructure. Led teams to create processes, establish and integrate systems, build customer knowledge base, and introduce Siebel CRM across the enterprise.
    IMPACT: — **Increased efficiency 40%.**
    — **Improved client satisfaction scores from 75% to 98%.**

- **BUSINESS DEVELOPMENT DIRECTOR**   Microdata Systems, Inc., 2002–2003
  (Interim Executive)   Chicago, IL

  Ignited stalled business through fresh ideas and innovative approaches to business turnaround, marketing, branding, product positioning, and pricing. Defined vision, created strategy, developed and launched tactical plans that were hailed by board and CEO as "practical, workable solutions to business problems."

  - Crafted branding/positioning strategy and developed a hybrid revenue model with a balanced mix of consulting and recurring revenue streams.
    IMPACT: — **Met strategic goal of growing product revenue to 35% of total sales.**
    — **Molded diverse and disparate product/service line into 5 branded practice areas.**

  - Created scalable business model that has fostered strategic growth in international markets.

- **FOUNDER/CEO**   Offshore Solutions, Inc., 1999–2002
                                     Corporate: Chicago, IL / Offshore: Bangalore, India

  Built successful offshore IT services firm, serving as middleman between U.S. firms and Southeast Asian service providers. Closely fit client needs to technology capabilities, managed client relationships at the executive level, and provided close oversight to ensure projects were completed on time, within budget, and with very high quality.

  - Achieved exceptional customer satisfaction, earning repeat business from 90% of clients.

  - Leveraging solid beginning and strong performance record, aggressively ramped up business development to build a durable contractual backlog.
    IMPACT: — **Grew pipeline from $500K to $3.5MM in less than 1 year.**
    — **Increased business value resulted in sale of the firm at 600% return on initial investment.**

275 Lakeshore Drive #7C, Chicago, IL 60611   drew.thomas@gmail.com ▪ 312-600-4548

■ **EARLY CAREER**   **Procter & Gamble, Inc.,** 1990–1999
                                                Cincinnati, OH / Bangalore, India

Advanced through Assistant/Associate Brand Manager positions supporting global growth of consumer products—laundry detergents, diapers, and dental care products. Selected for leadership role to launch *Oxydol* in India, achieving first-year results 50% above projections.

EDUCATION

MBA, 1995: Xavier University—Cincinnati, OH
BS, Computer Science, 1992: Xavier University—Cincinnati, OH
BS, Business Administration, 1990: Cornell University—Ithaca, NY

PROFESSIONAL, BOARD, & COMMUNITY AFFILIATIONS

- **Banking Industry**   Illinois Bankers Association
                          Midwest Banking Institute

- **International**   NASSCOM
                          Electronic and Software Export Promotion Council (ESC), India

- **Board Positions**   Chicago Council of Entrepreneurs
                          March of Dimes—Chicago Chapter
                          Naperville (IL) Chamber of Commerce

- **Community Groups**   Chicago Museum of the Avant Garde
  (Technology Advisor) Riverside Food Pantry
                          Chicago Education Council; Middle School Technology Forum

TECHNICAL EXPERTISE

- **Strategic Business-Technology Solutions**
  CRM / Sales Force Automation / Call Center Applications / VOIP Solutions
  Data Mining / Decision Support and Analytics Applications
  IT Infrastructure
  Vertical-Specific Business Applications / e-Commerce / Web Development
  Business Process Outsourcing

Drew Thomas

drew.thomas@gmail.com ▪ 312-600-4548
275 Lakeshore Drive #7C, Chicago, IL 60611

EXECUTIVE PROFILE

- **Relationship Management**
- **Business Process Outsourcing**
- **Business Development**
- **Revenue and Profit Enhancement**

Strategic and growth-oriented leader with broad expertise in business development, marketing, operations, and consultative solution-selling; 15-year track record of identifying and capturing new business opportunities, developing and maintaining marquee client relationships, and aligning products/services with strategic markets.

Sharp business focus complemented by customer orientation and strong foundation in strategic business-technology solutions. Deep expertise in outsourcing and offshore IT solutions for multiple industries.

Highest levels of integrity, ethics, business judgment, work ethic, and maturity.

- Strategic Planning / Tactical Execution / P&L
- Business Plans / M&A / Venture Capital
- Strategic Alliance & Channel Development
- Business & Technology Liaison
- Rainmaker Marketing Expertise

- Customer Acquisition, Retention, & Extension
- Customer, Vendor & Partner Relationship Management
- Deal Structuring & Contract Negotiation
- Cross-Functional Team Leadership
- Quantitative & Business Analysis

EXECUTIVE TEAM COMMENTARY

...Broad business perspective and extremely strong business acumen... The ability to architect and drive change... Action orientation with strong execution skills and drive for results... Strong influencing skills and tremendous personal energy and edge... Passion of a successful entrepreneur and the discipline of a seasoned executive... Externally competitive and internally team-oriented.

PROFESSIONAL EXPERIENCE

- **VP BUSINESS DEVELOPMENT**   **TransIT Services,** Naperville, IL, 2003–Present

Created and executed successful refocus/repositioning strategy for business services outsourcing firm.

- Drove revenues up 100% first year, 150% in last 18 months. Increased operating margins 25%.
- Increased operating efficiency 40% and improved client satisfaction scores from 75% to 98%.
- Generated $12MM VC funding. Participated in M&A analysis, selection, and integration (company purchased in fourth quarter 2005).

- **BUSINESS DEVELOPMENT DIRECTOR**   **Microdata Systems, Inc.,** Chicago, IL, 2002–2003

In interim executive role, ignited stalled business through fresh ideas and innovative approaches to business turnaround, marketing, branding, product positioning, and pricing. Grew product revenue to 35% of total sales.

- **FOUNDER/CEO**   **Offshore Solutions, Inc.,** Chicago, IL / Bangalore, India, 1999–2002

Built successful offshore IT services firm, connecting U.S. firms with Southeast Asian providers.

- Achieved exceptional customer satisfaction, earning repeat business from 90% of clients.
- Negotiated sale of the firm at 600% return on initial investment.

- **ASSISTANT/ASSOCIATE BRAND MANAGER**   **Procter & Gamble, Inc.**
  GLOBAL PROJECT LEADER   Cincinnati, OH / Bangalore, India, 1990–1999

EDUCATION

MBA, 1995: Xavier University—Cincinnati, OH
BS, Computer Science, 1992: Xavier University—Cincinnati, OH
BS, Business Administration, 1990: Cornell University—Ithaca, NY

Drew Thomas

September 20, 2005

Charles Champlain
Executive Recruiters of Chicago
249 West Wacker Drive, Suite 709
Chicago, IL 60610

Dear Mr. Champlain:

Building business by building relationships is my expertise. In business development, account management, and executive leadership roles with start-ups and established industry leaders, I have proven, over and over, that a customer-centric, partnering, solution-focused approach is the key to growth and success.

A few examples:

- At TransIT Services, I drove rapid revenue growth—$1 million to $3 million in two years—by deepening our relationships with major accounts, developing new solutions for their needs, honing our marketing strategy, and building strategic alliances with key players in niche markets.

- As an interim business development executive with Microdata Systems, I led a strategic refocus that enabled the company to achieve revenue targets and leverage the power of its brand.

- As chief strategist for a start-up firm providing offshore IT services, I quickly demonstrated the value of customer satisfaction and relationship building, achieving customer retention above 90%.

In brief, I am an experienced executive with deep expertise delivering technology and business solutions in diverse industries. I thrive in challenging environments where revenue acceleration is critical to business survival, and I am highly skilled in developing business, managing relationships, leading teams, and driving key initiatives from concept to completion.

Our success in building TransIT Services has resulted in our acquisition by a large complementary service—thus my search for a new opportunity where I can be a leading contributor to strategic growth by building, managing, and extending relationships with partners and customers.

If you know of a company that would benefit from my passion, expertise, and ability to deliver results, I would welcome your call.

Sincerely,

Drew Thomas

Drew Thomas

enclosure: resume

Drew Thomas

Business Development Executive

Strategic Focus ■ Relationship Management ■ Revenue & Profit Enhancement

October 3, 2005

Stanford McGraw
Executive Vice President
Midwest Financial, Inc.
191 Chicago Avenue
Chicago, IL 60615

Dear Stan:

I look forward to meeting you and Katherine later this week and the opportunity to discuss your new offshore business processing initiative.

To make our meeting as productive as possible, I would like to share some preliminary thoughts about how I can add value to your leadership team, deliver value to your internal customers, and help you rapidly achieve service delivery excellence. My interest is in a leadership role in the internal client management function, specifically as an internal evangelist for the organization, managing the transition and then the relationship with the various lines of business.

My experience shows that there are three key components for a successful offshore/outsourcing relationship: collaboration, communication, and coordination. Effectively executed, they ensure a clear focus on business objectives while building fruitful long-term relationships that support sustained growth. Leading the relationship management function for these kinds of complex, multicultural, global initiatives is what I do best.

I also offer deep expertise in managing, monitoring, and measuring processes and results and ensuring the consistent application of best practices.

In short, I have the skills and experience to ensure that this high-potential initiative delivers on its promises while benefiting Midwest Financial, its partners, and its customers.

I look forward to a candid discussion and your insight into this process.

Sincerely,

Drew Thomas

Drew Thomas

enclosure: resume

Drew Thomas

VICE PRESIDENT OF GLOBAL CLIENT SERVICES MANAGEMENT

YOUR CHALLENGE:

Building a successful offshore business-processing organization

MY VALUE:

My experience shows that the key to growing a successful offshore business-processing organization is to constantly work towards customer loyalty, ensure customer satisfaction, preserve revenue, and look for new opportunities to grow the existing relationships. Therefore, what will soon become critical for Midwest Financial is to consolidate its clients under a Global Client Services Management organization that will hold primary accountability for ensuring consistent service excellence. I think that I can help you by leading this organization. I am confident I can repeat the excellent results I attained in the past in similar environments.

PROPOSED SOLUTION:

Midwest Financial's GCSM organization, with a relentless pursuit of meeting clients' business objectives, would also ensure profit enhancement and top- and bottom-line growth objectives for Midwest Financial. The three key thrust areas for this organization could be:

- **Revenue Preservation**
  - Client Retention
  - Client Service Extension

- **Client Relationship Management**
  - Earning Client Loyalty
  - Ensuring Customer Satisfaction
  - Collaboration and Partnership
  - Internal and External Communication
  - Issue Resolution
  - Ensuring SLAs Are Met

- **Client Management Processes, Monitoring, and Measurement**
  - Standardizing Client Management Processes
  - Transition Management
  - Centralized Client Coordination
  - Monitoring Client Relationship
  - Measuring Client Satisfaction
  - Building and Following Best Practices

I am very keen to further explore this proposal with you and share additional details about how I can add value to your leadership team, deliver value to your customers, and help grow your revenues.

SYED RAMJEET

CFO ▪ SENIOR FINANCE EXECUTIVE

Made "the impossible, possible" for a number of Wall Street's leading financial firms.

Eighteen+ years' experience in finance management.	**Consistently deliver mission-critical results in finance** and in the technologies and teams that support finance. Supported hundreds of millions of dollars in revenue and income for world-class companies including W. J. Klein, Banque du Monde, and Smythe Byrd Hickman.
Deliver the "big wins" in corporate finance.	**Multimillion-dollar contributor,** driven by a visceral, "hard-wired" need to strategize, to innovate, and to disprove the words "It can't be done!" Gifted with the vision, determination, and skills needed for high-level, revenue-building strategies and tactics.
Supported $150+ million in accelerated growth.	**Recognized as key to development of an eventual $800 million revenue stream** for W. J. Klein, by strategizing and building foundation for firm's entire derivatives business, allowing comfortable yet aggressive growth from $0 to $150 million in annual revenues within first three years.
Created IT solutions for $70+ million business.	**Delivered and/or supported the creation of more than $70 million in revenue** for Banque du Monde through conception and development of an array of sophisticated strategies and tools for financial management.
Managed growth of multimillions in investments.	**Built $9 million personal portfolio in four years** and protected it from major loss during market downturn. Grew and managed holdings using personally developed proprietary computerized analysis and decision-making system.

EXPERTISE

- Corporate Finance Management
- Strategic/Tactical Planning & Execution
- Budget Planning, Development, & Control
- Domestic & International Tax Planning
- Operational & Financial Risk Management

- Operational & Financial Turnaround
- Investment Strategy & Transactions
- Treasury & Cash Management
- Equity & Debt Financing
- Investor & Banking Relations

- Financial Forecasting & Planning
- Financial Modeling & Analysis
- IT Strategies, Solutions, & Projects
- Quantitative & Qualitative Analysis
- Risk Analytics & Policy Formation

EXECUTIVE QUALIFICATIONS

Conceive and execute financial strategies—drive corporate growth, profitability, and value.

Provide "no surprises" decision support by implementing and enforcing financial accountabilities, controls, processes, and systems. Drive corporate development through sound investment strategies and transactions. Dissected thousands of companies' financials for investment purposes, identifying underlying risks, deficiencies, and opportunities that others missed.

Link business objectives with powerful enterprise-level IT strategies—business and technology translator and accelerator.

Adept at translating abstract mathematical concepts, theories, and methodologies into user-friendly finance and IT solutions that clearly support business need and enhance revenue generation. Conceived, developed, implemented, and managed technologically sophisticated systems and interactive, feature-rich software.

Innately wired for strategic and tactical thinking—formulate and execute corporate strategic plans.

Contribute true global perspective, intimate knowledge of global business (speak English, Igbo, and French), and acute insight in potential business impact of geopolitical, economic, industry, and cultural factors and events. Develop and execute high-level strategies, make high-stakes decisions, and combat mission-critical business challenges.

Respect and leverage human capital—motivate, mentor, and lead talented professionals.

Live the culture and lead by example. Direct productive cross-functional teams using interactive and motivational leadership that spurs people to willingly give 110% effort and loyalty. A trusted advisor, completely forthcoming, yet diplomatic and apolitical. Extremely high-energy and driven to make a difference, yet levelheaded with a calm demeanor and low-key ego.

111 Winding Road, Cheyenne, WY 82007 ▪ **Home: 307-393-2124** ▪ **Office: 307-404-9946** ▪ **sRamjeet@email.com**

PROFESSIONAL EXPERIENCE

PRESIDENT   **RAMJEET CAPITAL, INC., Cheyenne, WY**

2001 to Present

Executive Overview

Shell company, created as an organizational framework for managing personal investments in stocks, options, futures, commodities, FX, and other capital market offerings. Personally create and execute investment strategies, perform research and analysis, and manage the portfolio. Make investment decisions based on extensive knowledge of the market, using a proprietary IT-based trading model.

Personal Challenge

Take sabbatical, grow portfolio for personal and philanthropic wealth, and then reenter corporate space in CFO role.

Financial & Strategic Successes

- Grew $1 million investment into $9+ million, retaining 68+% value compared to NASDAQ's 78+% aggregate loss.

- Developed and built highly effective computerized proprietary trading model with automated decision-making component.

MANAGING DIRECTOR   **W. J. KLEIN COMPANIES, INC., New York, NY**
Global Derivatives Department

1995 to 2001

Executive Overview

Teamed with Senior Managing Director of Global Derivatives in department-level strategic planning, growth, and decision-making. Held direct accountability for providing IT-based analytics for this dynamic global business unit operating 24/7 in three continents (profit centers in North America, Europe, and Asia).

Led team of 25 finance and IT professionals. Provided front- and back-office operational support, and consulted and served internal customers—traders, marketing personnel, accounting (GAAP and statutory financial reporting), risk management, IT, networking, fixed income technology—worldwide.

Corporate Challenge

Support startup of global derivatives business—a W. J. Klein top priority. Hired to provide necessary mathematical models, develop related technology solutions, and contribute insight on business strategies.

Financial & Strategic Successes

- Credited with personal contributions to growing business from $0 to $150+ million in sales within three years (subsequently mushroomed to $800+ million by 1999).

- Conceived, designed, and managed development/rollout of specialized modeling software and decision-support tools directly tied to firm's ability to deliver accelerated growth to $150 million in three years and support further growth to $800 million.

- Software development delivered calculations, analytics, valuation, hedging, and risk management (cash flow, reset, interest rate, counterparty, volatility, basis, correlations, time value, convexity, etc.) for customized over-the-counter derivatives, deals, and portfolios.

- Led W. J. Klein to become an AAA-rated derivatives dealer (again supporting the ability for $150 million+ in accelerated growth) by showcasing the specialized technology and business practices to win confidence of the rating agencies.

- Formed and provided strong leadership to talented, robust team of professionals capable of meeting firm's short- and long-term technology needs.

---

111 Winding Road, Cheyenne, WY 82007 ▪ Home: 307-393-2124 ▪ Office: 307-404-9946 ▪ sRamjeet@email.com

PROFESSIONAL EXPERIENCE, continued

VICE PRESIDENT
Derivatives Department

BANQUE DU MONDE, New York, NY
1991 to 1995

Executive Overview

Developed and executed technology strategies and managed related R&D projects, budgets, and teams for a $70 million profit center of the U.S. branch of the second largest (assets) French bank. Managed operating systems, hardware, software, and interconnectivity for three offices operating 24/7 in global time zones. Led a team of five personnel involved in the development and implementation of derivatives software solutions.

Corporate Challenge

Convert a break-even business into a growth-focused, global business organization

Financial & Strategic Successes

- Created sophisticated interactive currency swap pricing/hedging system enabling generation of $15 million in annual business.

- Developed risk analysis/control solution, interest-rate swap pricing and hedging system, and seamless portfolio management capability for $70 million multi-currency derivatives portfolio.

VICE PRESIDENT
Interest Rate Products Group

SMYTHE BYRD HICKMAN, New York, NY
1985 to 1991

Executive Overview

Managed R&D activities, forecasted IT investment requirements, managed project lifecycles, and designed, developed, and implemented software solutions. Provided sophisticated, timely quantitative and analytical support to traders, marketing professionals, sales representatives, and operations personnel.

Promotional Track

Promoted to Vice President within three years. Originally joined major investment bank as Analyst in the Fixed Income Research department (1985 to 1988), providing decision support to institutional fixed-income sales and trading business. Covered mortgage-backed securities, corporate bonds, and government securities. Mentored and supervised Junior Analyst and educated sales representatives and traders on fixed-income business products, practices, and theories.

Corporate Challenge

Challenged to conceive, plan, and deliver the technological and decision support requirements of the $30 million Interest Rate Products Group.

Financial & Strategic Successes

- Succeeded in maintaining positive cash flow and neutral market position in unwinding the derivatives portfolio—without availability of treasury bill futures, government securities, and Eurodollar futures markets—as Smythe declared bankruptcy.

- Designed, developed, and implemented P&L calculation and analysis system and risk analysis and control solutions for $30 million interest-rate derivatives business.

- Facilitated $10+ million in annual revenue by creating interactive interest rate cap and floor pricing and hedging solution.

- Improved comprehensiveness, meaningfulness, and timeliness of analytics and decision support by assuming ownership of a portfolio of interactive, feature-rich proprietary technologies produced by the Fixed Income Research Department.

EDUCATION & LANGUAGES

MS, Computer Science, Cornell University, Ithaca, NY 1985
BA, Mathematics, University of Missouri, Rolla, MO 1983

Note: Coursework completed for PhD in Math
Note: Also satisfied requirements for degree in Statistics

Fluent in written and spoken **English.** Fluent in native Nigerian language of **Igbo.** Competent speaker of **French.**

SYED RAMJEET

CFO ▪ SENIOR FINANCE EXECUTIVE

Made "the impossible, possible" for a number of Wall Street's leading financial firms.

Eighteen+ years' experience in finance management.

Consistently deliver mission-critical results in finance and in the technologies and teams that support finance. Provide "no surprises" decision support, driving development through sound investment strategies and transactions. A high-energy, trusted advisor—forthcoming, yet diplomatic, and levelheaded. Motivational leader—spur teams to give 110% effort and loyalty.

Deliver the "big wins" in corporate finance.

Multimillion-dollar contributor, driven by a visceral, "hard-wired" need to strategize, to innovate, and to disprove the words "It can't be done!" Gifted with the vision, determination, and skills needed for high-level, revenue-building strategies and tactics. Contribute global perspective, intimate knowledge of global business, and acute insight in impact of geopolitical, economic, industry, and cultural factors/events.

Supported $150+ million in accelerated growth.

Recognized as key to development of an eventual $800 million revenue stream for W. J. Klein, by strategizing and building foundation for firm's entire derivatives business, allowing comfortable yet aggressive growth from $0 to $150 million in annual revenues within first three years. Supported hundreds of millions of dollars in revenue and income for world-class companies.

Created IT solutions for $70+ million business.

Delivered and/or supported the creation of more than $70 million in revenue for Banque du Monde through conception and development of an array of sophisticated strategies and tools for financial management. Adept at translating abstract mathematical concepts, theories, and methodologies into user-friendly finance and IT solutions that support business need and enhance revenue generation. Conceived and managed technologically sophisticated systems and software.

Managed growth of multimillions in investments.

Built $9 million personal portfolio in four years and protected it from major loss during market downturn. Grew and managed holdings using personally developed proprietary computerized analysis and decision-making system.

PROFESSIONAL EXPERIENCE

PRESIDENT, RAMJEET CAPITAL, INC., Cheyenne, WY　　　　　　　　　　　**2001 to Present**

Created an organizational framework for managing personal investments in stocks, options, futures, commodities, FX, and other capital market offerings. Grew $1 million investment into $9+ million, retaining 68+% value vs. NASDAQ's 78+% aggregate loss.

MANAGING DIRECTOR Global Derivatives Dept., W. J. KLEIN COMPANIES, INC., New York, NY　　　**1995 to 2001**

Direct accountability for providing IT-based analytics for global business unit operating 24/7 on three continents. Led team of 25. Credited with key role in growing business from $0 to $150+ million in sales in three years ($800+ million by 1999).

VICE PRESIDENT Derivatives Department, BANQUE DU MONDE, New York, NY　　　　　　**1991 to 1995**

Developed and executed technology strategies and managed related R&D projects, budgets, and teams for a $70 million profit center. Converted a break-even business into global business organization, enabling $15 million annual business.

VICE PRESIDENT Interest Rate Products Group, SMYTHE BYRD HICKMAN, New York, NY　　　　**1985 to 1991**

Conceived and delivered tech and decision-support requirements of $30 million Interest Rate Products Group. Maintained positive cash flow and neutral market position in unwinding derivatives portfolio when Smythe declared bankruptcy.

EDUCATION & LANGUAGES

MS, Computer Science, Cornell University, Ithaca, NY 1982　　　**Note:** Coursework completed for PhD in Math

BA, Mathematics, University of Missouri, Rolla, MO 1980　　　**Note:** Satisfied requirements for degree in Statistics

Fluent in written and spoken **English**. Fluent in native Nigerian language of **Igbo**. Competent speaker of **French.**

---

111 Winding Road, Cheyenne, WY 82007 ▪ Home: 307-393-2124 ▪ Office: 307-404-9946 ▪ sRamjeet@email.com

SYED RAMJEET

CFO ∎ **SENIOR FINANCE EXECUTIVE**

Made "the impossible, possible" for a number of Wall Street's leading financial firms.

Syed Ramjeet is a Wall Street veteran, a technology and finance expert, a millionaire, and a man who embodies the American dream. He is also surprisingly humble, committed to social contribution, and remembers his roots.

Born and raised in Nigeria and self-educated for many of his formative years, Syed Ramjeet taught himself calculus by the age of seventeen and received a college scholarship. Without friends or family, he came to the United States with $200 in his pocket and a determination to learn, succeed, and never return to Nigeria.

In less than two decades Syed Ramjeet earned his undergraduate degree from the University of Missouri, earned a master's in Computer Science from Cornell, completed Cornell's PhD coursework in math, and made groundbreaking multimillion-dollar contributions in finance and technology for three prominent Wall Street firms. He became a millionaire in his early thirties and went on to grow his personal investment portfolio to $9 million.

Mr. Ramjeet has more than twenty-two years' experience in finance management. While on Wall Street his technology and finance innovations supported hundreds of millions of dollars in revenue and income for world-class companies including W. J. Klein, Banque du Monde, and Smythe Byrd Hickman.

Known for "delivering the big wins," Mr. Ramjeet became a multimillion-dollar contributor, driven by a visceral, "hard-wired" need to strategize, to innovate, and to disprove the words "It can't be done."

Gifted with the vision, determination, and skills needed for high-level, revenue-building strategies and tactics, he contributed innovations that supported $150+ million in three-year accelerated growth for W. J. Klein—growth that mushroomed into an $800 million revenue stream through his work in strategizing and building the foundation for W. J. Klein's entire derivatives business.

Mr. Ramjeet created IT solutions for Banque du Monde that supported the creation of more than $70 million in revenue—he did this through the conception and development of an array of sophisticated strategies and tools for financial management.

Within his personal portfolio, Syed Ramjeet managed the growth of multimillions in investments, building a $9 million portfolio in four years and protecting it from major loss during market downturn. He leveraged and managed his holdings using a self-developed proprietary computerized analysis and decision-making system.

A visionary, Syed Ramjeet has a passion for innovation and idea generation combined with the ability to translate ideas between the tech and business sides and then implement those ideas to create revenue or solve a mission-critical problem. He can function seamlessly in multiple finance-related roles—crisis management, strategy creation, software development, turnaround management, and revenue generation—and has innate skill in defining and delivering metrics that foster accountability at individual and corporate levels.

Mr. Ramjeet has an intrinsic ability to be flooded with information, sift through it, experiment, and quickly determine a successful solution. He has said, "I am an excellent strategist and tactician. Indeed my brain seems to be wired for pattern recognition and strategic thinking. I enjoy shogi (Japanese chess), love unraveling complex business situations, and have been told I should have been an attorney."

After many successful years on Wall Street, and a number of years managing Ramjeet Trust, Syed Ramjeet is preparing for a new challenge in finance—that of CFO. Mr. Ramjeet has said, "I get my energy from making money—from creating a strategy, setting it to motion, experiencing the birth of the creation, and enjoying the success! With that in mind, the role of CFO is a logical next step and will draw upon my skills in finance, technology, leadership, and growth."

Mr. Ramjeet's inspiring story is one of massive and unremitting work and self-development leading to remarkable financial, career, and personal success—within only two decades of his arrival in America. He will bring the same drive for excellence to this new role. Using his skills in finance and technology as well as his principled, collaborative, vigorous, and disciplined yet flexible workstyle, Mr. Ramjeet is sure to create and support the highest levels of success for his new firm.

When reflecting upon his personal journey, Mr. Ramjeet is firm in his resolve: "In my teen years my values and character were formed. I identified and accepted the principle that no one owes me. I became self-reliant, hard-working, and strong. I held myself responsible for anything that might go wrong in my life, even if it was caused by lack of knowledge on my part."

Driven, yes, but also approachable and human. When asked to describe him, Syed's peers and reports portray him as "Kind, fair, apolitical, without a big ego." "Pleasant, very easy to work with, and not prone to get into petty squabbles." "Principled and strong—a straight shooter." "A man of substance, as opposed to hot air." "A bowl of energy."

Syed Ramjeet lives in Cheyenne, Wyoming, with his beautiful wife Tricia, two-year old son Jonathan, two dogs, and a cat. Not being risk averse, and trusting his judgment, he married Tricia within three weeks of their meeting and says, "A new dimension has been added to my growth as a human being." Syed enjoys playing and studying shogi, ballroom dancing (salsa in particular), and a wide variety of reading. Focused on spiritual and personal growth, he wishes to one day "have immense wealth that will enable me to fund foundations I create for humanitarian work."

Syed Ramjeet can be contacted at (307) 393-2124 or (307) 404-9946 or via email at sRamjeet@email.com.

SYED RAMJEET

CAREER SUCCESSES AND DISTINCTIONS
Made "the impossible, possible" for a number of Wall Street's leading financial firms.

STRATEGY, LEADERSHIP, FINANCIAL MODELING & IT

W. J. Klein Companies, Inc.
Managing Director – Derivatives

Situation
W. J. Klein made startup of a global derivatives business among its top priorities. To ensure success, the company hired me to provide necessary mathematical models, develop related technology solutions, and contribute insight on business strategies.

Action
To accelerate go-to-market cycle and avoid years it would take to write pricing, hedging, and derivatives portfolio management software, I purchased a solution (one I previously built at Smythe Byrd) and added new models for multi-currency derivatives analytics. This temporary solution enabled W. J. Klein to launch global derivatives business within 90 days. Later I researched third-party sources for IT building blocks, rolled out a new, highly scalable system less than seven months later, and transitioned system's custody from the vendor to my in-house IT team.

Impact & Analysis
Revenues of W. J. Klein's global derivatives business soared from $0 to $150+ million over three years, and turned a profit within the first full fiscal year. My principal and secondary mandates were huge, and I took them very seriously. During this period of time, I was literally working day and night to make sure all challenges were met, and I was able to influence members of my team to do the same.

ENTREPRENEURSHIP & FINANCIAL ANALYSIS

Ramjeet Capital, Inc
President

Situation
To gain maximum returns on personal investments and create a future philanthropy, I formed a private company.

Action
Originated and executed investment strategies, established finance and accounting structures (including proprietary software development), and applied my talents in technology, research, advanced analytics (qualitative and quantitative), and financial modeling to make informed, well-timed investment decisions.

Impact & Analysis
Grew my original $1 million investment into $9+ million within four years and protected the majority of assets during the downturn. I have always been a self-starter, and I leveraged my experience working with Wall Street firms. The vigor and intellectual stimulation of this pursuit keeps my knowledge and skills honed as I maintain knowledge of the marketplace, and I thrive on the challenge of analyzing key factors.

FINANCIAL ANALYSIS & RISK MANAGEMENT

Smythe Byrd Hickman
Vice President – Interest Rate Products Group

Situation
The firm's interest rate derivatives portfolio was suffering from lack of competent attention (key portfolio management personnel had suddenly left the company).

Action
Designed, developed, and implemented a complete portfolio management system based on proprietary pricing formulas with capabilities for daily P&L computation and breakdown for heterogeneous portfolio of over-the-counter derivatives and hedge instruments (swaps, caps, floors, swaptions, treasury bills, treasury notes, Eurodollar futures, etc.) and for exposition of risk.

Impact & Analysis
Delivered $30 million in new business and improved portfolio's manageability by upgrading risk analytics and stopgaps. Addressed operational performance issues by reengineering business processes, formulating policies, and creating controls that would mitigate future business risks related to knowledge management and employee attrition. I was, and continue to be, quick to assess, quantify, and control and/or mitigate financial and operational risks.

W. J. Klein Companies, Inc.

OPERATIONAL & FINANCIAL GOVERNANCE

Managing Director – Derivatives

Situation

W. J. Klein was suffering competitively because it was only rated "A" as a derivatives dealer.

Action

Rallied a few other senior executives to create a special-purpose derivatives subsidiary. Led the development of software solutions and implementation of operational procedures, as well as presentations and negotiations with rating agencies.

Impact & Analysis

Leveled competitive playing field by gaining "AAA" rating for W. J. Klein's derivatives subsidiaries—paving the way for growth and proving my ability to identify and act on significant strategic and competitive factors affecting a business.

Smythe Byrd Hickman

CRISIS & TURNAROUND MANAGEMENT

Vice President – Interest Rate Products Group

Situation

Smythe Byrd Hickman had suddenly filed for bankruptcy, placing the firm's bottom line, its interest-rate derivatives portfolio, and its customers, creditors, and shareholders at risk of huge losses.

Action

Focused on maintaining positive cash flow and market neutrality while systematically unwinding derivatives book without benefit of access to treasury and futures markets—an extremely complex challenge as collections and buy-outs had to be synchronized so as not to cause huge imbalance in portfolio market risk.

Impact & Analysis

Succeed in unwinding virtually entire $1+ trillion derivatives book while delivering returns to customers and generating $15+ million in profits to the firm. Composure rather than panic was my approach to this extremely complex, high-risk situation, where Wall Street was watching, concerned about a potential domino affect.

Smythe Byrd Hickman

BUSINESS & FINANCE STRATEGY

Vice President – Interest Rate Products Group

Situation

The firm was driven to capture revenue and optimize profitability from trading interest-rate caps and floors.

Action

I designed and developed a new system that used advanced mathematical equations to price caps and floors and compute hedges in the treasury and futures markets.

Impact & Analysis

Profits grew from $0 to $10 million annually over eighteen months. My strong entrepreneurial orientation was an excellent foundation for this initiative.

Banque du Monde

OPERATIONAL & FINANCIAL TURNAROUND

Vice President – Derivatives Department

Situation

Bank needed to accelerate growth, improve operational performance, and raise financial health to remain competitive and strong.

Action

Interconnected, consolidated, and leveraged combined resources (human capital, technology, "virtual" derivatives book) of offices in New York, Tokyo, and Paris. Replaced existing trading system with high-performance solution (based on one I designed and proved at Smythe Byrd Hickman), upgraded internal business process, executed cross-border business development initiatives (supported by new marketing tools), and championed globalization business culture.

Impact & Analysis

Converted a break-even business into a growth-focused, global business organization that generated $30+ million in revenue within one year, proving my ability to recognize and suggest business model changes that significantly affect top and bottom lines.

SYED RAMJEET

CFO ▪ SENIOR FINANCE EXECUTIVE

Made "the impossible, possible" for a number of Wall Street's leading financial firms.

September 25, 2005

Alan Rawlins, President
 Coast Capital
2497 Mission Hill Street
San Francisco, CA 94110

Dear Mr. Rawlins:

As a senior-level finance specialist with a history of big wins and a record of groundbreaking finance and technology contributions to a number of Wall Street's leading companies, I can help Coast Capital meet today's critical challenges.

How? I conceive and execute financial strategies that support corporate growth, profitability, and value; I powerfully link business objectives with future-forward enterprise-level IT strategies; I bridge the divide that often hinders business and technology communication; and I am skilled in crisis management and entrepreneurial thinking within organizations.

The following skills and achievements are predictive of the contributions you can expect should I become a member of your senior management team:

Expertise in both finance and technology, including an understanding of the culture and needs of technology, finance, and marketing professionals.

> At Smythe's Interest Rate Products Group, du Monde's Derivatives Department, and W. J. Klein's Global Derivatives Department, I laid the foundation for annual revenues of up to $30 million, $70 million, and $800 million, respectively.

Ability to get the job done, improvising if necessary, and using whatever resources may be available.

> At W. J. Klein I delivered—in months, not years—mission-critical products that became the foundation for an "immediate" $150 million derivatives business that eventually became an $800 million business.

Results-driven quantitative, analytical, and strategic thinking ability combined with extensive experience in a wide range of markets—equities, fixed income, currencies, commodities, futures, options—and knowledge of the culture and language of Wall Street, accounting, and the financial community.

> My entire career has been in the financial arena. I have helped Wall Street companies make money, and I have built a personal securities markets portfolio in the millions. My formal education is in rigorous disciplines—I hold an MS in Computer Science and have completed PhD coursework in math, both at Cornell—and my favorite hobby is shogi (Japanese chess).

Entrepreneurial skills and crisis management expertise.

> Entrepreneurial thinking in an organizational setting has been critical to my success in startup situations such as the founding of W. J. Klein's derivatives department or running Ramjeet Capital. Crisis management is a strength demonstrated by my successful post-bankruptcy unwinding of the Drexel derivatives portfolio.

Mr. Rawlins, my resume and a leadership profile highlighting key accomplishments are enclosed for your review. It is my firm belief that I can deliver exceptional outcomes to Coast Capital, and I look forward to discussing possible opportunities.

Sincerely,

Syed Ramjeet

Syed Ramjeet

111 Winding Road, Cheyenne, WY 82007 ▪ Home: 307-393-2124 ▪ Office: 307-404-9946 ▪ sRamjeet@email.com

191

Contributors:
Resume Writers and Web Designers

In addition to the two authors, a select group of professional resume writers and web designers contributed their work to this publication. We encourage you to contact one of these talented professionals if you seek assistance with your own career marketing documents.

Writers

These highly qualified professionals have earned a number of distinguishing credentials that include:

CCM — Credentialed Career Master
CCMC — Certified Career Management Coach
CEIP — Certified Employment Interview Coach
CERW — Certified Expert Resume Writer
CMP — Career Management Professional
CPBS — Certified Personal Branding Specialist
CPRW — Certified Professional Resume Writer
CRW — Certified Resume Writer
FRWCC — Federal Resume Writer/Career Coach
JCTC or IJCTC — International Job & Career Transition Coach
MCDP — Master Career Development Professional
NCRW — National Certified Resume Writer
PCCC — Professional Certified Career Coach

Arnold G. Boldt, CPRW, JCTC
Arnold-Smith Associates
625 Panorama Trail, Bldg. 1, #120, Rochester, NY 14625
585-383-0350
Arnie@ResumeSOS.com
www.ResumeSOS.com

Deborah Wile Dib, CPBS, CCM, NCRW, CPRW, CEIP, JCTC, CCMC
Executive Power Brand / Executive Power Coach / Advantage Resumes of NY
77 Buffalo Avenue, Medford, NY 11763
631-475-8513
debdib@executivepowerbrand.com
www.executivepowerbrand.com
www.executivepowercoach.com
www.advantageresumes.com

Kirsten Dixson, CPBS, JCTC
Brandego and Reach Branding Club
PO Box 963, Exeter, NH 03833
603-580-2208
kirsten@brandego.com
www.brandego.com

Michelle Dumas, NCRW, CPRW, CCM, JCTC, CEIP
Dan Dorotik, NCRW
Distinctive Documents
Somersworth, NH 03878
800-644-9694
resumes@distinctiveweb.com
www.distinctiveweb.com

Christine Edick, PCCC, JCTC, CEIP, CCMC
A Career Coach 4 U
2691 N. Vista Heights Rd., Orange, CA 92867
714-974-6220
christine@acareercoach4u.com
www.ACareerCoach4U.com

Louise Fletcher, CPRW
Blue Sky Resumes
Bronxville, NY 10708
914-337-5742
lfletcher@blueskyresumes.com
www.blueskyresumes.com

Louise Garver, MA, JCTC, CMP, CPRW, MCDP, CEIP
Career Directions, LLC
115 Elm St Suite 103, Enfield, CT 06082
860-623-9476
CareerPro@cox.net
www.resumeimpact.com

Gayle Howard, CPRW, CCM, CERW, CRW
Top Margin
PO Box 74, Chirnside Park, Melbourne 3116, Australia
getinterviews@topmargin.com
www.topmargin.com

Helen Oliff, CPRW, FRWCC Certified Executive Coach
Turning Point
2307 Freetown Court #12C, Reston, VA 20191
703-716-0077
Midwest Office 651-204-0665
helen@turningpointnow.com
www.turningpointnow.com

Don Orlando, MBA, CPRW, JCTC, CCM, CCMC
The McLean Group
640 South McDonough Street, Montgomery, AL 36104
Phone: 334-264-2020
yourcareercoach@aol.com

Tracy Parish, CPRW
CareerPlan, Inc.
PO Box 957, Kewanee, IL 61443
888-522-6121
resume@careerplan.org
www.careerplan.org
www.executivecareersolutions.com

Phyllis Shabad
CareerMasters
95 Woods Brooke Circle, Ossining, NY 10562
target@CareerIQ.com

Laurie Smith, CPRW, IJCTC
Creative Keystrokes Executive Resume Service
Gastonia, NC 28056
800-817-2779
ljsmith@creativekeystrokes.com
www.creativekeystrokes.com

Designers

The following professionals are leaders in the emerging field of web portfolio development and design.

Kirsten Dixson, CPBS, JCTC
Brandego and Reach Branding Club
PO Box 963, Exeter, NH 03833
603-580-2208
kirsten@brandego.com
www.brandego.com

Louise Fletcher, CPRW
Blue Sky Portfolios
Bronxville, NY 10708
914-337-5742
lfletcher@blueskyresumes.com
www.blueskyportfolios.com

Colin Fraser and Brandon Devnich
Lucky Marble Solutions Corp.
#2–15 Cadillac Avenue, Victoria, BC, Canada V8Z 1T3
866-943-5733
250-744-4357
brandon@luckymarble.com
www.i3dthemes.com
www.luckymarbletemplates.com

Career Resources

The following career resource are available directly from Impact Publications. Complete the following form or list the titles, include postage (see formula at the end), enclose payment, and send to:

IMPACT PUBLICATIONS
9104 Manassas Drive, Suite N
Manassas Park, VA 20111-5211
1-800-361-1055 (orders only)
Tel. 703-361-7300 or Fax 703-335-9486
Email address: info@impactpublications.com
Quick and easy online ordering: www.impactpublications.com

Orders from individuals must be prepaid by check, money order, Visa, MasterCard, or American Express. We accept telephone and fax orders.

Qty.	Titles	Price	TOTAL

EXECUTIVE JOB SEARCH

Qty.	Titles	Price	TOTAL
____	The $100,000+ Job Interview	$19.95	____
____	The $100,000 Resume	$16.95	____
____	Best Career Transition Resumes for $100,000+ Jobs	$24.95	____
____	Best Cover Letters for $100,000+ Jobs	$24.95	____
____	Best Resumes for $75,000+ Executive Jobs	$16.95	____
____	Best Resumes for $100,000+ Jobs	$24.95	____
____	CareerJournal.com $100,000 Plus Jobs	$16.95	____
____	Directory of Executive Recruiters	$49.95	____
____	Executive Job Search for $100,000 to $1 Million+ Jobs	$24.95	____
____	Executive Resumes: Marketing Yourself at $100,000+	$34.95	____
____	Haldane's Best Answers to Tough Interview Questions	$15.95	____
____	Haldane's Best Cover Letters for Professionals	$15.95	____
____	Haldane's Best Resumes for Professionals	$15.95	____
____	Haldane's Best Employment Websites for Professionals	$15.95	____
____	Rites of Passage at $100,000 to $1 Million+	$29.95	____
____	Salary Negotiation Tips for Professionals	$16.95	____
____	Sales and Marketing Resumes for $100,000 Careers	$19.95	____

RESUMES AND LETTERS

____	101 Quick Tips for a Dynamite Resume	$21.95 _____
____	201 Dynamite Job Search Letters (4th Edition)	$19.95 _____
____	Best KeyWords for Resumes, Cover Letters, and Interviews	$17.95 _____
____	Best Resumes and CVs for International Jobs	$24.95 _____
____	Best Resumes and Letters for Ex-Offenders	$19.95 _____
____	Best Resumes for People Without a Four-Year Degree	$19.95 _____
____	College Grad Resumes for $75,000+ Jobs	$24.95 _____
____	Competency-Based Resumes	$13.99 _____
____	Cover Letters for Dummies	$16.99 _____
____	e-Resumes	$11.95 _____
____	Expert Resumes for People Returning to Work	$16.95 _____
____	High Impact Resumes and Letters (8th Edition)	$19.95 _____
____	Military Resumes and Cover Letters	$21.95 _____
____	Nail the Resume!	$17.95 _____
____	Nail the Cover Letter!	$17.95 _____
____	Resume, Application, and Letter Tips for People With Hot and Not-So-Hot Backgrounds	$17.95 _____
____	Resumes for Dummies (2nd Edition)	$16.99 _____
____	Resumes in Cyberspace	$14.95 _____
____	Resumes That Knock 'Em Dead	$12.95 _____
____	Savvy Resume Writer	$10.95 _____
____	Sure-Hire Resumes	$14.95 _____
____	Winning Letters That Overcome Barriers to Employment	$17.95 _____

CAREER EXPLORATION, EMPLOYERS, AND RECRUITERS

____	25 Jobs That Have It All	$12.95 _____
____	50 Best Jobs For Your Personality	$16.95 _____
____	50 Cutting Edge Jobs	$15.95 _____
____	300 Best Jobs Without a Four-Year Degree	$16.95 _____
____	America's Top 100 Jobs for People Without a Four-Year Degree	$19.95 _____
____	America's Top Jobs for People Re-Entering the Workforce	$19.95 _____
____	Occupational Outlook Handbook	$18.95 _____
____	The O*NET Dictionary of Occupational Titles	$39.95 _____
____	Quick Guide to Career Training in Two Years or Less	$18.95 _____
____	Quick Prep Careers	$18.95 _____

JOB SEARCH STRATEGIES AND TACTICS

____	95 Mistakes Job Seekers Make and How to Avoid Them	$13.95 _____
____	America's Top Internet Job Sites	$19.95 _____
____	Change Your Job, Change Your Life (9th Edition)	$21.95 _____
____	The Ex-Offender's Job Hunting Guide	$17.95 _____
____	Guide to Internet Job Searching	$14.95 _____
____	The Job Hunting Guide	$14.95 _____
____	Job Hunting Tips for People With Hot and Not-So-Hot Backgrounds	$17.95 _____
____	Job Search: Marketing Your Military Experience	$16.95 _____
____	Jobs and the Military Spouse (2nd Edition)	$17.95 _____
____	Knock 'Em Dead	$14.95 _____

____	Military Transition to Civilian Success	$21.95 ____
____	No One Will Hire Me!	$13.95 ____
____	Quit Your Job and Grow Some Hair	$15.95 ____
____	What Color Is Your Parachute?	$17.95 ____

ASSESSMENT AND INSPIRATION

____	Aptitude, Personality, and Motivation Tests	$17.95 ____
____	Attitude Is Everything	$14.95 ____
____	Career Tests	$12.95 ____
____	Discover the Best Jobs for You (4th Edition)	$15.95 ____
____	Discover What You're Best At	$14.00 ____
____	Do What You Are	$18.95 ____
____	Goals!	$14.95 ____
____	I Don't Know What I Want, But I Know It's Not This	$14.00 ____
____	I Want to Do Something Else, But I'm Not Sure What It Is	$15.95 ____
____	Pathfinder	$14.00 ____
____	Seven Habits of Highly Effective People	$15.00 ____
____	The Success Principles	$24.95 ____
____	What Should I Do With My Life?	$14.95 ____
____	What Type Am I?	$14.95 ____
____	What's Your Type of Career?	$18.95 ____
____	Who Moved My Cheese?	$19.95 ____

DRESS AND IMAGE

____	Dressing Smart for Men	$16.95 ____
____	Dressing Smart for Women	$16.95 ____

INTERVIEWS, NETWORKING, SALARY NEGOTIATIONS

____	101 Dynamite Questions to Ask At Your Job Interview (2nd Edition)	$13.95 ____
____	Dynamite Salary Negotiations (4th Edition)	$15.95 ____
____	A Foot in the Door	$14.95 ____
____	Haldane's Best Answers to Tough Interview Questions	$15.95 ____
____	Interview for Success (8th Edition)	$15.95 ____
____	Job Interview Tips for People With Not-So-Hot Backgrounds	$13.95 ____
____	Job Interviews for Dummies	$16.99 ____
____	KeyWords to Nail Your Job Interview	$17.95 ____
____	Nail the Job Interview	$13.95 ____
____	Salary Negotiation Tips for Professionals	$16.95 ____
____	Savvy Interviewer	$10.95 ____
____	The Savvy Networker	$14.95 ____
____	Sweaty Palms	$13.95 ____

GOVERNMENT, INTERNATIONAL, AND NONPROFIT

____	Book of U.S. Government Jobs	$21.95 ____
____	Directory of Websites for International Jobs	$19.95 ____
____	Federal Applications That Get Results	$23.95 ____
____	Federal Resume Guidebook (3rd Edition)	$21.95 ____
____	FBI Careers	$18.95 ____
____	Global Citizen	$16.95 ____
____	Going Global Career Guide	$199.95 ____

_____	International Job Finder	$19.95	_____
_____	International Jobs	$19.00	_____
_____	Jobs for Travel Lovers	$19.95	_____
_____	Post Office Jobs	$19.95	_____
_____	Ten Steps to a Federal Job	$39.95	_____

SUBTOTAL   _____

Virginia residents (5% sales tax) ...   _____

Shipping/handling: $5 for first item ... $5.00

plus following percentages when SUBTOTAL is:

- $10-$99 — subtotal x 8%:   _____
- $100-$999 — subtotal x 7%:   _____
- $1,000-$4,999 — subtotal x 6%:   _____
- Over $5,000 — subtotal x 5%:   _____

TOTAL ENCLOSED ——————————————————

Individuals must prepay as follows:

❑ Check   ❑ Money Order enclosed for: $ _____

❑ Visa   ❑ MC   ❑ AmEx   ❑ Discover for: $ _____

Card:#_____ Exp:____/____

Signature _____

Approved organizations may submit official (signed) purchase orders for net 30-day payment terms:

Purchase Order enclosed: # _____

Signature _____

Bill To:

Name _____

Address _____

_____

Telephone:_____

Email:_____

Ship To (please specify a street delivery address):

Name_____

Address_____

_____

_____

Telephone:_____

Keep in Touch . . .
On the Web!

www.impactpublications.com
www.ishoparoundtheworld.com
www.travel-smarter.com
www.winningthejob.com
www.veteransworld.com
www.exoffenderreentry.com